FANZINES

FANZINES

THE DIY REVOLUTION

TEAL TRIGGS

CHRONICLE BOOKS
SAN FRANCISCO

This book is dedicated to my parents Edward Elmer Triggs
and Rae Janice Triggs.

First published in the United States in 2010 by Chronicle Books

First published in the United Kingdom in 2010 by Thames & Hudson
Ltd, 181A High Holborn, London WC1V 7QX

Library of Congress Cataloging-in-Publication Data available.

ISBN: 978-0-8118-7692-6

Manufactured in Singapore

10 9 8 7 6 5 4 3 2 1

Chronicle Books LLC
680 Second Street
San Francisco, California 94107
www.chroniclebooks.com

CONTENTS

CHAPTER ONE

A DO-IT-YOURSELF REVOLUTION: DEFINITIONS AND EARLY DAYS

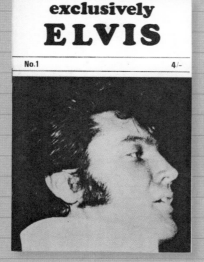

Fandom had its roots in the early genres of science fiction, rock and roll and Hollywood movies. British fanzine *New Worlds* (1930s–1997) is one of the longest-running science fiction publications. The rise of rock and roll set the stage for such musiczines as *Exclusively Elvis* (1969) – a bi-monthly first sold during an Elvis convention in Leicester, UK. *Western Trails Magazine* (*c.* mid-1970s) featured fan news about 1940s–60s Western stars, with this launch issue celebrating the Saturday matinee.

Walking into any fanzine symposium today one is immediately aware that the days of these small press publications are far from over. There is an air of excitement at such events, where fanzine editors and enthusiasts come to sell, buy or swap publications. Folding tables line the venue's walls, piled high with fanzines in all shapes, sizes and formats. Some fanzines are produced using desktop publishing, while many others are lovingly put together by hand using more conventional techniques such as scissors and glue. The atmosphere is fair-like, combining market trading with fanzine-making workshops, curated exhibitions and talks from zinesters themselves. This is a space where an invisible fanzine culture becomes visible.

From Underground to Overground

For the most part fanzines, or 'zines', remain hidden, flying beneath the radar of mainstream publishing and its conventions. Their production is often irregular, and distribution takes place at zine fairs, by word of mouth, through independent music shops or bookstores, or through the post. Zinesters (producers of fanzines) are less concerned about copyright, grammar, spelling, punctuation or the protocols of page layout, grids and typography, than about communicating a particular subject to a community of like-minded individuals. The print-runs vary in numbers. Some are limited editions of up to fifty, while others may be downloaded digitally from the Internet. It is hard to estimate how many fanzines are produced each year – although in the late 1980s, the *Guardian* newspaper reported that more than 10,000 titles of UK football-related fanzines alone were in publication, while in 1994 *Time* magazine reported that 20,000 titles were produced in the United States, a figure that was then growing at an annual rate of 20 per cent – 4,000 fanzines were sold in one month at one branch of the (now defunct) record chain Tower Records.[1]

The interest in small press publications and fanzines has increased over the last two decades, as evidenced by the plethora of international fanzine symposia and exhibitions and the increased number of book compilations of fanzines published by mainstream publishing houses. All of this started in the late 1990s, when there was a bustle of activity in America. At this time the range of topics and personal interests that zinesters were writing about came to light. Pagan Kennedy, a journalist and writer, was among the first to move from the underground into the overground, with her book *Zine: How I Spent Six Years of My Life in the Underground and Finally Found Myself … I Think* (1995), which was based on the writings in her own personal fanzine, *Pagan's Head* (*c.* 1988–94). Other fanzine producers soon followed in a publishing flurry that brought into the public consciousness, for example, insights into the everydayness of contemporary life as observed by Paul Lukas in *Inconspicuous Consumption: An Obsessive Look at the Stuff We Take for Granted, From the Everyday to the Obscure* (1996); Al Hoff's 'scavenging fun' at thrift stores in *Thrift Score* (1997); the antics of America's temporary work industry as viewed by Jeff Kelly in *Best of Temp Slave!* (1997); and, notably, from Chip Rowe, producer of *Chip's Closet Cleaner* (1989–), *The Book of Zines: Readings from the Fringe* (1997). This book still sits alongside an accompanying website that continues to provide an updated resource with practical 'how-to' advice, fanzine directories and interviews with producers.[2]

This process of moving from 'below critical radar' into mainstream publishing houses was not without its critics or controversy. By 1997, some within the do-it-yourself community were accused of selling out, by trading on the DIY ethos for commercial gain. Fanzine producers are in a unique position, at the same time author, editor, publisher and designer; they are subcultural insiders and embrace the ethos of a DIY community. Despite fanzines being amateur publications, their producers have become their own makers of cultural meaning, taking part in the construction of the very pop culture that they critique. With this in mind it is no wonder that critics have expressed concerns that mainstream publishing would 'endanger the alternative, anti-establishment viewpoint that makes zines unique', and asked: are these 'the last days of Pompeii for the zine world?'[3]

The graphic language of 1960s and 1970s fanzines formed the basis for the 'design' of zines to come. John Ryan, editor of this special offset edition of the Australian comiczine *Boomerang* (1970s), is pictured in front of his comics collection. On the cover of *Aware Magazine* (1977), produced by Steve Kolanjian, is a session photograph of Fleetwood Mac, whose discography and history appear inside. Bob Dylan appears on the cover of issue four of *Crawdaddy!* (1966–2003), often credited as the first publication of pop music criticism.

On the other hand, it is not uncommon for fanzine producers to have intentionally used fanzines as a testing ground before entering into professional careers as journalists, photographers or graphic designers. You have only to look at established British media figures such as Jon Savage (*Bam Balam* and *London's Outrage* to weekly music press and then to *The Face* and on to national press and television) and Danny Baker (*Sniffin' Glue* to *NME* and BBC Radio) to get the idea. In the United States, James Romenesko (*Obscure*, 1989–99) runs spin-off indie websites The Obscure Store and Reading Room (1998–) and MediaGossip.com (1999) and a page on the journalism site PoynterOnline (1999–), which have attracted a regular readership from 'people obsessed with newspapers'.[4]

Some fanzines have undergone a parallel transition. *Giant Robot: Asian American Pop Culture and Beyond* (1994–), for example, began as a modest fanzine in Los Angeles created by former punk-rock zine producers Eric Nakamura and Martin Wong. With the help of a loyal fan base and a self-confessed DIY ethic *Giant Robot*, with its Asian pop culture focus, went from being a fanzine in the form of a stapled-and-folded photocopied 'digest' of 240 copies per issue to a fully blown bi-monthly magazine sold in all good bookstores. By 2001, its producers had also turned *Giant Robot* into an established brand label with retail and gallery spaces in New York and San Francisco. *Bust*, 'the voice of the new girl order', is another title that had its roots in fanzine popular culture. Created in 1993 by Debbie Stoller, Laurie Hanzel and Marcelle Karp, this few-hundred-run photocopied fanzine was part of a new wave of feminist publications reacting against the established women's magazines such as *Cosmopolitan* and *Glamour*; others were *Hip Mama* (1997–), *Bitch* (1996–), *Bamboo Girl* (1995–) and *Rockrgrl* (1995–2005). Within five years *Bust* was a glossy magazine with female pop stars on its covers and a national circulation of 20,000. Other fanzines have made the jump to the mainstream, including the football fanzine *When Saturday Comes* (1986–), which proved there was a huge audience for a wittier take on football and which influenced

media cover elsewhere (for example British television's *Fantasy Football League*). The British style bible *i-D* (1980–) took everyday subcultural street clothing and turned it into a glossy fashion cult. And finally, *Cheap Date* (1997–) – tagline: 'antidotal antifashion for thinking thrifters' – produced by Kira Jolliffe and courting such high-profile fashionistas as Sophie Dahl, Anita Pallenberg and Erin O'Connor, is now published in the mainstream, with a Russian edition. All these examples of zines that started off small and made it big are the exception rather than the rule, but they show what can happen when an idea catches the zeitgeist.

The on-going debates have not deterred other zinesters from turning to mainstream publishers, nor the mainstream itself from co-opting the fanzine as a popular cultural form. In the 1990s, it seemed that everywhere you turned faux fanzines were being published by large multinational companies. The fanzine as a graphic form was co-opted – moving from an authentic, edgy, political underground into the world above as an item now imbued with commercial hipness. *Dirt* was brought out by Warner Brothers, *Slant* emerged out of Urban Outfitters, and *Full Voice* was published as part of the Body Shop's advertising campaign celebrating the body and self-esteem in 1997. A year later, the Portland-based advertising agency Wieden & Kennedy drew upon its local community and interest in DIY American culture to produce *U Don't Stop* for Nike.[5] Conversely, *Us! The Fiat Fanzine* (2009–), produced by British design group This is Northstar, presented the fanzine as a way to 'build a sense of community and brand loyalty': its use of matt paper and unusual illustration is clearly rooted in the graphic language of fanzines.

Fanzines have even made it on to television. *Our Hero* (2000–02) was a hit television series that aired in Canada, in which the lead character, Kale, wrote a fanzine about her life as a seventeen-year-old with her two best friends. In the Nickelodeon cartoon *Rocket Power* (1999–2004), one of its main characters, Reggie, publishes her own zine, dubbed appropriately 'The Zine'. Fanzines have also played a

Fanzines are critical spaces free from conventional constraints. In *Travellin' Fist* (1989), Dan Koretzky complains about the lack of mainstream publishing venues and the low quality of rock criticism. Greg Shaw's commitment to raising the profile of rock journalism in *Who Put the Bomp!* (1970–79) is evident as he observes a shift to a more discerning fan and collector. Jamie Reid's *Suburban Press* (1970–75) provided an early experimental aesthetic of gritty photocopied imagery that suited his Situationist-inspired critique of Croydon's urban development.

supporting role in such novels as *Hard Love* (1999) by Ellen Wittlinger and *Tales of a Punk Nothing* (2006) by Abram Shalom Himelstein and Jamie Schweser, whose narrative about the punk scene in Washington, DC is constructed through the use of fanzines and letters.

One of the earliest studies on fanzines was written by the German-born American psychiatrist Fredric Wertham, titled *The World of Fanzines* (1972). In 1982 when Mike Gunderloy began to produce the bi-monthly catalogue *Factsheet Five* (later edited by R. Seth Friedman), a readily identifiable fanzine community started to emerge, reinforced by the publication of multiple fanzine compilations in the 1990s. By the late 1990s fanzines had become a serious subject for academic study, and such books as Stephen Duncombe's *Notes from the Underground: Zines and the Politics of Alternative Culture* (1997) and Bob Dickinson's *Imprinting the Sticks: The Alternative Press Beyond London* (1997) led the way for a broader appreciation of what had been a subcultural phenomenon.[6]

Yet the do-it-yourself authenticity fostered by early fanzine producers has not necessarily been lost. Zinesters today maintain an enthusiasm for and commitment to the fanzine form as a way of expressing their individual concerns, their rants on politics, their loves and hates, their desires and disappointments. The authentic resides in the authorial voice, where the personal is political and not beholden to global corporations. Zinesters continue to operate on the margins of the mainstream. They disregard the traditions of professional design studios and the conventions of literary publishing houses. Rather than conforming, zinesters are defining and 'manufacturing' their own identity and representing this through their writing and DIY image-making. Referring to fanzine editors as producers or makers introduces new ways of thinking about the producer as a 'popular author' and the fanzine as an 'autobio/graphical object'.[7] Through the DIY nature of their production, fanzines take on an enhanced value in how they contribute to and reflect a broader everyday cultural experience.

Wertham describes fanzines in his 1972 study as a 'novel form of communication', arguing that they have a unique place in the history of communication, design, journalism, publishing and popular culture. Fanzines are documents of a social history framed by political, economic and cultural contexts. Wertham observes that fanzines 'exist as genuine human voices outside of all mass manipulation'. He argues that these voices 'deserve to be heard'.[8] Fanzines are also about a relationship that is formed between producers and readers, where the readers may also be producers but most certainly are fans sharing similar interests. Fanzines may be considered as 'virtual' spaces where producers and readers unite in communities of interest or dissent. Perhaps the most visible evidence of this process is in football, or soccer, where each club may have a number of separate fanzine titles, yet have a collective voice that can have a real impact on club decisions – for example, concerning ticket prices or club regulations.

Just as important are the form of the fanzine and the way it has been made, both elements that feed into our understanding of what is being communicated. This includes the design of the layout (often visually 'chaotic'), the choice of typography (either handwritten or, as with early fanzines, typewritten or using rub-down lettering), and production techniques (whether mimeographed, photocopied or computer-generated). Mimeographing and photocopying are both methods of duplicating, the former using a stencil fitted around an inked drum, the latter using the now prevalent form of xerography. With the rise of computers in the 1980s, producers began to use desktop publishing packages to generate their texts and layouts. More recently producers have discovered – or rediscovered – the art of letterpress printing. Fanzines are usually sized to be held easily in the hands, although sometimes a producer will use oversized broadsheet formats. Occasionally they might resemble more three-dimensional objects and incorporate recycled objects or materials, such as old vinyl single records. Advances in technology over the last few years have also, for better or worse, changed how we view fanzines, with online or digital forms.

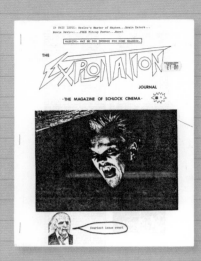

This book focuses primarily on British and American fanzine production, using fanzines from other countries as specific examples throughout to punctuate certain points about stylistic approaches or shared themes. Some non-Anglo-American fanzine titles are written in English (or in dual languages) rather than in a producer's first language – partly as a way of ensuring wider distribution and links with other fans internationally. The selection of fanzines contained within this book reflects the author's position as a design historian and also as a fanzine collector, and as such the book is by no means an exhaustive study, presenting simply 'a' history of fanzines rather than pretending to be a definitive textbook on the subject.

Defining and Positioning Fanzines

The term 'fanzine' is the conflation of 'fan' and 'magazine', and was coined by the American sci-fi enthusiast and zine producer Louis Russell Chauvenet in 1940 in his hectographed fanzine *Detours* (1940s, USA), when he declared his preference for the term 'fanzine' rather than 'fanmag' as the best shortened version of 'fan magazine'. (Hectograph was an early twentieth-century printing method that used glycerin-coated layers of gelatin to make limited copies.) Other producers followed and adopted the term readily to describe a mimeographed publication (using a more up-to-date production method of duplicating) devoted primarily to science fiction and superhero enthusiasts.[9] By 1949, the term was in common use and was included as a formal entry in the *Oxford English Dictionary*.

'Fanzine' itself first appeared abbreviated to 'zine' sometime in the 1970s, describing a photocopied, stapled, non-commercial and non-professional, small-circulation publication. Wertham differentiates fanzines from the underground press and little magazines while at the same time acknowledging there is some 'fluidity in the boundaries of these publications'.[10] He defines 'underground' as being 'in opposition' or 'anti-establishment', with the emphasis on the social–political. Some of the more recognized examples of the underground or counter-cultural press include *Oz*, *IT*, and *Frendz* from the 1960s and 1970s. On the other hand, little magazines are concerned with 'mainstream literature', and are often 'avant-garde' and publish experimental works.[11] Early literary figures to have contributed to or edited little magazines include Max Eastman (*The Masses*), T. S. Eliot (*The Criterion*), Ezra Pound (*Poetry: A Magazine of Verse*) and James Joyce (*The Little Review*).

Wertham describes the salient characteristics of fanzines as being 'dependent upon their independence', fostering free expression without censorship, and their producers not seeking mass circulation.[12] Cari Goldberg Janice defined zines in 1992 in relationship to what they are not – small press, underground press or alternative press. She proposed that while integrally linked to these movements, 'a zine is anything that is published on a non-commercial basis … anyone can publish a zine – that's the main attraction'.[13] A few years later, Duncombe defined zines within the context of 'a rapid centralization of corporate media', arguing for their political independence and localization. In 2002, Chris Atton proposed fanzines as sites for cultural production and described the fanzine as 'the quintessence of amateur self-published journalism'.[14] In all cases, zine producers and scholars alike acknowledged that fanzines build and promote DIY communities.

Historian George McKay defines DIY culture as being 'youth-centred and -directed clusters of interests and practices', and makes the links between alternative culture and the DIY ethos explicit.[15] He considers the way in which DIY direct action is in keeping with ideas about 'self-empowerment' through campaigning and lifestyle politics. Zine producers have followed suit. However, there is another way of looking at DIY that does not emphasize the oppositional or subcultural framework: what if, for example, a housewife from Virginia or from Hertfordshire produces a zine about collecting Pez dispensers? True, the very act of creating such a zine could be seen as a challenge to mainstream consumer culture, but at the same time it is not coming from a counter-cultural position.

L'Incroyable Cinema (1969–c. 1971), a precursor to today's 'media zine', ran for 5 issues, printed in Manchester on an old Multilith 1250 press. The first issue of *TCM* (1986) contains articles on DIY home-recording and reviews of Victoria Wood's performance as well as a centrefold of comedian Tony Hancock. *Penetration* (1976–c. 1977) has articles on rock stars Ted Nugent and Dave Brock, with a photo-collage essay on Motörhead reminiscent of the essays in John Holmstrom's *Punk* fanzine.

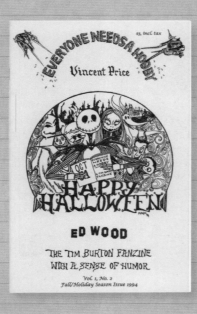

Diana Rigg (1986) gives a nod to the British star of *The Avengers*; this musiczine about 'spiky pop groups' has a particular reference to post-punk and retro culture (note the checkerboard mock-1960s DC Comics header). *Everyone Needs a Hobby* (1994-n.d.) is a tribute to director Tim Burton and celebrates such films as *Ed Wood* and *Edward Scissorhands*. *The Complate Monty Python* (1978-79) is an extensive resource for information on the Pythons' work, including photographs, records, films and interviews with Python members.

Fanzines are disseminated to like-minded 'fans', whose interests may range from science fiction, sport and music, to television, thrift shopping and beer-drinking. They have, for example, flourished in the underground music scene; they form part of the thrift-shop culture; they have been mouthpieces for animal rights groups; and they may serve, equally, as personal diaries for young teenagers growing up and interested in a range of issues and concerns. Early on in the history of fandom, Wertham noted that fanzines 'are sincere and spontaneous'.[16] Larry Bob, the producer of the now-defunct queerzine *Holy Titclamps* (1989–2003), has described the zine 'as a labor of love, producing no profit, and frequently a loss, of time at least'. He continues, 'information is the reason a zine exists; everything else, down to the paper it's printed on, is there to convey information.'[17]

Although providing an exact definition of the term 'fanzine' is somewhat problematic as shifts in historical context, genres and producer definitions must be taken into account, we may define fanzines as non-commercial, unofficial, amateur publications that are politically self-conscious and can form an important communication network for alternative cultures. They may be photocopied or printed, or in electronic form as 'e-zines' or downloadable from websites as pdf files. They are forums in which their producers articulate their view of the world around them. The main areas of consideration include a fanzine's format and layout, its method of distribution, a specific producer's motivation and the intent and context of the text.

We may also propose that the fanzine is a continually evolving form of communication. What it is attempting to communicate – whether personal or political – is determined by how it is put together as much as by what it is trying to say. For many fanzine producers, a politics of resistance is communicated visually through its graphic language, which has become integral, if not vital, to the development of a subcultural discourse. This is most evident in late 1970s punk fanzines – notably in *Sniffin' Glue* (Mark Perry, 1976–77, UK), *Search and Destroy* (V. Vale, 1977–79, USA) – and, later, in riot grrrl fanzines

of the 1990s, in which a similar graphic language is used, but this time with a feminist twist – for example *Jigsaw* (Tobi Vail, 1988–, USA), *Bikini Kill* (Tobi Vail, Kathi Wilcox and Kathleen Hanna, early 1990s, USA) and *Girl Germs* (Allison Wolfe and Molly Neuman, early 1990s, USA). In both cases, the political intent of the producer is reinforced through a graphic language of dissent – breaking all of the rules about design layout, typography and readability.

For others, the fanzine is a space for personal experimentation, which also remains free from the conventions of traditional forms of writing and/or design practice. In these personal fanzines, or 'perzines', authors document the most intimate details of their lives, generating personal narratives and thereby unique autobio/graphical snapshots. In this way there is a holistic relationship between the autobiographical and the graphical. There is a preoccupation with the handmade, which often manifests itself through the use of DIY media such as ribbons, stickers, different-coloured papers, crayons and felt-tip markers. The academic Anna Poletti has observed of perzines that 'the practice of self-making through zine-making is particularly momentary'. In other words, zines reflect a slice of life at a particular time, characterized as they are by 'out-of-date contact details, continually changing titles, the common use of pseudonymns or just first names…' and quickly dating DIY production methods.[18] It is within this context that a distinct graphic language emerges, born out of an individual's handwritten scrawled text, uniquely dysfunctional typewriters and cut-and-paste collage imagery.

Fanzine genres that draw on the perzine format include horror (*The Vincent Price File*, 1996–n.d., UK), music (*Bye Bye, Duffel Boy*, Pete Green, 2009–, UK) and queer (*Ricochet! Ricochet!* Colette and Patrick, 2005, UK). While they focus on topics of which their producers are fans, perzines are typified by a focus on the 'self' as the subject of discussion. For example, David Greenberger's humorous observations as an activities director at a nursing home have been the focus of *The Duplex Planet* (1979–, USA), while *Nancy's Magazine* (Nancy Bonnell-Kangas, 1983–*c.* 1994, USA) gives us insights into the author's life

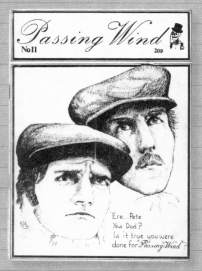  

Iconic English style unites these three zines. *Passing Wind* (c. 1978–c. 1981) takes a satirical look at British culture, with an interview with Peter Cook, a cartoon about Oxford's Bodleian Library and pen pal requests from Magdalen College, Oxford. *The Way Ahead* (1984) is a modzine about 'Modernism: from scooters to fashion and music' and includes advice on fashion for mod girls. Singer Adam Ant appears on this mini-zine. *Panda Eyes* (2009), with a first print-run of 150 issues sold over the internet.

as a librarian. In other perzines, Ayun Halliday reveals the realities of motherhood in *East Village Inky* (1998–, USA); Cindy Crabb shares her daily (and often emotional) life experiences in *Doris* (1991–, USA); while *Toast and Jam* (Rachel Kaye, 1997–98, UK) dealt with often heart-rending tales of eating disorders. In all cases, there is an intimacy to the writing, and visually individual stylistic approaches to match. Zine producers choose to create rather than just consume the culture around them.

Fanzines as Graphic Objects

Up to this point we have examined fanzines in terms of their role as a vehicle for alternative or underground communication. But the fanzine is also a graphic object, in which its form and the DIY process by which it is produced provide some understanding of a history of design and popular culture. The fanzine looks the way it does because it is created by a single producer conflating the roles of author and designer. This opens up the possibilities for experimentation in terms not only of a fanzine's editorial direction but also of its graphic sensibility, both unencumbered by the kind of self-censorship that would pertain in the mainstream. For example, when a publication is owned by a corporation then it generally has to conform to a corporate strategy, and that might involve content compromises to avoid upsetting advertisers or to prevent conflict with aspects of corporate business interests (how many glossy women's magazines have had to spike stories about animal experimentation in the cosmetics industry?). By contrast, the production methods adopted by zine producers – such as the photocopier or desktop publishing – allow the producer to have more freedom in putting together the zine in his or her own way, often without consideration of conventional design rules or aesthetics.

In the graphic design profession, debates around graphic authorship came to the fore in the mid-1990s, focusing for the most part on a designer's practice and process of self-publishing. Critic and designer Michael Rock's seminal essay, 'The designer as author' (1996), and

subsequent discussion in 'Fuck Content' (2005), provided a platform for re-evaluating the role the designer might play in mediating between form and content. This went some way in legitimizing the designer's voice as equal to that of other privileged forms of authorship. Rock's proposition was that the object as a form could be considered as a 'kind of text itself'. That is, design principles such as 'typography, line, form, color, contrast, scale, weight' become devices by which a story might be told. This opens up for discussion ways of understanding the graphic object not only by what it means but by 'how it means'.[19]

Such an approach may be applied to the study of fanzines. Meaning is constructed not only through visual images, but also through the symbiotic relationship between image, text and the graphic form itself. Collectively these elements communicate ideas and themes, and also subtly shape readers' attitudes, opinions and beliefs. Fanzines actively engage with popular cultural texts. The 'poaching' and re-contextualization of mainstream newspaper articles, photographs in collage form and other mainstream media elements create an 'urgency of resistance' and an 'urgency of personal engagement'.[20] The use of the photocopier (or mimeograph and duplicator in early fanzines) reinforces the sense of immediacy of the message. (The duplicator, often referred to as a 'ditto machine', was invented in the 1920s and gave a characteristic aniline purple text.)

Writing about the value of fanzines as historical objects, scholars often draw on the work of Walter Benjamin and his essay 'Author as Producer' (1934). Duncombe explores this in relationship to a 'politics of form'; fanzines are positioned 'within the condition of the production of culture that constitutes an essential component of their politics', but also 'within' the very conditions of the culture in which they are produced. The way in which fanzines are amateur productions suggests they are already situated in opposition to mainstream publishing and its conventions. At the same time fanzines are designed to be ephemeral: they are produced quickly and cheaply using copy-paper and lo-fi production and printing processes, with irregular publication dates and

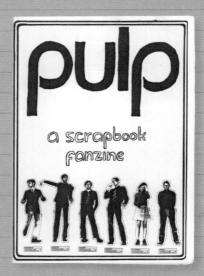

The international impact of
the British music scene is
demonstrated by these zines.
Considered the authoritative
resource, *Where's Eric!* (1992–)
is a desktop-published zine
produced by Clapton fans,
boasting a readership today
in 42 countries. *Weller Is
Back* (1991) was the third Paul
Weller fanzine to emerge out
of Dundee, and printed news
clippings, gig reviews, and
features on a Jam tribute
band. *Pulp* (2004) is a second
printing of a collection
of clippings and reviews of
Jarvis Cocker and Pulp.

limited print-runs and distribution. This leads Duncombe to suggest that the form is operating 'against the fetishistic archiving and exhibiting of the high art world and for the for-profit spirit of the commercial world'.[21]

This all goes towards defining a fanzine 'style' that also refers to the individual traits distinctive to the fanzine producers themselves. In other words, fanzine 'style' operates on two levels. On the one hand, it adopts style as a form of prevailing 'symbolic resistance' to the dominant culture, while on the other hand, it announces individual styles about difference on a more local or personal level. Style denotes a way in which a shared language is formed and a community identifies itself.

At the same time, the form of production 'has encouraged many readers to produce their own publications'.[22] This is an interactive process that forms an integral part of the DIY attitude of the movement. Duncombe describes it as a 'participatory cultural production and organization', where the producer and the reader are both active in the creation of the message. The visual and text-based language that the producer uses to address the reader of the fanzine tells us something about the identities of both the producer and the reader. It also suggests something about the assumed relationship between them.

A Brief History of Self-Publishing

Fanzines have played a key role in the evolution of fandom and alternative printing histories. Born out of the traditions of nineteenth-century political broadsheets, pamphlets, self-publishing and amateur printing, as well as of the underground counter-cultural publications of the 1960s, fanzines are part of an alternative press history. The fanzine as a self-publishing form stretches as far back as the publications of the radical social critics of the French Revolution. Thomas Paine's political pamphlet *Common Sense* (1776), for example, is often cited as an early example. The literary self-publisher, poet and engraver William Blake produced his *Songs of Innocence* in 1789, with poems illustrated by lavish engravings – a sort of forerunner to the contemporary artzine.[23] Other historical roots for fanzines include little

magazines, which emerged in force in Britain and the United States around 1910 as a form of non-commercial, self-published literary publication. The focus tended to be on experimental poetry, fiction and criticism. *The Dial,* published by Margaret Fuller and Ralph Waldo Emerson (1840–44), is often cited as one of the precursors to the zine form of publishing.[24] Although short-lived and having a limited readership (shared characteristics with today's fanzines), it nonetheless became an influential, if not controversial mouthpiece for the literary, philosophical and religious writings of the Transcendentalist Club in Boston, Massachusetts. Another early influential little magazine was *The Germ* (January–May 1850), which ran for four issues and provided a forum for Britain's nineteenth-century Pre-Raphaelite group of artists and writers. Here, poems and literary texts sat alongside drawings as a place where artists themselves could express their opinions about the nature and principles of art.

In the United States the formation of amateur press associations (APAs) during the nineteenth century facilitated the publication of amateur papers alongside the writings of amateur journalists. The model was for subscribers to send in their own pieces of work to a central collection point where all the works would then be collated and redistributed to members. Warner, writing in his book *All Our Yesterdays* (1969), makes mention of the amateur journalist Howard Scott, who in the 1870s issued a publication called *The Rambler* – which as an APAzine speculated about scientific developments and also fan conventions (for example in September 1879 the editor reports on the plans for the WAPA – 'a nineteenth-century amateur journalism group whose full name is lost' – convention in Chicago).[25] Such enthusiasm led the way for the development of communities of interest (especially in science fiction), where we find some of the inspiration for today's zine networks and communities.

However, it is not until the early twentieth century that we begin to see the formalization of some of these early visual characteristics, which help to establish a readily identifiable form. It may be suggested

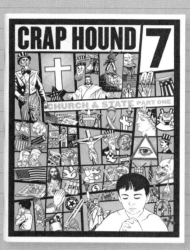

Lobster Telephone (1980s-90s) was a 'cyberfunk art terror' zine whose subject was social degradation, symbolized visually through its chaotic layout and low-fi print quality. *Lower than Dirt* (1996) was a limited edition of 150 copies. Its editor, Richard Santos, creates a series of photo collages from mainstream press stories about murder suspects, popular shootings and conspiracy theories. Sean Tejaratchi's *Crap Hound* (1994-) is a 96-page clip art zine, this issue focusing on black-and-white religious and patriotic imagery.

that what we might consider a graphic language of fanzines has its roots in two main areas: one that draws from the forms, techniques and contexts of artistic and literary practices such as Dada, Fluxus and Surrealism; and a second one based primarily in the intentions of political and counter-cultural activity as found in Situationism from the 1950s and 1960s, in the underground radical press and in the music and subcultural movement that came to be labelled punk in the 1970s.

Nico Ordway comments on the emergence of the post-World War I art movement Dada, arguing for recognizing the Dada artists' self-published journals as the 'first proto-zines': that is, zines 'produced for the pleasure of their creators and provocations of readers, ignoring or satirizing all canons and standards of journalism'.[26] Dada had a direct impact on the visual language of fanzines and specifically those produced during the punk period beginning in 1976. Illustrations and advertisements were cut out of the newspapers and popular magazines of the time, and re-presented using collage techniques. The collage approach, which juxtaposed 'found' imagery with photographs and texts, reinforced the Dadaists' attack on the dominant culture of the time. Such an approach generated an 'aesthetic of rebellion' that matched the Dadaists' contempt for bourgeois sensibilities.[27]

Self-publishing continued into the 1950s with a form of underground publishing characterized by works that were typed, mimeographed or Xeroxed in the tradition of what the Soviets had coined *samizdat* publishing.[28] Although the idea of samizdat has a long history, in the 1950s it meant clandestine DIY magazines distributed via anarchist networks in opposition to post-Stalin governments.

In the United States and Western Europe, fanzines are often affiliated with the underground press and the counter-cultural movement of the 1960s, though there is a distinction to be made. While fanzines sit comfortably within the domain of the underground they are not considered part of the underground press movement of the 1960s and 1970s. The relationship between private and public spaces helps to differentiate the two types of publications. The underground

press, for example, often entered into the consciousness of the 'public' realm, whereas fanzines remained essentially 'private' in that they were produced by fans for fans. This meant that traditionally fanzine producers blatantly disregarded copyright or censorship regulations while the underground press was more susceptible to the libel laws – laws from which fanzines tended to be sheltered by remaining firmly out of sight within their underground spaces. However, with the rise in profile of many fanzines in the 1990s, the threat of libel cases has increased, with some producers facing charges of copyright infringement in their appropriation of corporate imagery in challenging the rise of consumer culture.

Despite this distinction, the graphic language of the counter-cultural publications was not lost on fanzine producers. Counter-cultural broadsheets of the 1960s and 1970s such as *It*, *Frendz* and *Oz* created a visual mix of styles, colours and techniques, the result of each spread having been designed by a different person. Designers and illustrators also relied on their vast collections of comics, cartoons and illustrations as inspiration for collages, which ultimately captured the spirit of psychedelia and the rough edge of rock and roll. But this was also the result of new technologies such as the IBM Golfball typewriter and the more cost-effective printing method of offset lithography, which gave designers and printers a new-found freedom. The resulting experimentation created, in part, an attitude reflected in the density of overlapping colour, collaged images and typographic legibility in the production of fanzines that carried from the 1970s well up to the present day.

Fanzine Genres Pre-1976

One way of looking at the history of fanzines is through the development of genres, specifically early fan writing as found in science fiction, music and comics. Genres are created as a result of a number of fans locating themselves within subjects of interest. R. Seth Friedman, for example, in the metazine *Factsheet Five* (1982–98), one of the more substantial

Independent women find a place in fanzines in one way or another. *Spilt Milk* (1996), produced by two sisters, used riot grrrl-inspired 1950s images of teenagers and hand-drawn doodles. *Katy Keene Magazine* (1979-83) was dedicated to Bill Woggon's comic book *Katy Keene*. The singer Madonna was the subject of the Italian fanzine *Like a Virgin* (c. 1990s) and featured an interview with the diva herself. *Danzine* (1995-2003) was an 'adult' quarterly zine for exotic dancers and workers in the sex industry.

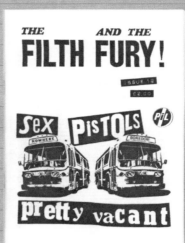

Punk attitude and design outlasted the 1970s. One of the first queercore punk zines, *Outpunk* (1992–97) was produced on a Mac LC 475 using QuarkXpress, Adobe Photoshop and Microsoft Word. In the DIY spirit, *Lip Gloss* (c. 2009) produced homemade badges that were attached to the cover of the zine. Retro punk imagery – here, Jamie Reid's image for the Sex Pistols – featured on the front of *The Filth and the Fury!* (2000) to coincide with the opening of that film in London.

fanzine review publications, formalized the fanzine taxonomy in order to organize the vast array of material that he received for each issue. Friedman reveals in the publication's October 1995 editorial that in that year alone he had produced five issues reviewing a total of 6,258 zines.[29] By the end of its run, *Factsheet Five* reviewed fanzines under the generic categories of quirky, medley, fringe, music, punk, grrrlz, personal, science fiction, food, humour, spirituality, politics, queer, arts and letters, and 'comix'. With the advent of electronic zines, Friedman also introduced a digital category.

A history of the contemporary incarnation of fanzines begins within the science fiction genre. Duncombe, like Wertham before him, argues that fanzines emerged as a 'distinct medium' with the rise of science fiction clubs in the 1930s.[30] Writers would publish in order to 'share science fiction stories and critical commentary', including some now notable authors such as Ray Bradbury and Arthur C. Clarke. The earliest amateur sci-fi fanzine to be established was called *The Comet* (1930) and was edited by R. A. Palmer for Chicago's Science Correspondence Club, while the earliest-established science fiction professional magazine, or 'prozine', was titled *Amazing Stories* and edited by Hugo Gernsback. It was Gernsback who introduced the idea of publishing readers' letters in the magazine, thereby providing a catalyst for early science fiction fan communities. Readers' letters were of particular importance to science fiction fan publications and were a precursor to the process of connecting readers and creators in contemporary fanzines. Ray Bradbury published his first story in his own fanzine, *Futuria Fantasia* (1939–41). Warner suggests that Bradbury's publication was well edited, though it included spelling mistakes; it was printed in green mimeograph ink to represent the colours of 'Technocracy' – a future society shaped by its technology.[31] In the UK, *The Futurian* was published in Leeds (1938–40) by J. Michael Rosenblum and included fiction poems and articles from 'leading sf fanz of the day', one of whom was Arthur C. Clarke.[32]

These early publications were created as 'handwrittenzines' or 'carbonzines', each copy being produced individually, or duplicated copies made from a handwritten or typewritten original. Robert Hansen suggests that offset lithography has been used throughout the history of science fiction fanzines, although less frequently owing to cost. The Gestetner ink duplicator (a stencil printing process developed by David Gestetner in the late nineteenth century) was used until about 1980 when photocopying began to become the preferred production method.[33] Like most fanzines, sci-fi fanzines had print-runs of around 100–250 copies and were produced either on a duplicator or on hectograph or mimeograph machines. Warner reports that some popular science fiction zines, such as *Le Zombie* produced by Bob Tucker, had only 150 copies for distribution.[34]

The first Trekker fanzine began in 1967, a year after the start of the first run of the cult science fiction television series *Star Trek*. Fanzines included *Spockanalia*, which appeared in New York City as a ninety-page mimeograph with staples. Spock himself, the actor Leonard Nimoy, wrote a letter that was published in the issue 'wishing them luck'. Fanzines with a high profile at fan conventions included *Terran Times* (1969–early 1970s), *Thrall* and *Beyond Antares* (both early 1970s). Other contemporary science fiction television programmes such as *Doctor Who* and *Blake's 7*, and such Hollywood films as *Planet of the Apes* and (to a lesser extent) the *Star Wars* series, have generated cult followings and corollary fanzines.

Developing alongside the science fiction fanzines were the comic book fanzines. In some cases, comic fanzines would cross over, covering aspects of both genres and their fandom. David Kyle's fanzine *Fantasy World* (1936–n.d.) created, as its subtitle suggested, 'Cartoons of Imagination' as science fiction comic strips. The first British comic fanzine, *EC Fan Bulletin* (1953) – a mimeographed and limited-run fanzine for the small publisher Entertaining Comics – was produced by Bhob Stewart and inspired by science fiction fanzines. A year earlier in the United States, Superman was celebrated in Ted White's fifty-copy

edition *The Story of Superman* (1952), and Jimmy Taurasi's *Fantasy-Comics* (early 1950s) appeared, bringing together the genres of science fiction and Entertaining Comics' horror books.[35]

Just as contributors to the science fiction fanzines often became professional writers and artists, so comics zinesters followed a similar path. Future comics luminaries who got their start drawing for the early fanzines included Paul Neary and Brian Bolland. Noted as the first 'true comics fanzine' by Robert M. Overstreet in his *The Overstreet Comic Book Price Guide* is *Alter Ego*, which appeared in 1961 and through its readers' pages 'influenced profoundly the comics fan movement'.[36] In the UK in the 1960s comic titles flourished, including *Ka-Pow* (1967), *The Komix* (1963), *Conclusion* (mid-1960s), *Seminar* (1970), *Heroes Unlimited* (Anthony Roche, 1967–n.d.) and *Unicorn* (Mike Higgs and Phil Clarke, 1971). These fanzines dealt primarily with fantasy characters and superheroes – although in issue 4 of *Unicorn* its editors reproduced articles by Earl Gottschalk, Jr. from the *Los Angeles Times West* magazine, on 'comix', the underground X-rated comics of the period. This period represented a second wave of fan momentum, responding to the 'Second Heroic Age of Comics', as it is often dubbed, with its revival of the costumed hero.

Comic zines were important for the way in which they rediscovered old comics that were forgotten, overlooked or hard to find. They created an auteur scene around comics – especially with Jack Kirby, the creator of many superheroes, whose particular style of drawing was celebrated by a dedicated fan base. The fanzine producer maintains a unique position towards the comics, often concerned with the minutiae of fandom – highlighting inconsistencies in comic book stories, debating which the best publishers might be (Marvel or DC…?), and often taking an ironic but highly focused position on their hobby.

In music fanzines of the 1960s, the graphic language of cut-and-paste, hand-rendered type and/or Letraset (rub-down lettering) was starting to provide hints of a recognizable fanzine style that would fully emerge in the 1970s. At this stage, however, we see typographic

approaches strongly influenced by the designs offered by the underground broadsheets. Fanzines covered such musical genres as psychedelic, classical, jazz, country or pop, as well as specific groups or solo artists, including Elvis, the Beatles, Dusty Springfield and David Bowie. Early in the 1950s, music fanzines were prevalent in the United States; *The Rambler* (1957–58), devoted to folk music, ran for nine issues, while *Jazz Fan* (1958), edited by Bill Harry, ran for fourteen. Fanzines came into their heyday with the early rock-and-roll scene and emerged out of the traditions of early science fiction publishing.

But it was a new breed of music fans in the 1960s who took the form of the fanzine to its next level – both visually and in terms of journalistic tone. *Crawdaddy!* was the first magazine of American rock and roll and was started in February 1966 by Paul Williams, who had as a teenager been a science fiction fanzine producer. *Crawdaddy!* featured stories on Bob Dylan, Simon and Garfunkel, Donovan, Jefferson Airplane, the Rolling Stones and other rock musicians and predated the founding of *Rolling Stone* magazine. The term 'fanzine', according to Williams, was picked up by rock amateur publishers to describe their publications. However, *Crawdaddy!*, though similar to the format of science fiction fan publications, had aspirations to be a professional music magazine. The fact that Williams explicitly stated that the entire contents were copyrighted underlined this aim for mainstream recognition. *Crawdaddy!* sold for 25 cents and subscriptions were $1.00 for four issues. It was produced from 1966 to 1968 and then irregularly from 1993 to 2003, with Williams describing the publication in the latter era as 'definitely a fanzine'. It was sold as double-sided photocopies and used underlining, crossing out and typewriter texts, with occasional use of handwritten headlines.[37]

Mojo Navigator (1966–67) was a second and equally important American rock fanzine, founded by Greg Shaw, a West Coast record-collector. Shaw had been active in science fiction fandom in the 1960s and is cited as having introduced the term 'fanzine' into the vocabulary of music fandom. He defined fanzine in this case as a term 'for mags

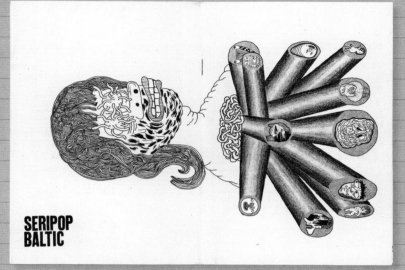

The lack of constraints in the fanzine format affords emerging artists space to experiment and to publish new works. *Seripop Baltic* (2009) is a contemporary collaboration between DIY artists, writers and zinesters, created as a one-off response to an exhibition by Montreal artists Seripop at the Baltic Centre for Contemporary Art in Gateshead, England. James Pallister's *Meat Magazine* (2004–) provides a biannual forum for up-and-coming writers and artists. This themed issue takes as its subject national identity.

which were about single bands or branches of the rock family tree. Other less specific publications he called genzines.'[38] Shaw went on to edit *Who Put the Bomp!* (1970–79), which ran for twenty-one issues, providing a forum for serious fans and professional critics who had something to say about the new music scene and record-collecting. The first few issues contained six pages of mimeographed typewritten texts and were produced with a print-run of thirty-five copies; from issue 4 a standard format was used (cover, table of contents, editorial, readers' pages, band and fanzine reviews, and feature story) and the size increased to twenty-two pages, using three-colour mimeography. Early American rock-and-roll zines such as this were to have an impact in terms of both content and form on subsequent music zines, including punk. The link is explicit in the case of, for example, fanzine producer Jonh [sic] Ingham, who was assistant editor and art director of *Who Put the Bomp!* and who moved to London in 1976, where a year later he would start the punk fanzine *London's Burning*.

Another zine, *Bam Balam* (1974–*c*. 1980s), was published quarterly by Brian Hogg in Dunbar, East Lothian, Scotland, employing a typographic treatment of the title that referenced 1960s counter-cultural psychedelia. The drop shadow and outline letterforms were hand-drawn and organic in their construction – a visual representation of the mid-1960s' sounds of garage and freakbeat. *Bam Balam* was a training ground for journalists, including Jon Savage, who remarks that the fanzine had 'an unacknowledged but important influence on British punk'.[39]

In the case of these genre fanzines – science fiction, comics, music – it may be argued that fans are constructing a hierarchy of taste. Their knowledge is highly specialized, whether it be a science fiction fan obsessing about Arthur C. Clarke, a comic fan celebrating Jack Kirby, or a music fan idolizing Elvis. It is here where the fan becomes an elitist – someone who knows what is in 'good taste' within his or her peer group. In a similar way, Thomas McLaughlin has proposed, 'zine writers and editors may legitimately be thought of as "elite fans", fans who have

accumulated the textual and historical expertise that places them above the average couch potato…'.[40] It is this specialist knowledge that has a significant role to play in unpacking how popular culture is understood, but is also critiqued in both textual and visual forms.

So Zines Are…?

We began with a description of a zine fair, and have explored some of the ways in which zines have moved from the underground into a more mainstream consciousness. This process has roots in the history of fandom and the formation of fan genres. However, it is also clear that when zines more latterly have made a more mainstream impact it is their DIY 'charm' that is at stake. If there is a stereotype of a zine in 2011 then it is of a photocopied, roughly hewn production, probably produced by a lone and slightly awkward youth. This is what the mainstream media focuses on: this is what they make television shows about. But equally clearly, those early roots have given rise to an infinite variety of zines, serving a hugely varied demographic. This book acknowledges that the 'zineness' of zines is crucial, but it also points to the potential of the form outside of narrow pigeonholes. The DIY revolution is here to stay.

Shocking Pink!!

YET ANOTHER   60p

SICK AND TWISTED?

Young Women's Magazine

WOW!!!!!

ZAP!

IT'S OUR CHOICE

Including
FIGHT EVIL! FIGHT ALTON!   A JACKIE INSERT
CUTTING CRITICISMS OF SOCIETY TODAY.
EXCLUSIVE POSTCARD FROM MICHELLE SHOCKED.

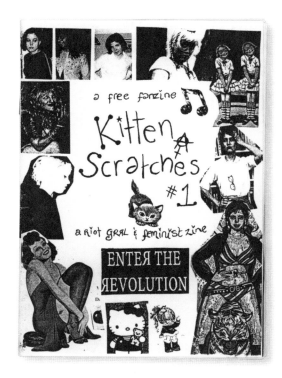

The DIY politics of the feminist movement resonates in *Shocking Pink* (1981–82, 1987–92), which became a voice for young women in the UK on issues such as sex, violence against women and queer politics. *Kitten Scratches* (1999) provided a more recent 'call to revolution' as part of the second-wave British riot grrrl movement. *DIY Life Zine* (2010) is a downloadable zine encouraging people to take their lives and communities into their own hands; subjects include unschooling, self-defence and barefoot living. *Beer Can Fanzine* (1999) is a photocopied fanzine that continues the tradition of punk DIY graphics.

NO⁶

NO NO

NOTHING IS TRUE

OMSK

JACKO BACKO

JACKSON; HEAVEN SENT?

LADS

WOMANS SPOT

HOLLY WOOD

SEA MONSTER

ISSUE NUMBER FOUR
MAY 1996
BI-MONTHLY
ONE POUND
+50p
THE *ONLY* MAGAZINE

NEGATIVE REACTION

—We got no values
No: 1 Feb '77 20p

IAN DURY
The Jam
Climax
plus reviews

BOO!

PRICE TWO QUID

MAKE YOUR OWN DAMN ALCOHOL

EASY AND CHEAP WAYS TO MAKE ALCOHOL AT HOME
COMPILED BY JARROD   ILLUSTRATED BY LAURE

THE COMPLETE **Soapmaker**

Tips, Techniques & Recipes for Luxurious Handmade Soaps

Norma Coney

the ABBREVIATED version

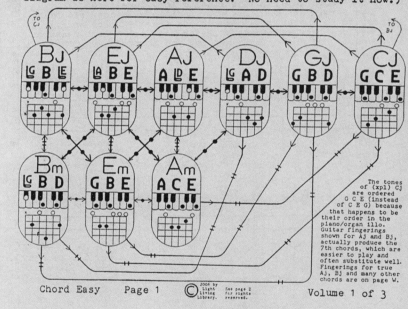

5th edition, full version, $5. Other versions described on p.Z.
Light Living Library, POB 190-ce, Philomath OR 97370-0190

CHORD EASY

HOW TO CHOOSE CHORDS. If you can play a melody or hum it true,
you can select chords to accompany it. This booklet can help
beginners start, and help the experienced expand harmonic
horizons. It can help you choose chords for almost any song:
old, new, popular, obscure - or one you compose.
    If you already know that most music has 12 tones per
octave labeled A B♭ B etc, and if you are able to jot down a
melody you know, continue below. If not, go to page Y.

CHORDS are combinations of tones that sound pleasing if played
together or in rapid succession. Two types of chords are used
most. I call them j chords and m chords. There are 12 of
each, one for each of the 12 tones per octave. Each j or m
chord consists of 3 tones. Example (xpl): Gj consists of G
and B and D tones. (More about terminology on page W.)
    Nine chords are enough to accompany well most pop/rock/
folk songs. WHICH 9 (of the 12 j and 12 m chords), depends on
how a song is played. This diagram gives the 9 chords for
songs played so they end with Gj; plus the tones in those 9
chords, and piano/organ and guitar fingerings. The connecting
lines show which chords most often follow one another. (This
diagram is here for easy reference. No need to study it now.)

The tones
of (xpl) Cj
are ordered
G C E (instead
of C E G) because
that happens to be
their order in the
piano/organ illo.
Guitar fingerings
shown for Aj and Bj,
actually produce the
7th chords, which are
easier to play and
often substitute well.
Fingerings for true
Aj, Bj and many other
chords are on page W.

Chord Easy   Page 1   Volume 1 of 3

While 1970s punkzines were generally
photocopied, the first issue of *Negative
Reaction* (1977-78) was printed using offset
litho, but it still drew on an emerging punk
aesthetic of typewritten texts and hand-
scrawled lettering. In *Nothing Is True*
(1992), featuring political rants on war and
misinformation, Letraset typefaces are
used to replicate the aesthetic of cut-out
lettering. In the satirical magazine *Omsk*
(c. late 1990s) the hand-rendered cover drawing
reinforces the cartoon-like character of
Michael Jackson. Camilla and Fred Deakin
moved the fanzine aesthetic into the 1990s
with the Acid House fanzine *Boo!* (early 1990s),
using overprinted fluorescent colours and
psychedelic lettering. The DIY spirit is
fostered in the three 'how-to' fanzines:
Make Your Own Damn Alcohol (2005), *The Complete
Soapmaker* (1997) and *Chord Easy* (2007).

Novae Terrae (1936–39), founded by Maurice K. Hanson for the Nuneaton branch of the Science Fiction League, went on to become the official mouthpiece for the Science Fiction Association (SFA) in 1937. It ran for 29 issues until it was renamed *New Worlds* in 1939. Many of the early covers were provided by Harry Turner, an early Royal Air Force radar technician and artist who had an early interest in science fiction and wrote his own fan magazine in the early 1940s.

Red Ink (early 1970s) was a satirical zine produced by Newcastle Universituns Socialist Society, which spoofed university life and the politics of the time. A quarterly comiczine, *Heroes Unlimited* (1967–n.d.) was produced on a Gestetner duplicator. The genres of comics and science fiction come together in this cover illustration, where the library of the future is a place where bodies rather than books are lent out. *KRLA Beat* (1965–68) was a zine compilation of newspaper articles on bands and music.

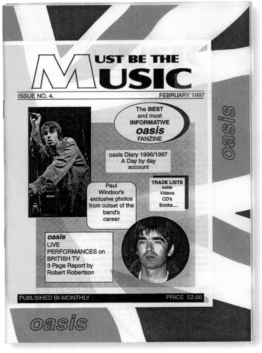

Pop music is one of the most prolific fanzine
genres. *Creep* (1990s) provided a forum for
commentary on 1990s bands, while at the
same time referencing the content of zines
outside the music scene, publishing clip
art from Sean Tejaratchi's *Crap Hound*. Suede
fans were treated to this double issue of
Glamourpuss (1996). The Oasis-inspired *Must
Be the Music* (1996–99) was a promotional zine
that ran 12 issues: the bi-monthly publication
boasted a readership of more than 2,000.
MaximumRocknRoll (1982–), a punkzine, began in
1982 as a newsprint booklet inside *Not So Quiet
on the Western Front*, a compilation album on
the Alternative Tentacles record label. This
authoritative publication is still going,
and to date more than 300 issues have been
published.

MAXIMUMROCKNROLL

ISSUE #221

OCT. 2001 $3.00

BORDERS
£2.75

THE NIGHTMARE CONTINUES...

...tales from the G-8 protests in Genova.

TOTALITÄR·SIN DIOS·RITCHIE WHITES·THE WONTONS·TRUE NORTH
REMAINS OF THE DAY·BOTTLES AND SKULLS·SOOPHiE NUN SQUAD

SLASH

VOLUME TWO NUMBER TWO   NOVEMBER 1978   FIFTY CENTS

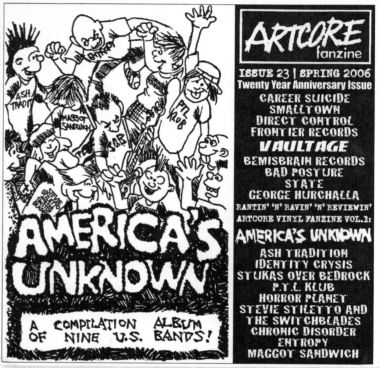

Slash (1977–80) was a highly respected US West Coast punk music broadsheet, with contributors from other zines including Tony Drayton (*Ripped & Torn*), Jon Savage (*London's Outrage*) and cartoonist Gary Panter (*Jimbo*). Meanwhile on the East Coast, *Punk* (1975–79), founded by John Holmstrom, featured a mix of British and American bands – here, punk princess Patti Smith. Some credit the title with giving punk music its name. *International Anthem* (1977–81) was produced by the anarchist collective Crass, whose hard-hitting agit-prop political messages were more counter-cultural than punk but who inspired generations with their views on animal liberation, human rights and government injustices. This issue of *Artcore* (1986–) celebrates its twentieth anniversary with a vinyl fanzine – a combined 40-page print zine and compilation album of nine rare or unreleased American punk rock and hardcore bands.

Following pages The format, offset-litho printing and monthly publication hark back to some of the early science fiction newsletters. *The Celestial Toyroom* (1976–) is a *Doctor Who* newsletter that claims to have reached more than 1,000 fans. The free two-page newsletter *Your Mornings Will Be Brighter* (c. 1990s) kept local fans up to date with listings of gigs held in and around Folkestone, Kent, England.

THE Celestial Toyroom

Number 7   July '79

INVASION

CUP FINAL DAY was more noticeable this year for the exodus of people away, rather than to the country's capital city, when DOCTOR WHO fans rendezvoused for the annual DWAS invasion of Blackpool. Whilst London might well be the base for the Society Executive, and venue of PANOPTICON III, Blackpool can be regarded as the Northern centre of Doctor Who fandom, with the largest of two exhibitions in Britain featuring props costumes and hardware from the programme.

MORE THAN 40 Members of the Society, from far afield as the Surbiton Local Group and West Midlands 'Beyond Cygnus-A' had collaborated and booked out an entire hotel. Organiser, J. Jeremy Bentham, who drove a mini-bus of fans up to Blackpool from London was overwhelmed at the success of the Weekend, and is hopeful of further activities in the future amongst the Society 'hard-core'.

WHO

PUTS HIS FOOT IN IT

OCEANS IN THE SKY - the film made by the D. W. A. S. drama dept. is now complete, bar the special effects. Premiered at the Tom Baker Pen-Pal Club Social Event on May 26, the full version is hoped to be ready for PANOPTICON III.

The film has taken three years to make at a cost of £3,000. The sets include a magnificent TARDIS console which was made by Reg Spillet who also plays a part in the film. The whole of the TARDIS interior was built on a stage cannibalising existing materials. An original score has been written for the soundtrack by Tunbridge Wells D. W. A. S. Member Mark Ayres. A version of the original television theme will be used to open the adventure concocted by Owen Tudor and Paul Howden-Simpson. 'Oceans' boasts a cast of 20 actors, including Leo Adams as 'The Doctor'. Leo is a professional actor of 30 years and had his own rep company.

The last session was filmed in a sewage works with Mr. Adams having some unfortunate accidents with the co-ordination of his feet in relation to the nature of the location, which broke up his co-star, Diane Woodley.

There is already a poster available of the film, and a paperback book is planned explaining how the film was made.

IMPORTANT ANNOUNCEMENT
ALL MEMBERS WITH MEMBERSHIP CODES BEGINNING "8 A G" PLEASE SEE 'RE-APPLICATION TO MEMBERSHIP' LETTER ENCLOSED, AS THIS IS THE FINAL EDITION OF CT OF YOUR PRESENT YEAR.

SUMMER REPEATS
The repeat this summer of 'The Pirate Planet' seems much more certain, with probably that well-known cure for insomnia, 'The Androids of Tara' to follow.

Just six weeks after booking for the convention opened we have been forced to close our registration files. 375 of you have registered and this response is intensely heatening. However, we do still have 16 places left for Sunday only and if you wish to register please send £3.50 to Deanne with a registration form and sae. Now an apology to those Members who have had to wait a few weeks for confirmations of their registrations. This was because the accomadotion was massively over-subscribed. Happily, we have been able to extend this facility. As regards to paying for accommodation please send your cheque/postal order payable to Deanne as soon as possible. Whenever you write with a query on the convention it would help us if you could quote your convention number. The good news is that we will almost definately be able to show the entire first story consisting of four full episodes. Several guests have replied to our invitations including Dick Mills, Graham Williams and Douglas Adams. If you are unable to come we can offer supporting Membership costing £1.00 for which you will recieve all bulletins, a copy of the convention booklet and a badge. If you want to take this up, please write to Mark enclosing an sae, with your cheque/PO payable to Deanne. Lots more next month!
David, Deanne and Mark.

WRITERS POOL MEETING

The venue: 287 Carlton Hill, Nottingham. The purpose: The launching of the third edition of COSMIC MASQUE. On May 26 at the home of John Peel, an interesting discussion followed the official launching of the third Writers Pool publication. One topic of discussion was the way the Doctor had changed and it was decided that the transisition from Hartnell to Troughton was a rejuvenation-the body returning to an earlier age. Troughton was changed into Pertwee by the Time Lords. His cells destroyed by the Metebellis Spider, the Doctor was as good as dead. Even the power of the TARDIS could not repair his body and effect a rejuvenation. Cho Je came to his rescue and regenerated the cells of his body and he became a younger, different personality. But what will happen to the Doctor next time?

LATE NEWS
LOCAL GROUP ANNOUNCEMENT

We are pleased to announce the official opening of our eleventh Local Group: Michael Nicholson, 25 Long Bank, Birtley, Chester-le-Street, County Durham. A full list of the existing Local Groups is on page two and three.

May 1990 ... May 1990 ... May 1990 ... May 1990 ... May 1990 ... May 1990 ... May 1990 ... May

YOUR MORNINGS WILL BE BRIGHTER

FREE ... FREE ... FREE ...   FREE .... FREE ... FREE ...

The Arena, Vienna

What a momentus year mighty '90 is turning out to be – Tyson knocked out, the West Indies beaten in the first test on their own soil, Liverpool beaten by Crystal Palace in the F.A. Cup semi final, Mandela free, Thatcher (or Torture as one Austrian is to pronounce it) with her back to the wall, a new era unfolding in Europe, Poll Tax anger swelling up ... and Folkestone four-piece TREES spreading their gospel overseas, hot on the heels of their three-date "Hit the North" weekend and first local gig of the new decade.

It's Friday 13th and all is well. Heathrow Airport is woken from its slumber by the arrival of Matt Goss, chased by a bevy of emotional girls; there's a party from Sheffield United Football Club present as well, cult-hero of the 70's Tony Currie amongst their ranks.

I have a very tight schedule ... my plane to Munich is delayed by half an hour ... I'm going to miss my train ... but no, the train's late as well, perhaps the Germans are human after all.

Vienna's indoor Arena is a Marquee-style venue, indeed Mark E.'s The Fall play here the next week. The gig starts at 8pm and goes on until 5am, it's quite a rave, there's about 500 people present.

TREES are on fifth out of six, due on at about midnight after CLOUDS OVER CHRYSLER (from Linz in Austria), the excellent BOMB CIRCLE and OCCIDENTIAL BLUE HARMONY LOVERS, both from Vienna; and German/American hardcore act SPERMBIRDS. The band are tired, the acts go on for longer than had been expected, they finally hit the stage at 1.30am; by now the crowd has mingled, but there's still an expectant faithful to entertain, radio

airplay of their "Love Child" EP had gone down well. Those who witness the spectacle insist that it will go down in legendary terms within the city.

TREES vocalist Jason MacKenzie has been mysteriously left out of Sounds' "Rock Nutters" series so far, tonight he's demented, revelling in the clean air and friendly atmosphere of a city he's clearly taken to, dancing around his large stage. Tonight he's making the Viennese whirl in their city of Mozart, Beethoven, Schubert and the Strauss family. Guitarist Richard Carlile is also in party mood, signing autographs, pulling some extraordinary faces and even contributing some backing vocals. There must be something in the air.

The band are called back for The Doors' "L.A. Woman" and The Stranglers' "Pretty Face" and then it's goodnight Vienna. Tom Jones' "It's Not Unusual" is left out of the set tonight, now that would be breaking down the cultural barriers a little too far.

....

THE SHEDS unveiled their new line up at a Hunt Sab benefit gig at Bottoms in Folkestone on Good Friday. Bass player Dave "DJ" Jones left the band at the end of last month. They acted quickly to switch drummer Matthew "Mole" Lambert to bass and recruit new drummer Michael Warren (also of Big Blue Dirt Box, formerly of The Cutlery). EPIDEMIC and THE SKYDOGS completed the line up that night. See the new-looked SHEDS at Heroes in Folkestone on Wednesday May 9th.

All enquiries to: RICHARD MURRILL, 9 Gainsborough Close, Folkestone, Kent CT19 5NB.

SPEED KILLS!

#7
$4.50

futurism/virgil exner/fsa/unwound/art&text
BONUS 10" phonorecord featuring: back off
cupids, flying saucer attack, a handful of dust,
and portastatic

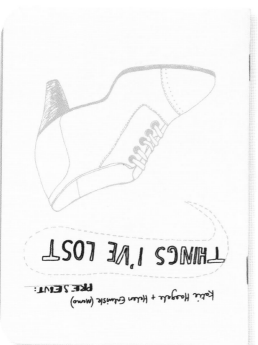

Without conventional publishing constraints, fanzines can take on different formats and methods of production. *Speed Kills* (1990s) follows in the tradition of 1970s punk fanzines that inserted flexi-discs into their page: here a 120-page newsprint fanzine accompanies the 7-inch vinyl. *Things I've Found/Things I've Lost* (2009) is a 25-copy limited edition split zine, opening from both front and back, with two screen-printed front covers and interior pages on pink photocopy paper. This zine reads in two directions, enumerating items that the producer has found by the side of the road plus others that have been lost. The 1980s Swedish fanzine *Straight from the Grooveyard* includes a cassette tape featuring top Swedish garage and psych bands such as Roky Erickson, Crimson Shadows and Creeps.

Hand-rendered typography features in this set of fanzines spanning the 1960s and 1970s. This 1998 issue of *Freak Beat* (1980s–90s), produced by Richard Allen, founder of the now defunct Delerium Records, harks back to the counter-cultural imagery and typographic treatment of the original European rock music genre of the 1960s. Inserted into the zine is a 1987 flexi-disc featuring the Steppes' only full version of their single 'History Hates No Man'. This edition of Paul Williams's classic rock fanzine *Crawdaddy!* (1966–2003) includes pieces by future rock luminaries Jon Landau and Sandy Pearlman, as well as photographs by one Linda Eastman – soon to be Linda McCartney. Published twice a year, *Bam Balam* (1974–c. 1980s) was a 1960s pop music fanzine, which Mark Perry credits as predating by four issues his own influential punkzine *Sniffin' Glue*. This issue includes items on Manfred Mann, the Beach Boys and Buffalo Springfield. *Sniffin' Flowers* (1977–n.d.) was produced as a literature and art zine by Sue, Simon, Andrew and Jackie as their 'first excursion into tha' depths of print…'. It features an interview with British writer Michael Moorcock, who talks about his early career and his first contribution to a fanzine at the age of eleven.

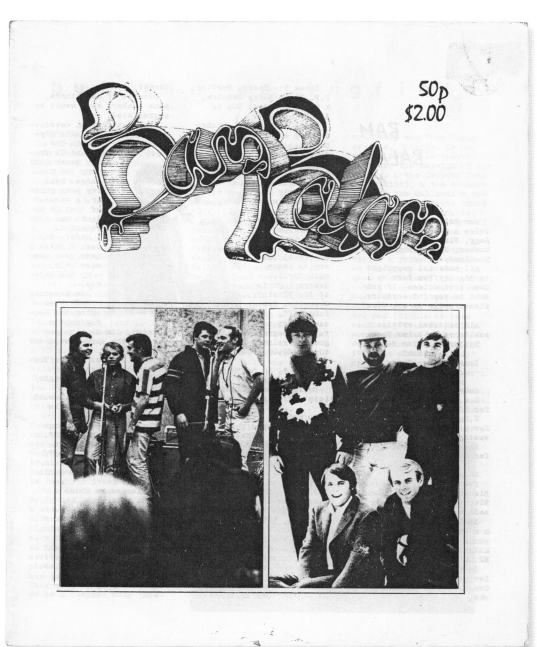

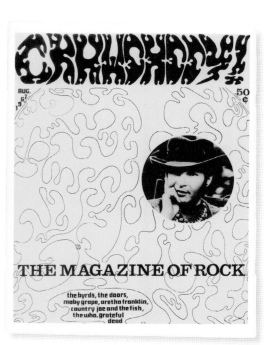

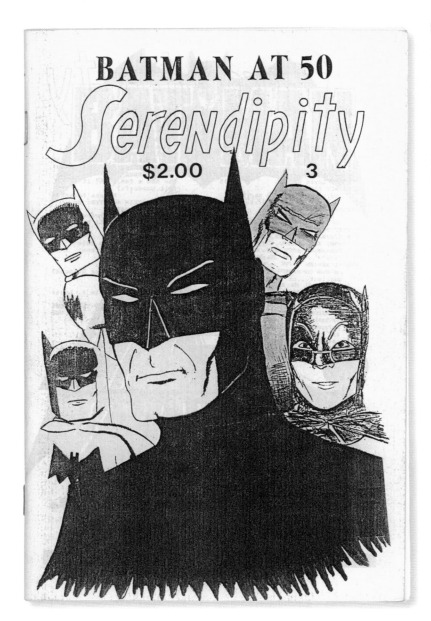

The 1980s fanzine *Serendipity* looks back to the previous decade's television shows, such as *The Man from U.N.C.L.E.*, *Batman* and *Star Trek*. In this issue *Batman*'s fiftieth birthday is celebrated with drawings of the inner workings of the Bat Cave. *Fear and Loathing* (early 1990s–) is one of the longest-running and most influential punk fanzines in the UK (issue 61 was released in 2010), with densely typewritten text and colour-copied covers. With many of their issues, inserts for indie-label 7-inch singles were also included – this issue, it was the American female punk band N.Y. Loose, helping them to develop a UK fan base. *Revolting* (1993–n.d.), 'a publication to raise social awareness and human potential', is printed on recycled paper. It was a zine that focused on political injustices: this issue also has articles on recycling, sustainability and environmental concerns.

Console (1980s) was a *Doctor Who* sci-fi
zine that contained reviews of the British
television show as well as examples of
original scripts. It also offered a 'Console
Quiz' crossword puzzle for the diehard
fan. *Typography Papers* (1996–) was a formal
exercise for students at the University
of Reading, looking at ways of presenting
typography for reading; it formed a precursor
to the academic series 'Typography Papers'.
Funk n' Groove (1990s) featured Erik Estrada,
star of the American cop show *CHiPS*, on the
cover of its first issue. The obsession of the
zine's co-producers for 'collecting, idolizing
and worshipping the greatest stars and icons
of the last three decades' is reflected in
their nostalgic references to, for example,
The Brady Bunch and Boy George.

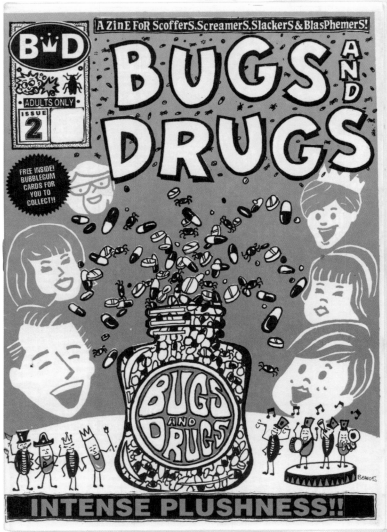

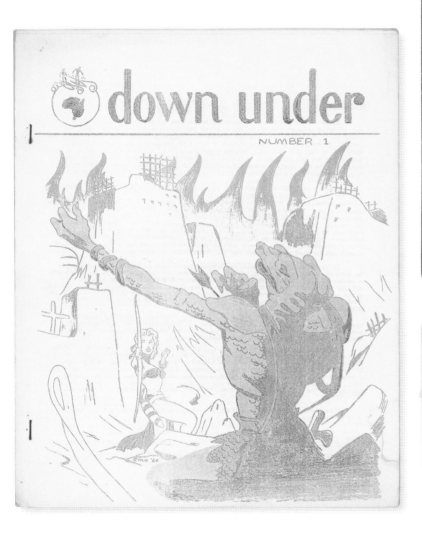

Illustration was always key to fanzine covers: *Punk and Disorderly* (1990s) has a provocative punk drawing on its front cover, *Bugs and Drugs* (1992–96) an 'adults only' warning. *Brumble* was published for the 1965 convention of the Birmingham Fiction Group. *Le Collectionneur de Bandes Dessinées* (1977–2008) became a leading publication on comic-strip historical research. The Australian *Down Under* (mid-1960s) was devoted primarily to comics and fandom coming out of Australia and England and was distributed internationally. *FOOM* (1973–78), or 'Friends of Ol Marvel', was a Captain America Marvel comic fanzine with early contributions by Stan Lee. This final issue of *Comics Unlimited* (1970–79) billed itself as a comics-oriented article zine.

The *Space Times* (1950s–60s) cover illustration by Harry Turner is drawn directly on to offset litho plates and printed in mahogany and green inks. *Thanks for the Memory* (c. 1977–c. 1980) was a *Doctor Who* fanzine that celebrated the English actress Elisabeth Sladen, who was known for her three-year role as the investigative journalist Sarah Jane Smith in the popular British television series. *Personal Log 01* (1980s) was a non-profit, fan-written fanzine dedicated to *Star Trek*, with a print-run of 200 copies: the cover depicts Lieutenant Uhura, who features as the main character study for this issue of short stories and poems. The comiczine *Heroes Unlimited* (1967–n.d.) was originally written about American superheroes, but in this issue its editor asks readers for their thoughts on including one article per issue on British comic superheroes or fantasy characters as well.

Comiczine producers continued to dedicate
their publications to both mainstream
superheroes and underground comix characters.
The Komix (1963) comprised John Wright's
original stories, plus reviews of other
zines. Inspired by science fiction zines
and devoted to American superheroes. *Ka-Pow*
(1967-n.d.) also included a comic strip by Mike
Higgs. *Nightmare* (1969) was a fantasy- and
comiczine, containing reviews of now-cult
films, records and comic conventions. Five
hundred copies of the comix showcase split
zine *Dead Duck/Corpsemeat Comix* (1991) were
produced, reprinting two seminal strips.
Dead Duck (1988) and *Corpsemeat Comix* (1983).
Zum! (1991-c. 1993) was a UK small press zine
that featured articles, reviews and strips
from the world of alternative comix. *The
Golden Age Fanzine* (1970s) featured Marvel
superheroes and also the history of detective
comics. The professional publication *Graphic
Story World* (1971-73) had contributing editors
across the world.

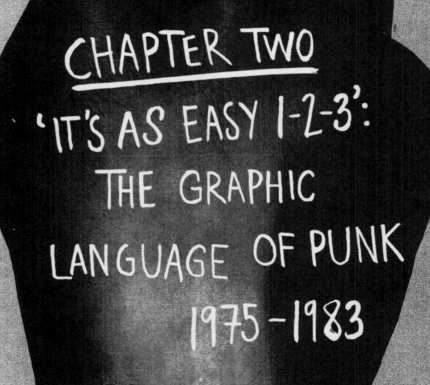

CHAPTER TWO

'IT'S AS EASY 1-2-3':
THE GRAPHIC
LANGUAGE OF PUNK
1975–1983

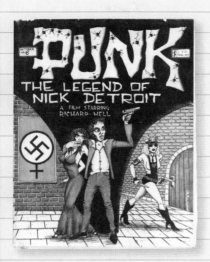

The Situationist-inspired *Suburban Press* (c. 1970) used cut-up graphics and agit-prop images to present a distinct anti-design graphic language, which would help define a British zine style. In the United States, *Punk* (1975-79) founded by John Holmstrom, combined punk and comics to 'galvanize a movement'. Mark Perry's first issue of the punkzine *Sniffin' Glue* (1976-77) focused on The Ramones' London gigs and credits the band's song 'Now I wanna sniff some glue' as inspiration for its title.

Identifying the specific moment when punk began is difficult, as is a precise definition of the term. Mark Perry, founder of the punk fanzine *Sniffin' Glue*, suggested in issue 1,

> nobody can define punk-rock, it's all about rock in its lowest form – on the level of the streets. Kids jamming together in their dad's garage, poor equipment, tight clothes, empty heads (nothing to do now you've left school) and model-shops. Punk-rock's all those things.[1]

The first wave of punk has generally been accepted to have had a three-year life span, beginning with the depression and drought of 1976 and ending with the death of Sid Vicious of the Sex Pistols in 1979.[2] On the other hand, punk should not be defined entirely by the career of the Sex Pistols – however influential they may have been – nor by the history promoted by their manager and publicist, Malcolm McLaren. Critics such as the American journalist Greil Marcus would argue that in the United States it began in New York around 1973–74, well before the Sex Pistols, with such bands as Television and the Ramones. Punk's second wave continued into the 1980s with the rise of anarcho-punk, street punk, hardcore and the neo-fascist punk movements.[3] Punk fanzines aligned themselves to these new categories of punk politics, providing a new wave of fanzine activity. In the 1990s and 2000s punk continued to thrive in its various forms, spurred on by newer publications such as *MaximumRocknRoll* (1982–) and *Punk Planet* (1994–2007) (both USA).

Defining Punk Agendas

Punk was not only about music and class politics, but also had an impact on fashion, fine art, film, comics, novels and, of course, fanzines. Mark Perry had developed his own brand of 'punk journalism', for example, and he actively encouraged others to participate in 'having a go yourself'. Punk fanzines also served another, equally important purpose. During the early rise of punk, many fans considered them to be the only reliable way of disseminating information about the music and the movement itself. Dave McCullough, a one-time fanzine producer and then a journalist for the music paper *Sounds*, reported in 1979 on the position of British fanzines:

> you didn't know where to look in case you were being 'sold out'. You could actually 'look up to' an "institution" like *Sniffin' Glue* and at least TRUST that they were going the whole way. It gave you The Word and put what the press said (which you always *did* suspect) in a rigid perspective.[4]

Perry was very much aware of his new-found position as a punk provocateur and of the influence he had on other fanzine producers. He speculated that the success of his fanzine was due to the fact that he was honest and told readers exactly what he thought, using a graphic language adopted from American rock-and-roll fanzines. In punk as in other genres, fanzines were written for and produced by those 'in the know'. They had first-hand experience as participants at the gigs and were often allowed access to backstage. They interviewed bands directly, frequently getting an exclusive story. Although punk was almost immediately picked up by the national and music press (the first review of a Sex Pistols gig was written by Jonh [sic] Ingham and published in *Sounds* in April 1976) the stories in the mainstream press were often sensationalized. Punk was viewed as frightening and aggressive, with tabloids such as the *Daily Mirror* and the *People* using scare stories to criticize the morals of the burgeoning youth culture.

Punk fanzines may have been driven by political agendas, including class politics and critiques of mainstream political ideologies, but they also reflected the fact that punk had emerged from a position of knowingness about artistic practice and its history. Legs McNeil in particular, co-founder of *Punk* magazine (1975–79), traced punk back to the antics of art-world provocateur Andy Warhol, and other critics too have argued that fanzines had their stylistic origins in Warhol's *Interview* magazine, which represented 'the same sense of slapped together necessity' and the same '"artless" reproduction of every spoken word'.[5]

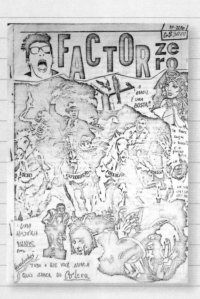

Punk obsessions varied internationally. *Search & Destroy* (1977–79), which came out of San Francisco from editor V. Vale, featured an interview with the American writer William Burroughs. The first Brazilian punkzine was *Factor Zero* (1980–81), which had a passion for South American bands and comics (the DIY graphic language was clearly borrowed from the British model). *Total Control* (1977) was a small booklet about The Clash included in the first German punk fanzine, *The Ostrich* (late 1970s).

Perry and McNeil thus provide two starting points not only for exploring the potential difference in writing styles of punk but also for defining the graphic language of punk fanzines.

A Graphic Language of Resistance

Can we identify a graphic language of resistance? Resistance, in this case, is taken to mean a 'refusal to comply', as in, for example, resisting authority. Stephen Duncombe suggests that through the process of resistance we are freed from the 'limits and constraints of the dominant culture'. In turn, 'cultural resistance' allows us to 'experiment with new ways of seeing and being'.[6] In fanzines this may be represented through content, or graphically, or both, where rules and prescriptions are disregarded intentionally. Such strategies are easily understood within the subculture and so provide a focal point and help to establish a community of like-minded individuals.

Punk fanzine precursors that began to define what a distinctive graphic language of punk might be include Jamie Reid's *Suburban Press* (1970–75) – a Situationist-inspired publication that, along with *Sub* magazine and *King Mob*, provided a bridge between the hippie press and punk fanzines.[7] Situationists 'characterized modern capitalist society as an organization of spectacles', arguing that 'people are removed and alienated not only from the goods they produce and consume, but also from their own experiences, emotions, creativity, and desires'.[8]

Reid established the connection visually between Dada, Situationism and punk, suggesting that 'probably Dada's finest moment was [when it was] on the streets and accessible to working class kids'.[9] He described his job as being graphically to translate and simplify the Situationist use of political rhetoric and jargon. For example, *Suburban Press* critiqued local council politics and contextualized it with excerpts from Situationist graphics and texts. The cover of *Suburban Press* No. 1 (1970) uses a dot-patterned image of a suburban house with the idealistic slogan 'Fresh from the Suburbs', playing on the location

of Reid's press in Croydon, Surrey, as well as making ironic comment on the 'capitalist ideal'. The publication uses typewritten texts created on an IBM 72 typewriter.

While Jamie Reid and others were exploring the possibilities offered by Situationism and the graphic languages of other art movements, a second source for a fanzine language was emerging. Mark Perry's *Sniffin' Glue* (1976–77) was so influential that tributes to his success were witnessed in the way the fanzine itself was referenced graphically: for example the second issue of *Murder by Fanzine* (c. 1983, Scotland) pastes a flyer promoting issue 6 of *Sniffin' Glue* over the head of a guitar-player, thereby rendering him anonymous. Nonetheless Perry is careful not to accept the 'first fanzine' tag, instead citing earlier rock-and-roll publications such as Greg Shaw's *Who Put the Bomp!* (1970–79) and Brian Hoggs's *Bam Balam* (1974–c. 1980s) as precursors to his own.

Despite an emerging set of punk 'conventions', which included the small, stapled format, 'spontaneous' page layout, the production values of the photocopier, and a mixture of typographic treatments such as cut-and-paste, 'ransom notes', and handwritten and typewritten letterforms, each fanzine maintained an individualized approach. The manner in which the graphic marks, visual elements and their layout were presented reflected not only the message, but also by default the individual hand of the fanzine producer. This is evident in a comparison of covers from three of the more prominent fanzines produced in the late 1970s. Charlie Chainsaw, for example, in his first issue of *Chainsaw* (1977–85, London) used stencil letters for the title and a series of cut-out newspaper texts collaged with a photograph of the Sex Pistols and a reference to its namesake, an image from the poster of the film *The Texas Chainsaw Massacre*. Mark Perry in the July 1976 issue of *Sniffin' Glue* employed his own quickly produced handwriting scrawl, where letters were all caps and visually presented in the same weight. And Tony Drayton's *Ripped & Torn* (November 1976–79, Glasgow) took a more formal approach, combining one photographic image of

The regions of Britain had their own spin
on punk. *Ripped & Torn* (1976-79), produced
by Tony Drayton, ran for 18 issues, moving
between Glasgow and London. For a while it
was a serious competitor to *Sniffin' Glue*.
City Fun (1977-84) was produced in Manchester,
England, and was initially run by a collective,
providing early coverage of Factory Records
and the Hacienda Club. *Alternative Sounds*
(1980-81) ran for 18 issues and focused mainly
on the Coventry music scene with such bands
as The Silence, but also covered other English
Midlands towns.

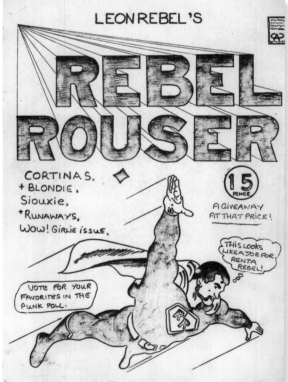

Friendly and sometimes not-so-friendly rivalry characterized the tone of the punkzine heyday. *In the City* (1977–80), one of the more famous productions, complains about the number of zine producers who sold out to join the music press, including journalists Danny Baker and Dave McCullough. The focus for this issue is the anarcho-punk band Crass (logo by David King). Mick Mercer's *Panache* (1976–92), one of the longest-running punkzines in the United Kingdom, emphasizes its 'value for money' by playing with cut-out advertising. In *Rebel Rouser* (late 1970s) Leon Rebel's hand-drawn effort offers a punk poll to keep readers interested.

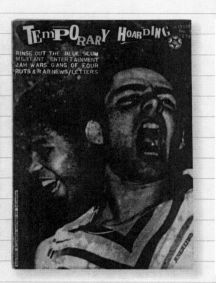

Almost as soon as punk emerged it was co-opted by more mainstream interests. *Anarchy in the UK* (1976) was a broadsheet published by the Sex Pistols' management, Glitterbest, as a collage of photographs and news clippings about the band. *Trick* (1977) was another broadsheet, more akin to *Sounds* or the *New Musical Express*, and included a range of advertisers. Designed by a group of graphic designers, *Temporary Hoarding* (1976–81) was the mouthpiece of Rock Against Racism with a circulation of 12,000 in 1979.

the Damned with handwritten upper- and lower-case lettering in a hierarchical sequence from the title, the stories promised inside to the smaller, self-effacing tag lines: 'This is Too fantastic … buy it Now'. These examples, in spite of their individual handling of the basic graphic notation of fanzines, established overall a recognizable punk identity.

Post-1979: Anarcho-punk

By the 1980s a vocabulary of punk had been absorbed into fanzine production. But a more radical strain of politics was becoming evident. The graphic language that followed promoted a more aggressive and provocative approach, as, in the 1980s, the second wave of punk gave rise to more aggressive and visual styles. The most interesting of these were centred around the anarcho-punk movement. This was a politically committed strain of the subculture headed by the band-cum-commune Crass. Crass were responsible for a number of publications and fanzines, including *International Anthem: Nihilist Newspaper for the Living* (1977), which featured text by Penny Rimbaud and the remarkable photo-collages of Gee Vaucher. These were reminiscent of the work of political artists John Heartfield and Hannah Höch, and the fanzine's format was similar to the previous decade's counter-culture broadsheets.

Other fanzines similarly made much of anarchist iconography. *Cobalt Hate* (1984) utilized the circle A in inventive fashion, and the crowded, claustrophobic appearance of the cover mimicked the anger of the hardcore anarcho-punk music. Its front cover made explicit the producer's political leanings with hand-rendered slogans and phrases such as 'nihilism.propeganda', 'Black Flag Anarchists' and 'Police opression: Police Faschism'. The intentional misspellings and hand-scrawled writing conveyed a sense of immediacy and irreverence towards publishing conventions. This added another level to the punk aesthetic.

Other fanzines would follow in the 1990s in the United States. *Profane Existence* (1989–2008), for example, was founded in

Minneapolis, Minnesota, and was one of the largest of the anarcho-punk fanzines in North America. During this period, it took on numerous formats – eight-page magazine, broadsheet newspaper, perfect-bound book – depending on editorial positions and budgets. *Profane Existence* now exists only via the Web (although fundraising events provide a glimmer of hope for the relaunch of the print version), and continues with international coverage of the anarcho-punk movement and its related community and lifestyle news, including DIY health care, self-help primers and, of course, politically aware music.

Punk Sites of Resistance

Thus, we can speak of fanzines as places of cultural 'resistance'. They offer fans a 'free space for developing ideas and practices', and a visual space unencumbered by formal design rules and visual expectations.[10] Fanzines embraced punk's do-it-yourself attitude. As one member of the punk community reflected, 'our fanzines were always clumsy, unprofessional, ungrammatical, where design was due to inadequacy rather than risk'.[11] Yet as the plethora of punk-inspired fanzines materialized, a unique visual identity emerged, with its own set of graphic rules and a do-it yourself approach, neatly reinforcing punk's new-found 'political' voice. Malcolm McLaren, manager of the Sex Pistols and self-proclaimed creator of punk, was quick to point out, '"Anarchy in the UK" is a statement of self-rule, of ultimate independence, of do-it-yourself'.[12] As if to punctuate this point graphically, the producer of the punk fanzine *Sideburns* (1976) famously provided a set of simple instructions and a diagram of how to play three chords – A, E, G – alongside the command 'Now Form a Band'. As with its music and fashion, punk advocated that everyone go out and produce a fanzine. As independent and self-published publications, fanzines became vehicles of subcultural communication and played a fundamental role in the construction of punk identity and a political community.

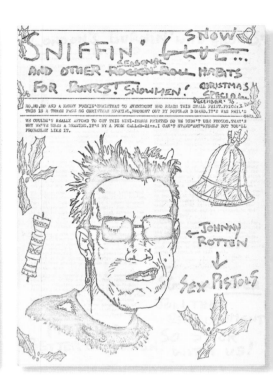

While Jamie Reid and others were exploring the possibilities offered by Situationism and the graphic languages of art movements, a second source for a graphic fanzine style was emerging. *Sniffin' Glue* (1976–77) by Mark Perry et al. has been credited as the first British punk fanzine. It ran for 14 issues and incorporated a spiky aesthetic made up of typewriter lettering, handwriting, cartoons (for example by Savage Pencil) and photographs of gigs (for example by Jill Furmanovsky). Issue 1 identified itself as 'for punks' and as a mouthpiece for their music and anger: it had a run of 50 copies. By the last issue in 1977, the zine had a circulation of between 10,000 and 15,000. Although Perry claimed to have been inspired by previous rock-and-roll publications, he succeeded in initiating a DIY style that captured the zeitgeist and that provided a counterpoint to the mainstream music press.

SNIFFIN' GLUE...
AND OTHER ROCK'N'ROLL HABITS, FOR A BUNCH OF BLEEDIN' IDIOTS! NOVEMBER '76.

If you actually like is rag you must be one of the idiots we write it for. Price:

EDDIE AND THE HOT RODS
LIVE AND ALBUM REVIEWS.

THE SUBWAY SECT PLUS CHELSEA

CHAINSAW

M.J. WELLER

BLURT   SURGICAL PENIS KLINIK   PLUS...The Dancing Di Midnits & the Lemon Boys, Anarchy, Cartoo Plasmatics (Ugh), and lots of bad taste!

NO. 11   30p

Two of the more visually interesting successors to *Sniffin' Glue* were *Chainsaw* (1977-85) and *Panache* (1976-92). The former, created by Charlie Chainsaw, ran irregularly for 14 issues, with later examples experimenting with an innovative use of colour covers. It also featured ugly but vivacious illustrations and cartoons by Michael J. Weller and Willie D. Also characteristic was the missing letter 'n' from its typewritten text, which was filled in by hand.

Following pages *Panache* was created by Mick Mercer as a 12-page, stapled and photocopied publication that flaunted its typographic mistakes, overcrowded pages and grainy photographic images. Its entertainingly claustrophobic style reflected a fan's desire to pack in as much information as possible.

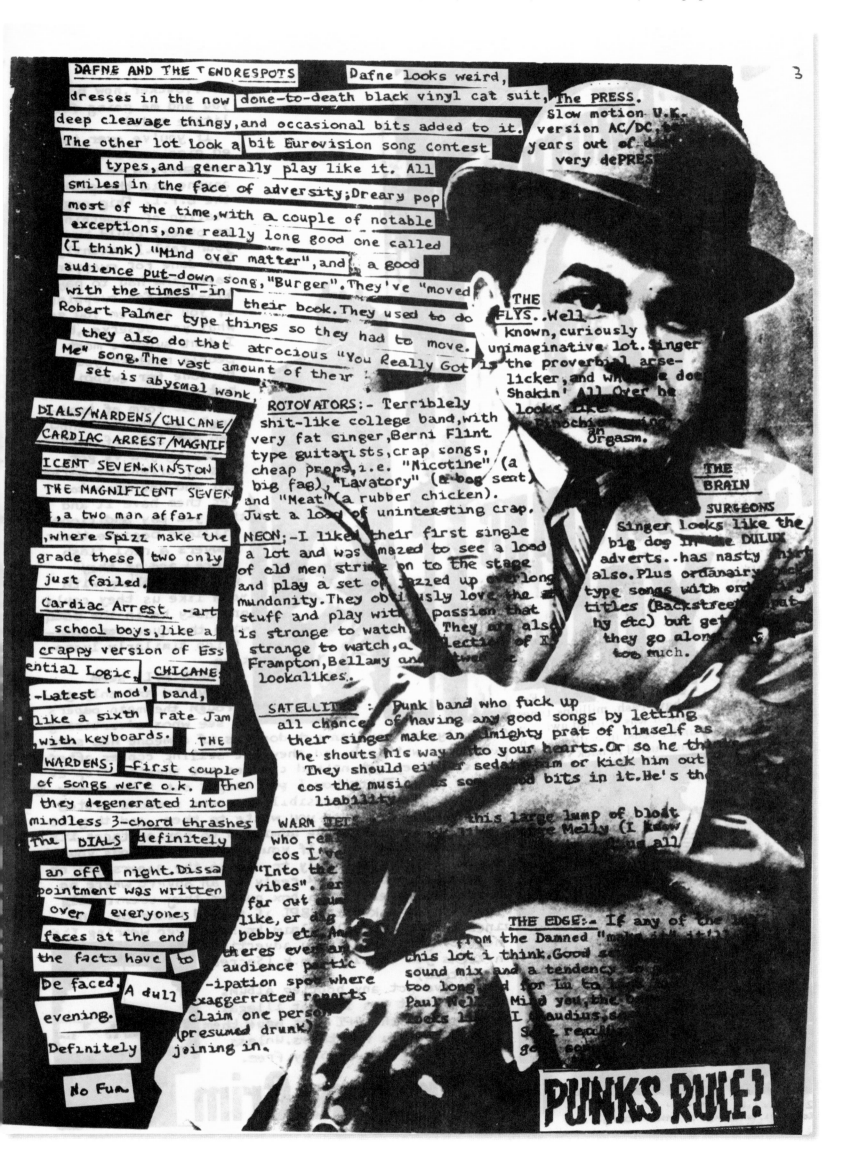

3

DAFNE AND THE TENDRESPOTS Dafne looks weird, dresses in the now done-to-death black vinyl cat suit, deep cleavage thingy, and occasional bits added to it. The other lot look a bit Eurovision song contest types, and generally play like it. All smiles in the face of adversity; Dreary pop most of the time, with a couple of notable exceptions, one really long good one called (I think) "Mind over matter", and a good audience put-down song, "Burger". They've "moved with the times"-in their book. They used to do Robert Palmer type things so they had to move. they also do that atrocious "You Really Got Me" song. The vast amount of their set is abysmal wank,

The PRESS. Slow motion U.K. version AC/DC, years out of d... very dePRES...

THE FLYS.. Well known, curiously unimaginative lot. Singer is the proverbial arse-licker, and when he does Shakin' All Over he looks like Pinochio having an Orgasm.

DIALS/WARDENS/CHICANE/ CARDIAC ARREST/MAGNIF ICENT SEVEN-KINSTON **THE MAGNIFICENT SEVEN**, a two man affair, where Spizz make the grade these two only just failed. **Cardiac Arrest** -art school boys, like a crappy version of Ess ential Logic. **CHICANE**: -Latest 'mod' band, like a sixth rate Jam, with keyboards. **THE WARDENS**; -first couple of songs were o.k. then they degenerated into mindless 3-chord thrashes The **DIALS** definitely an off night. Dissa pointment was written over everyones faces at the end the facts have to be faced. A dull evening. Definitely

No Fun.

ROTOVATORS:- Terriblely shit-like college band, with very fat singer, Berni Flint type guitarists, crap songs, cheap props, i.e. "Nicotine" (a big fag), "Lavatory" (a bog seat), and "Meat" (a rubber chicken). Just a load of uninteresting crap. **NEON**;-I liked their first single a lot and was amazed to see a load of old men stride on to the stage and play a set of jazzed up overlong mundanity. They obviously love the stuff and play with a passion that is strange to watch. They are also strange to watch, a selection of Frampton, Bellamy and between lookalikes.

SATELLITES: Punk band who fuck up all chances of having any good songs by letting their singer make an almighty prat of himself as he shouts his way into your hearts. Or so he thinks. They should either sedate him or kick him out cos the music has some good bits in it. He's the liability.

WARM JETS ...this large lump of bloat ...re Melly (I know ...cos I've ...us all "Into the vibes". ...er far out ...like, er dig bebby etc. An theres even an audience partic -ipation spot where exaggerrated reports claim one person (presumed drunk) joining in.

THE BRAIN SURGEONS Singer looks like the big dog in the DULUX adverts..has nasty shirt also. Plus ordanairy rock type songs with ordinary titles (Backstreet Apat hy etc) but get they go along too much.

THE EDGE:- If any of the from the Damned "make it" it'll this lot i think. Good sound mix and a tendency too long ed for Lu to Paul Well. Mind you, the looks like I Claudius, s Se requ go so

PUNKS RULE!

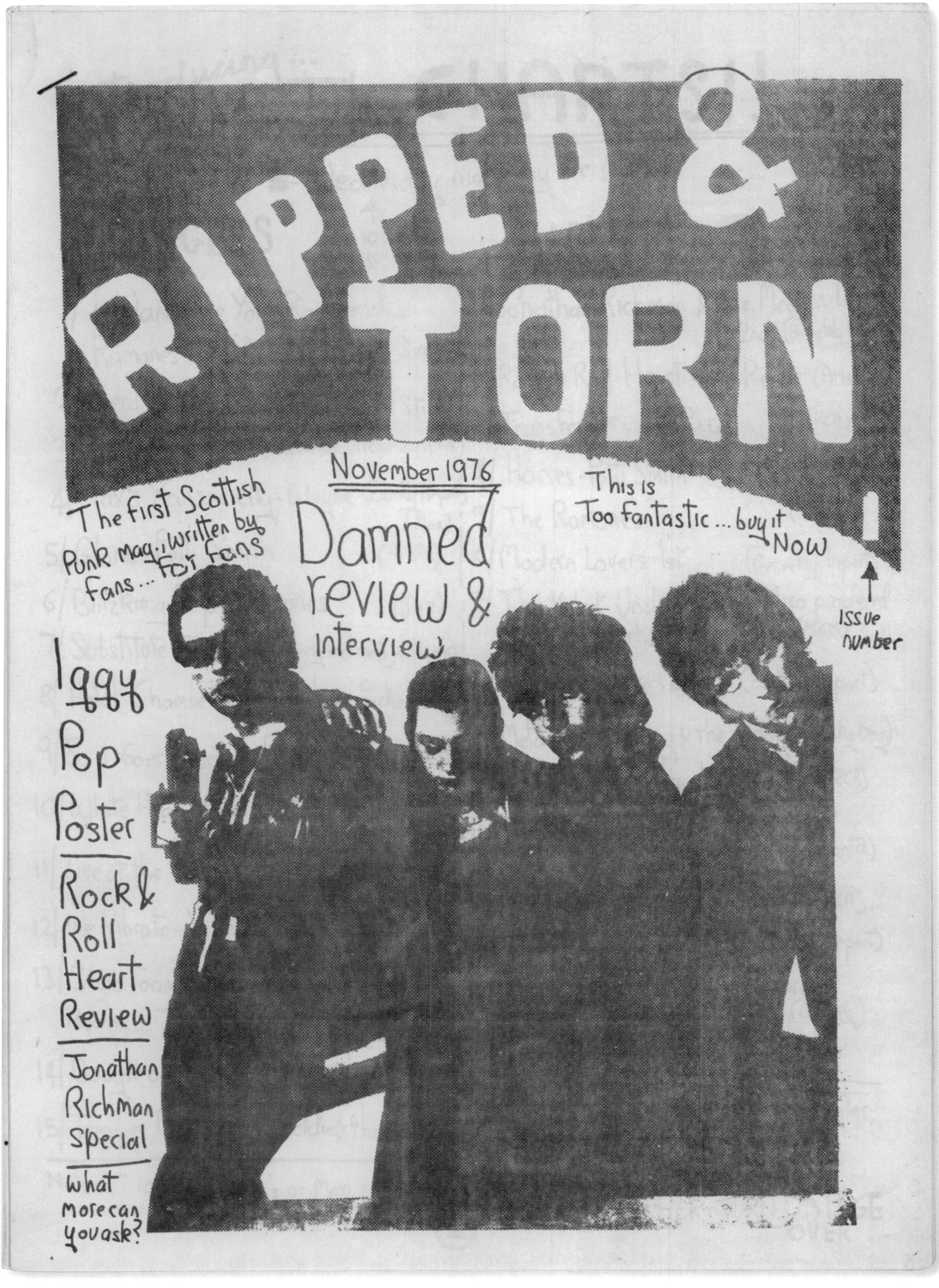

RIPPED & TORN

The first Scottish
Punk mag. written by
Fans... for Fans

November 1976

Damned
review &
interview

This is
Too fantastic...buy it
Now

issue
number

Iggy
Pop
Poster

Rock &
Roll
Heart
Review

Jonathan
Richman
Special

What
more can
you ask?

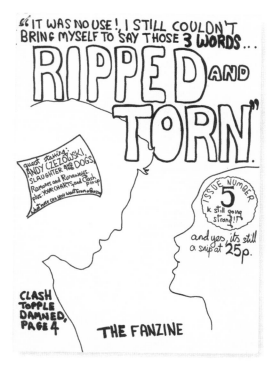

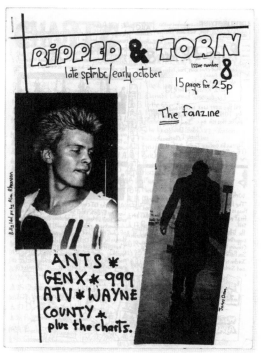

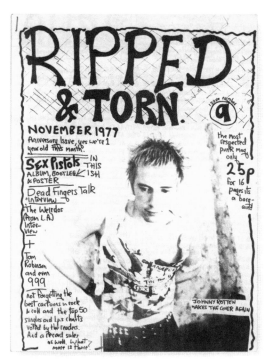

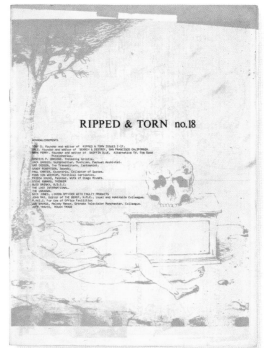

Ripped & Torn (1976–79) by Tony Drayton covered the punk scene in both Glasgow and London. Often excluded from punk histories, this zine was at the time recognized by other producers as a front-runner, partly for its attempt to offer a broader understanding of punk's political agenda. Probing interviews were its stock in trade. The title appeared with numerous variations (handwritten, gothic-type lettering, etc.), while covers invariably featured a photograph of the punk icon of the moment. The final issue consisted of a compilation of rants from other zinesters, including V. Vale, Mark Perry and Jon Savage.

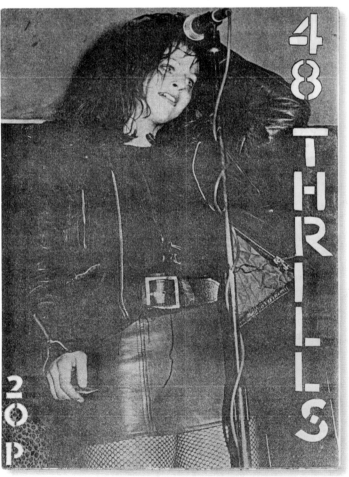

48 Thrills (1977) was first produced on a duplicator and its author, Adrian Thrills, presented it explicitly as an alternative to mainstream music magazines *Sounds* and *NME* (ironically he would later become a professional music journalist). To mark the difference, spontaneity was key: near the end of issue 1, the typewritten text turns into handwriting. *Bondage* (1976) was produced by 'Shane', as in Shane MacGowan, later of the Pogues. Jonh Ingham's *London's Burning* (1976) was an early fanzine for Clash fans. The oversized *Dayglow* (c. 1978) kept to the punk aesthetic: producer Steve May asks 'Who the hell wants to be professional?'

Another mix of British regional zines. *Kleenex* (1979) celebrated the music of the Swiss female post-punk/new wave band of that name. *Dada* (late 1970s) compared punk to Dada and had an art-school feel. *Punkture* (1977) reported on the Midlands scene and was printed by the North Staffs Polytechnic Student Union. It had an obsession with the commercialization of the punk look and its exploitation in such shops as Harrods. *Another Tuneless Racket* (1978), which came out of Glasgow, complains about the region being the 'ultimate in programmed boredom'. *Confidential* (1977) features an article with music-press writer Caroline Coon and reviews the Dead Boys at Watford.

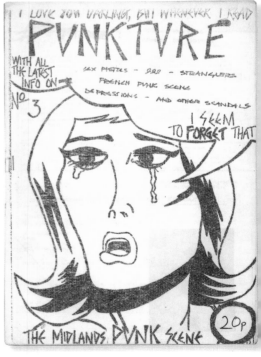

number 2

20 pence

CONFIDENTIAL

ERATION X...CLASH...RICHARD HELL...RUNAWAYS...TALKING HEADS...DEAD BOYS...NEWS....

RRY BITHNELLS HOT LICKS...CAROLINE COON...RAMONES...PISTOLS...AMW...BETHNAL........

/.......REVIEWS....FAX....PIX....INFO...EXTRA WHAKY EDITION...3rd WORLD WAR........

Situation 3 (1977) amusingly asks, 'Music papers: will they ever take over from fanzines?' with reviews of mainstream music papers. *Situation Vacant* (c. 1978) includes articles and interviews with Ultravox and Throbbing Gristle. Alan Anger, a journalist and vocalist for the group the Rowdies, produced *Live Wire* (1978), which ran for 19 issues, and also *Live Wire or Pretty Vacant* (c. 1978), which playfully questions if this is 'a new mag, or is it another attempt to disguise *Live Wire*'. *More-on-Four* (1977), by Sarah Shosubi with a cover photograph by Crystal Clear, differentiated itself by means of its oversized format and black overprinted on yellow copy-paper.

MORE-ON-FOUR
1977 rock + Roll + more-

25p.

SAT'DAY NIGHT
in THE CITY
OF THE DEAD

GENERATION X

THE LURKERS

THE ADVERT

THE MODELS

Ultravox!

ISLAND

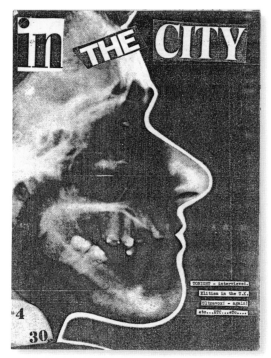

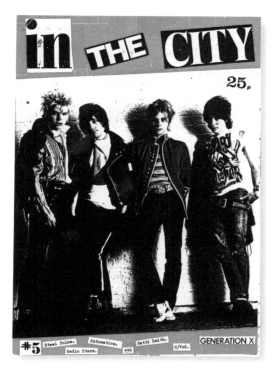

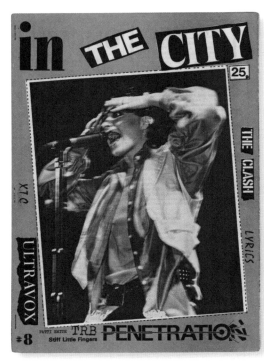

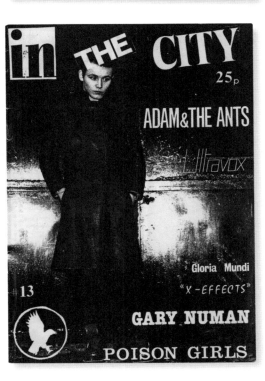

In the City (1977–80) by Francis Drake et al. took an often acerbic look at the London scene. Issue 5 reports on a controversy sparked by Patti Smith holding a 'press conference just for fanzines', and how *In the City* was snubbed after writing a letter to Smith asking to conduct an interview with her without any intervention from her record company. Graphically, the zine was notable for its use of colour-photocopied covers (not cheap at the time) and standardized logo. Like many other punkzines, *In the City* was distributed at the independent record store Rough Trade in west London.

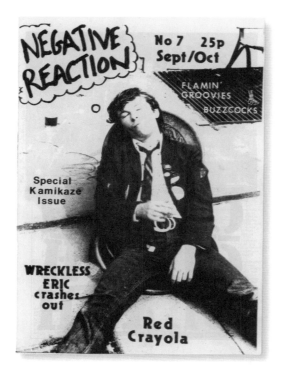

Taking a more professional approach, Jonathan Romney, producer of *Negative Reaction* (1977), had the zine printed by Labute Printers in Cambridge and distributed by Phoenix Magazines; the layout is in a more conventional three-column grid. *Positive Reaction* (1979), from Northern Ireland, mentions the possibility that the zine will be sold in Toronto. *Kids Stuff* (1977–c. 1978) acknowledges that 'David Bowie is Now music'. *Suspect Device* (1979) asks, 'Where's Captain Kirk?' *Slash* (1977–80) was a large-format tabloid from the Los Angeles punk scene, which gave rise to punk label Slash Records; this issue features the Damned and the Screamers.

slash

VOLUME ONE NUMBER ONE   MAYDAY ISSUE 5/77   FIFTY CENTS

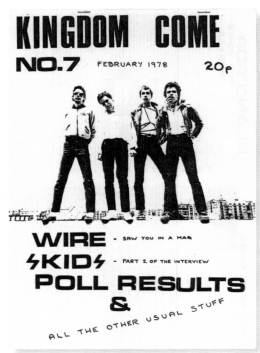

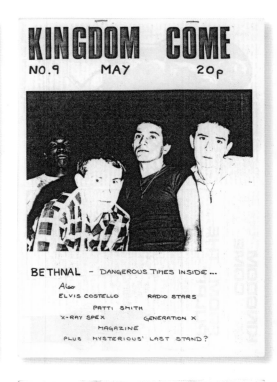

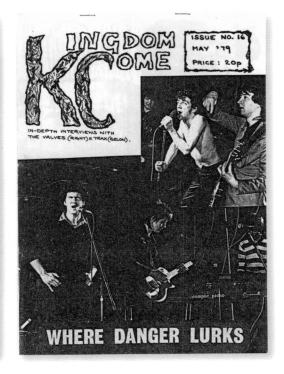

Kingdom Come (1977–*c.* 1979) was by Johnny Waller from Fife, Scotland, another zinester who became a professional journalist. Despite receiving criticism from other zines for having 'no visual appeal', it was not without design interest. For example, the front cover is in portrait format but the interior pages are landscape. The Scottish scene is well represented (with larger bands like the Skids and unknowns like the Belsen Horrors) but there is also room for regular punk fare. Issue 12 was notable for letters from Charlie Chainsaw (*Chainsaw*) and Mick Mercer (*Panache*) extolling the virtues of zines as sites for experimentation.

KC15

KINGDOM COME
MARCH '79   20p

photo credit: ALAN WILD

GAYE ADVERT: cover girl
is just one of the many well-known punk stars not featured this issue. Instead, we concentrate on the young, inexperienced but promising acts who are the real new wave; the real neighbourhood threat – we hope! Most of them you won't have heard of, but that doesn't mean they aren't worthy of your attention. The action starts on page 2
INSIDE:– FREEZE, PRATS, DELETED, FAKES, VERTICAL SMILES, CUBS, VALVES, **SWELL MAPS**, BARBS, SWITCH, MEMBERS, LETTERS PAGE.
PLUS A CHANCE TO WIN A FREE TRIP TO ROCHDALE WITH THE DELETED AS THEY RECORD THEIR "ELECTRIC HEAT" EP. (page 4)

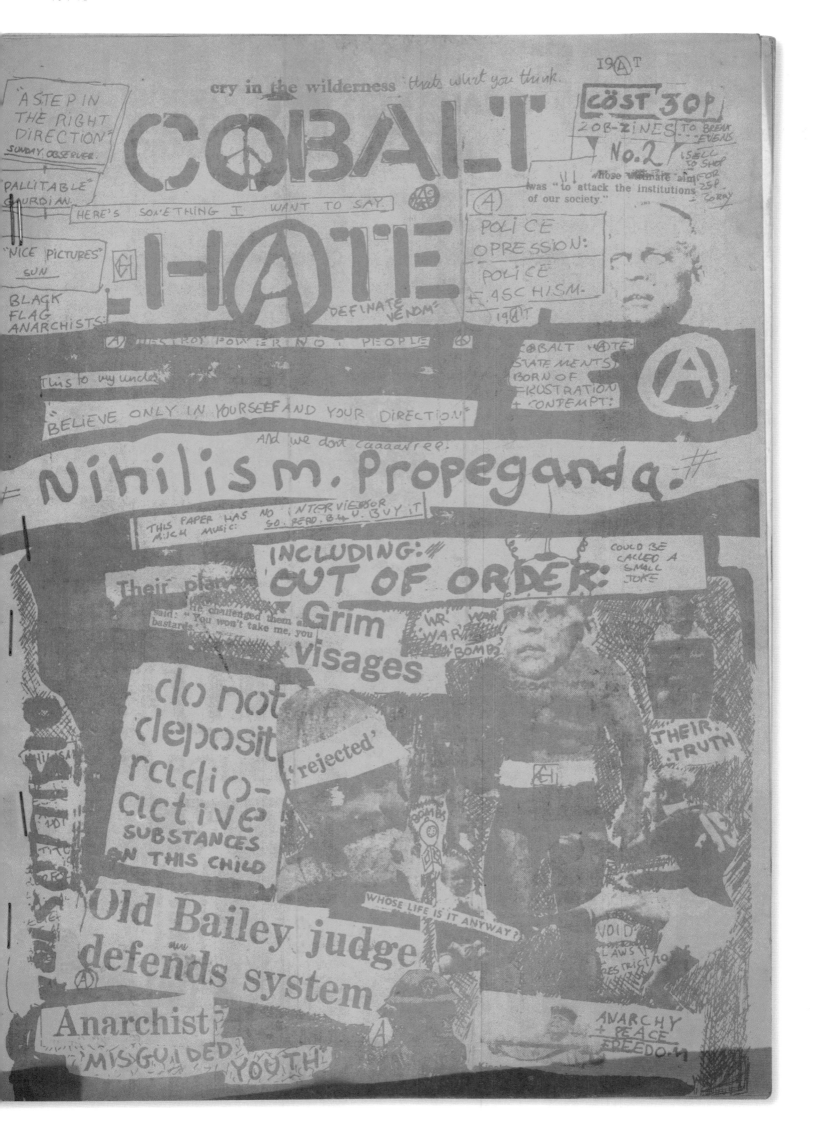

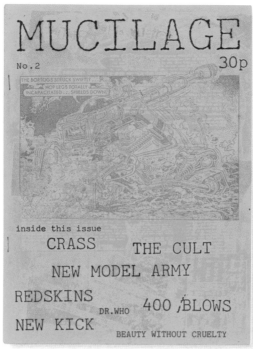

By the 1980s anti-Thatcher politics were coming to the fore in the United Kingdom, often in the form of coverage of the anarcho-punk scene. *Cobalt Hate* (1984) is an example: a chaotically laid-out anarcho-punk fanzine made up of collage, newspaper headlines, slogans and handwritten and stencilled type. Its message beyond the music was 'destroy power, not people'. *Mucilage* (c. 1984, front and back covers) was produced on the zine's own Mucilage Press, where other fanzines were also printed cheaply. Its interview with Crass became a classic of its kind (and was later reproduced on the band's own website). *Blam!* (1981) used typography in an unusually up-front way on its covers; bands featured in issue 1 include Young Marble Giants and Wah! Heat. *4th Wall Theatre of Hate* (1981) came into being to promote and encourage anti-nuclear activity through music, linking musicians, anti-nuclear activists and audience. The first national event was with the Thompson Twins, and there were also tours organized to coincide with CND demonstrations in London.

Anarchism informed the development of a graphic language of 'shock' that was both provocative and political. *Inx Blotch* (c. 1981, front and back cover) reported on skirmishes between skinheads and Asians in Southall, west London. The cartoon-strip cover of *Transformation* (1980; front and back cover shown) focused on the troubles in El Salvador. *Stödge* (n.d.) juxtaposed Hitler, the Pope and news images with photographs of police brutality. *NN4 9PZ* (c. 1979–80) took in local radical bands but left its back cover for a classic piece of agit-prop. *Communiqué 2* (1980) promised 'large doses of anarchist propaganda'.

Communiqué 2

A SYSTEM WITHOUT A SYSTEM

Nihilistic Vices

total oblivion is the answer₀₀₀₀

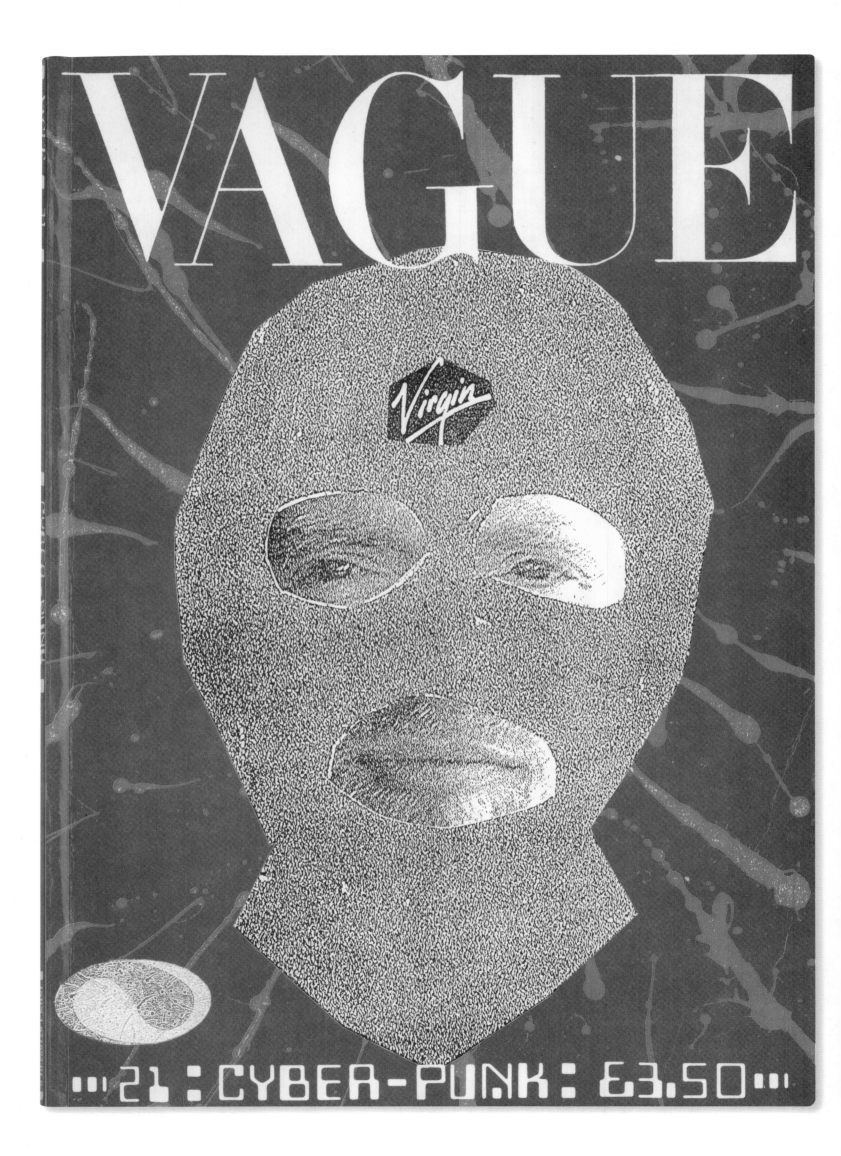

VAGUE

∙∙∙21 : CYBER-PUNK : £3.50 ∙∙∙

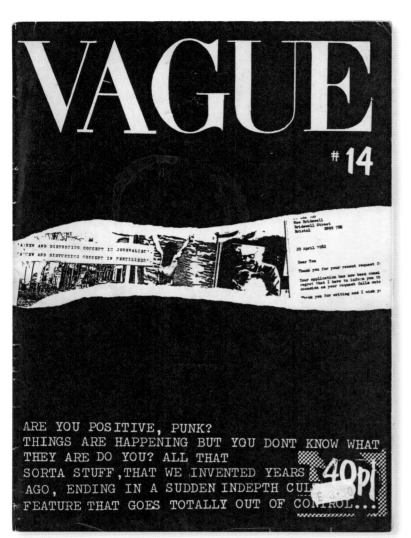

Tom Vague's name has become closely associated
with London history and psychogeography.
His long-running publication *Vague* (1979–)
is a forum for discussions of Situationism,
anarcho-punk and 'the decay of the spectacle'.
Design has always played a key role in this
fanzine (for example, the 'Branson' cyberpunk
cover by Jamie Reid and Joe Ewart): even in
its earliest days the chaotic layouts were
overprinted with fluorescent colours. In the
1980s this was the first fanzine of its kind
to be perfect-bound.

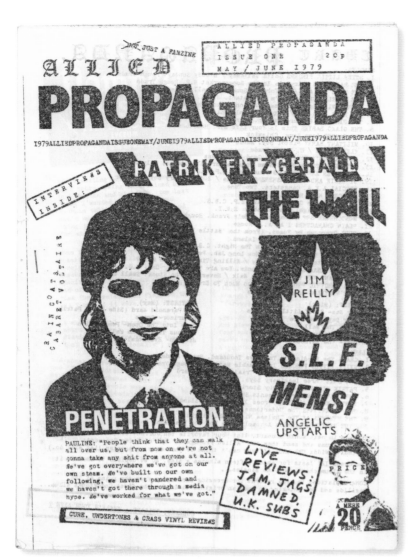

A mixture of typographic juxtapositions gives *Allied Propaganda* (1979–mid-1980s) its own unique style, while the interior subverts the conventions of reading by placing the editorial in the middle of the fanzine. *Cross Now* (*c.* 1980s), with its free flexi-disc, relies on a more graphic use of red and yellow crosses. In this issue it interviews legendary British DJ John Peel. The logo for *Grinding Halt* (1979–*c.* 1980) plays with a juxtaposition of upper- and lower-case letterforms and the cover clearly takes delight in the different type styles used for various band names. In a similar vein, *Safety in Numbers* (*c.* 1978–80s) renders a stylized title using a DIY ransom-note approach. The cover shows a mod holding what appears to be a Crass banner. *Mental Children* (1980) makes the case that women are no longer ornaments and contributed actively to the punk music scene. This cover image is a colour photocopy depicting three members of the Slits, half-dressed, bathing in an idyllic forest clearing, from the sleeve of their first album.

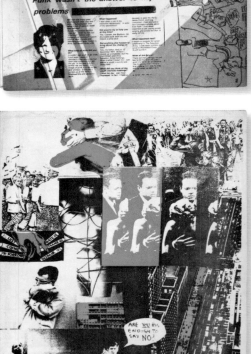

Post-punk zines started to experiment with style and content. *Guttersnipe* (*c*. 1978– *c*. 1979, front and back cover) was printed at the Printshop at Telford Community Arts (Shropshire, UK), providing a different kind of visual aesthetic from its photocopied counterparts. The use of red and black makes for an interesting variation on the ransom- note trope. *Rapid Eye Movement* (1979–*c*. 1990s, front and back cover) was an industrial- culture post-punk fanzine, which in later incarnations became a series of collected volumes. The cover is stark and self- consciously arty (taken from a screen-print image), though the contents include some standard music fare, including Chelsea and 'token mods'.

RAPID EY-E MOVEMENT

30p

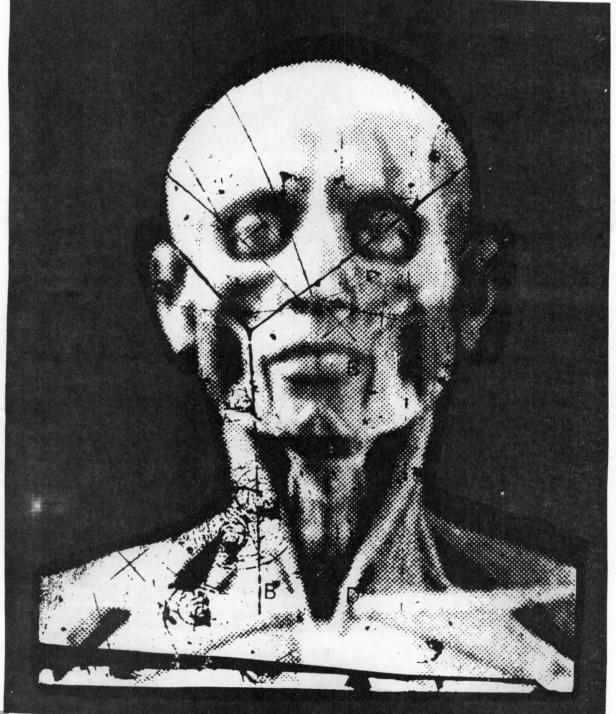

Winter '79 * Issue 1 * 34 pages * Scritti Politti *
Mark Perry * Patrik Fitzgerald * the Pirahnas *
Nicky + the Dots * Tony Parsons + Julie Burchill *
Chelsea * Token Mods & loads more!!

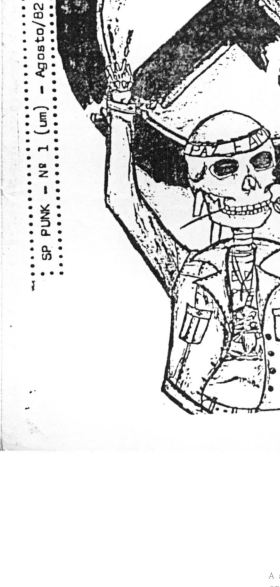

Não queremos guerra.
Também não acreditamos,
que com a páz e o amor,
alguma coisa ira mudar.
Queremos união e luta
para a vitória de

nossos ideais.

A spread of Brazilian punkzines. Under an oppressive regime the emergence of punk in Brazil was sporadic, fuelled by reports from the 1977 British punk scene in *Pop* magazine. Things took off in the 1980s after the festival 'O Começo do Fim do Mundo' ('The beginning of the end of the world') held in São Paulo in 1982. This was attended by more than 3,000 punks and 20 bands and sparked a plethora of fanzines. Home-grown bands and their affiliated zines included *Alerta Punk* (1983), with a cover borrowed from a Gary Panter illustration, *Espectro do Caos* (1980s), *SP Punk* (1982) and *Atentado* (1983).

The aftermath of punk gave rise to a less angry aesthetic, but a similar graphic language was often retained. *Adventures in Reality* (1980–c. 1981) ran for ten issues and was produced by Alan Rider. This issue included a flexi-disc by the band Attrition. *It Ticked and Exploded* (1979–c. 1980) came out of Paisley, Scotland, and highlighted local bands, such as the Zips. This issue includes letters by Tony Drayton (*Ripped & Torn*) and Johnny Waller (*Kingdom Come*). *Black & White* (1979–80), produced in Dublin, was unusual for letting the bands write the copy while the editors designed the layout. *The Poser* (c. 1980s) was a post-punk photozine, with this issue featuring the Mo-Dettes, the Ruts and Iggy Pop. Unusually, it offered photos for sale, printing thumbnails to choose from, plus advice for aspiring gig photographers. *Out of Print* (1979) from East Sussex, England, features the Swell Maps and Siouxsie and the Banshees. The editorial draws attention to the different photocopy paper that is used throughout, and makes succinct comment on the competition: 'I hate Sounds; NME is shit; Melody Maker? Aaargh! Wipe your bottom.' *Leamington's Love Letter* (1981) contained poetry and cartoons with a political bent as well as articles on the local anti-nuclear movement. This issue promises 'an interview with Ronald Regan [sic]' and 'more lies'. *No More Masterpieces* (1979) from Liverpool was produced by future rock journalist Paul Mathur (who would discover Oasis) and featured a variety of punk and post-punk artists. This issue calls for the formation of a fanzine co-op. *Today's Length* (c. 1980s) was a zine of a different kind, with visual essays presented in loose-leaf form, punctuated by ironic takes on cosmetic and tobacco advertising. Its producers included Malcolm Garrett and Joe Ewart, who would later become luminaries of the graphic-design world.

The line between DIY zines and professional publications was often slim. Some zines became mainstream over time, such as *Jamming!* (1979–86). *Flipside* (1977–2000) from Los Angeles shifted from a fanzine approach to more glossy covers towards the end of publication. Professional punkzines included *Bomp!* (1970–79), from California, edited by rock journalist Greg Shaw (previously of *Mojo Navigator*). *Zig Zag* (1969–*c.* 1980s) first came to favour as a UK rock magazine and was later revamped in punk guise.

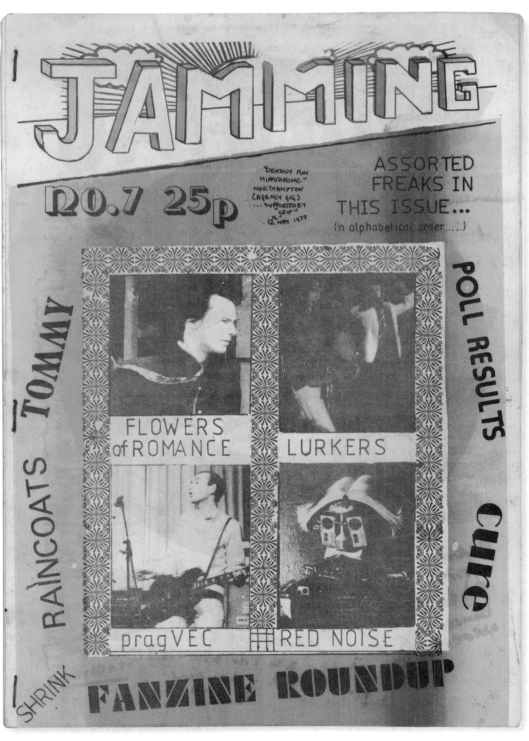

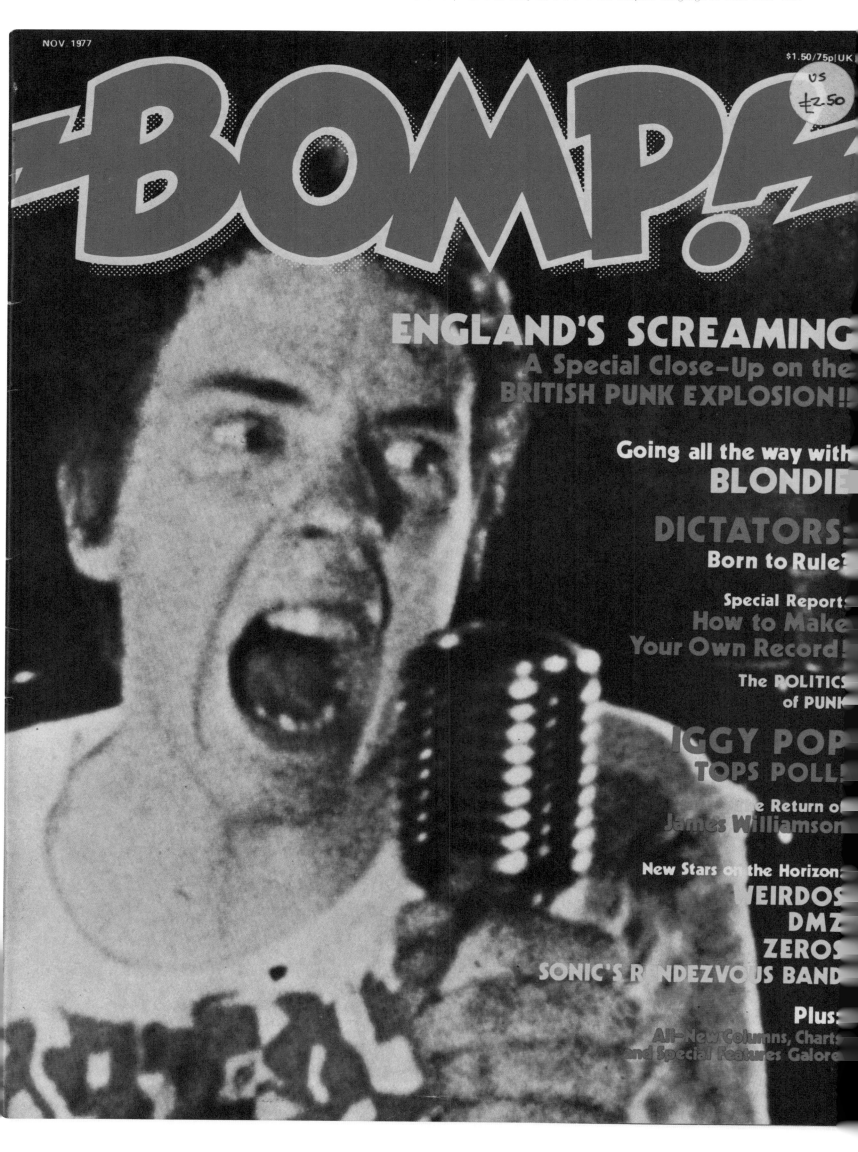

NOV. 1977

$1.50/75p(UK)

US £2.50

BOMP!

ENGLAND'S SCREAMING
A Special Close-Up on the
BRITISH PUNK EXPLOSION!!

Going all the way with
BLONDIE

DICTATORS:
Born to Rule?

Special Report:
How to Make
Your Own Record!

The POLITICS
of PUNK

IGGY POP
TOPS POLL!

The Return of
James Williamson

New Stars on the Horizon:
WEIRDOS
DMZ
ZEROS
SONIC'S RENDEZVOUS BAND

Plus:
All-New Columns, Charts
and Special Features Galore

CHAPTER THREE

LIBERATED SPACES: SUBCULTURES, PROTEST AND CONSUMER CULTURE

1980s – 1990s

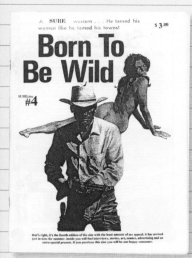

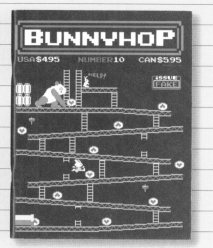

SUREzine (c. 1997-n.d.) was
a music- and perzine from
Melbourne, whose producer
remarks that 'my spleen
has never been exposed so
thoroughly'. *Ben Is Dead*
(1988-99) was a Los Angeles-
based zine by Deborah 'Darby'
Romeo, whose confessional
tone of writing and pop
culture commentary made
it one of the notable
publications of the 1990s.
Bunnyhop (1995-c. 2000s)
is perhaps best known for
receiving a 'cease and desist'
notice from Matt Groening
for copyright infringement
of his character Binky.

With the rise to power of Margaret Thatcher and Ronald Reagan in the late 1970s and 1980s, a new era of 'free market' economics was born. On one hand, this encouraged small businesses to develop, which some saw as a co-opting of the individualistic DIY urge that had occurred during punk. On the other hand, the 'greed is good' culture that took over the financial districts in both the United Kingdom and the United States provided the zine producers with a target.

The rhetoric of the marketplace was one that 'equated the freedom to spend money with broader political and cultural freedoms', in the words of cultural historian Frank Mort.[1] Along with this new financial liberation came the concept of selling a lifestyle. As the journalist Andrew Marr reflects, the 1980s resulted in the thinking that 'we are what we buy'[2] – in other words it was a time when people consumed not only products but also the aspirations that the advertising campaigns sought to convey. It was all about 'conspicuous consumption', taste and fashion, 'the cultivation of the self'.[3] Consumption became cultural practice, and fanzine producers both capitalized on this and critiqued it mercilessly.

Meanwhile, co-option by the mainstream was continuing. In the United Kingdom, lifestyle magazines emerged, providing a different take on youth culture, including *The Face* (1980–2004), the '80s fashion bible' founded by Nick Logan; and the one-time zine and self-consciously titled 'style bible', *i-D* magazine (1980–), founded by Terry Jones. These publications bridged the gap between post-punk and a new kind of youth subculture – rave. Their graphic form reflected the fanzine aesthetic – the streetwise attitude of DIY photography, illustration, typewritten texts and so on. Just as the music press in the 1970s had co-opted a *Sniffin' Glue*-style aesthetic, so now these new style magazines tapped into the more sophisticated look of the consumer-era zines. Similarly in the United States, *Details* (1982–) founded by Annie Flanders (and later sold to Condé Nast), was ostensibly a New York fashion and club magazine, but also riffed on themes and aesthetics borrowed from the zine scene.

Consuming Dance Culture

The rave scene gave rise to newly valorized occupations such as 'DJs, club organizers, clothes designers, music and style journalists', according to sociologist Sarah Thornton.[4] These positions carried with them 'subcultural capital', which, according to Thornton, 'can be objectified or embodied' within the objects that surround the scene but also took the form of 'being "in the know"'.[5] Fanzines played a role in the circulation of that knowledge: as carriers of current slang and the latest fashion trends, and critiques of club and dance music. Take for example, *Gear* (c. 1991), produced by Camilla Deakin (later a journalist for *The Face*), which provided insightful commentary on London's club culture scene, highlighting bands' intentional and media-conscious use of 'high profile, coke snorting' bribery campaigns involving clubs and PR companies, and health warnings against 'the chosen drug of our culture', Ecstasy. *Gear* often took advantage of its position 'below critical radar' to flout libel and copyright laws. At the same time, the 'epitome of cool' was represented in articles on, for example, the duo Diana Brown and Barry K. Sharpe, who was also founder of Duffer of St George, the clothing label that informed 'the look for the 90s soul-boy'.[6] The distinctiveness of *Gear*'s graphics, created by Fred Deakin, also captured a particular club-culture visual style now affiliated with club flyers and music festival posters; a desktop-publishing version of 1960s retro, hippie, counter-cultural and psychedelic typography using in its layout overprinted block areas of acid colours.

Another example was *Boy's Own* (1987–92), the first acid house fanzine, which covered also 'football, funk and left-wing politics'. The zine's producers, Terry Farley, Andy Weatherall, Cymon Eccles and Steve Maize, emerged out of the decade's DJing and house music scene. Farley also had an interest in the Liverpool-based football fanzine *The End* edited by Peter Hooton (band member of The Farm), which 'blurred the lines between football, pop, booze, drugs, left-wing politics and fashion'.[7] Hooton's approach influenced *Boy's Own*'s editorial direction, while at the same time, designer Dave

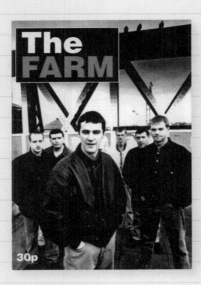

The rise of the northern England indie/dance music scene initiated a plethora of related zines. *Halcyon Daze* (1989) was a zine for Happy Mondays fans 'guaranteed to thrill, titillate and burn rather well when winter arrives'. *The Farm* (1990s) promoted a more professional magazine approach; contributors included, in this first issue, members of the band. *Debris* (1983–89) was produced by Hacienda nightclub DJ and journalist Dave Haslam, who captured the emerging Manchester music scene.

Little's distinctive logo and series of covers quickly established a brand identity.

Meanwhile, outside the capital, *The Herb Garden* (1990s, Leeds) *Ace of Clubs* (1990–n.d., Manchester) and *Ribena* (1990s, Essex) covered rave and dance culture. *Ace of Clubs* producer Gareth Jones, who used club nights to promote the fanzine, reflects that his zine 'was a northern version of London's *Boy's Own* mag'.[8] Eventually the popularity of the club nights meant that Jones had to discontinue the fanzine and focus on his business. In Leeds, *The Herb Garden* editor, David Gill, remarked, '… if you bother to look hard enough, you will find some roots of popular culture [here]… the north is no different to anywhere else.' Essentially a 'satirical tipsheet', *The Herb Garden* mirrored the lifestyle of its readership, 'with tasteless send-ups of overpaid DJs, overpriced clubs, overrated artists and the kind of PR-based dross found in most style magazines'. Its first issue was a parody of a special-issue format of *i-D*.[9] By the mid-1990s, *The Herb Garden*, was printing in excess of 2,000 copies and transformed itself into a monthly magazine while maintaining its acerbic editorial position. In a 1995 interview, Gill assured his readership that moving into the mainstream would not deter his original editorial approach, commenting, 'We have this Apple Mac program called "Fanzine Check". When you finish an article you put it through and it adds 30 spelling mistakes and 20 swear words.'[10]

The north of England was also notable for zines picking up on the way in which rave/acid house was merging with indie rock. Many were affiliated with the Manchester's Hacienda Club, including the Happy Mondays zine *Halcyon Daze* (1989), which became a focus for the 'Madchester' scene.

Another regional publication was *The Faced* (1990s), which came out of Exeter and documented the thriving rave scene as it was taking place. Its newsletter-like approach took special interest in the moral panic around the emerging scene, and the way in which ravers were increasingly depicted in the media as 'folk devils'. This backlash would eventually contribute to the introduction of the United Kingdom Criminal Justice and Public Order Act in 1994.

Spiral Tribe was a collective responsible for hosting free parties and outdoor festivals, known as raves. These dance and acid house events (an extension of the Ibiza club scene of the mid-1980s) took over disused warehouse spaces or farmer's fields for impromptu gigs – the details of which were often released just before the event to avoid police detection. As one DJ wrote: 'Instead of money and power, rave called for empathy, intimacy, spirituality and the joy of losing yourself in the crowd.'[11] Just about every zine of the period references Spiral Tribe's work, and the collective itself gave rise to several publications that were zine-like.

It is true that in general zines specific to rave culture were less prevalent than during punk/post-punk. The music critic Simon Reynolds observed: 'Apart from *Boy's Own,* there was next to no fanzine documentation of the scene as it happened. People were too busy having fun. But it was a creative period for short-term artefacts like T-shirts, flyers, and club design.'[12] There were other exceptions, as we have seen, but this remains one of the sparser periods in zine history.

America and Anti-Capitalism

The 1980s and 1990s witnessed a boom in DIY fanzine production centring on critiques of capitalism, and although there were British examples, this phenomenon was primarily the product of the 'home of consumerism', the United States. As zinesters positioned themselves on the margins of the dominant culture they were able to freely editorialize against what they saw as its vices. Thus the critiques of capitalism tended to take on a very personal aspect, mixing the tradition of autobiographical perzines with something more political. As Stephen Duncombe remarks, 'the personalization of politics is one way in which zinesters confront the distance between themselves and a mainstream political world in which they effectively have no say.'[13]

THE FACED

ISSUE 4   FREE

JULY 92

The free party scene this year has become reminiscent of those fine old days of the mad, mental pay parties of the late eighties. An indication of the way things were going cmae with one of last years final summer parties in September at an old B&Q superstore on the outskirts of Stroud. Around 8,000 people congregated for that one. Blocking off much of the centre of Stroud itself with car stereos pounding, and bobble hats bobbling.

This year started earlier than ever, with a number of small parties kicking off in late February, and early March. But the real beginning and portent of the future came at Lechlade where a crowd of between 10,000 and 15,000 took over the common for the weekend, and three or four different soundsytems supplied the entertainment.

Just a couple of weeks later rumours of a big party began circulating, as the media geared up for its pre-solstice hippie watch. The anniversary of last years legendary Chipping Sodbury party was due on the late-May Bank Holiday. However the land on which that had taken place was injuncted, and things took on a rather farcical look as the police in several counties desperately tried to move travellers out

of their jurisdiction and into their neighbouring forces. When Castlemorton became a potential venue, the fate of the Common was sealed by a well timed news report which pinpointed its exact location for party people nationwide. The initial small group of travellers who had taken the land, was joined by other small groups, then by the soundsystems, and inevitably by the 'ravers'. The police tried to portray the way the party evolved as a carefully orchestarted plan laid out by some massive drug dealing organisation, falling prey to the kind of cospiracy theory that is normally developed by our side. In fact it was purely coincidental that just about every free party soundsystem in the country chose to put in an appearance at Castlemorton. But what a coincidence!! The names are send a thrill down the spine of any self-respecting free party person. CIRCUS WARP, D.I.Y, SPIRAL TRIBE, BEDLAM, CIRCUS IRRITANT, CIRCUS NORMAL, TECHNO TRAVELLERS, RUFF KREW. Its enough to reduce even the most hardened 'rave cabbage' wearer to tears of joy. Over that weekend upwards of 20,000 to 25,000 people experienced the delights of what has to be the biggest

and best free party so far. Strangely, it was not the shear size of the event which sparked the massive media coverage, but rather the proximity of the local residents to the site. It was not the best place to hold such a gathering, however arguably more suitable sites had had to be abandoned in the run up to the festival as the police passed the buck. As a result of the locals being so close to the site, and because they had been bombarded by media stereotypes and police lies, a massive level of paranoia developed amongst them, until they seemed to picture themselves as the white suited , petrol hoarding good guys in Mad Max 2, and the partygoers became the masses of leather-clad barbarians hungry for their blood, children, livestock and toilets, not necessarily in that order. furthermore the availabilty of drugs which the police usually tend to ignore or cover up, perhaps in fear of revealing how they have failed to inflict the 'rule of law'upon us, was on show for all to see.

In the end however it was not the drugs or the noise that became the central issue. It was literally the shit that hit the fan. The product of some 20,000 bowels. Indeed this was a complaint that had some

Next Issue: Roger Cook , Peoples Hero, or fat bag of pus?

ACE OF CLUBS

ISSUE No. 1 – 'THE CHICKEN OR THE EGG EDITION' – 100p

Ace of Clubs (1990-n.d.) was a 'club mag' that featured emerging DJ stars such as Pete Tong and also a 'swap shop' for the collectors of club flyers. *The Faced* (1990s) was a 'free' acid house newsletter out of Exeter, England which reported on the thriving rave scene and the 'free party sound system' collective Spiral Tribe. *Gear* (c. 1991) was an early clubzine that combined popular culture journalism with bold psychedelic graphics.

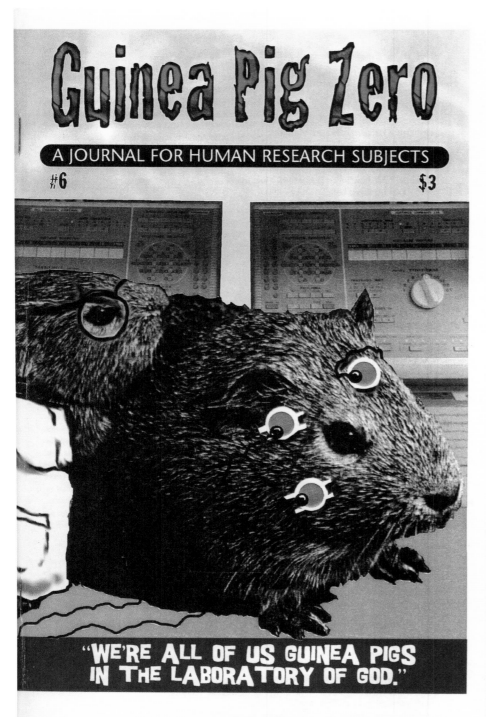

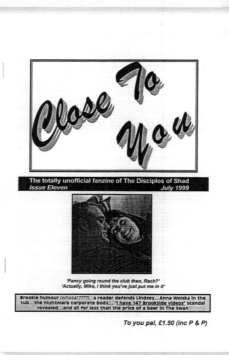

Guinea Pig Zero (1996–2001), produced by Robert P. Helms, was 'an occupational jobzine for people who are used as medical or pharmaceutical research subjects'. Contributors included Dishwasher Pete (of *Dishwasher* fame) and others who had volunteered for drug experiments, and debates focused on the ethical questions related to research using human subjects. *Close to You* (1990s) was an 'unofficial' mouthpiece for the British soap *Brookside*. *Screaming to Be Heard* (1988–n.d.) was a comedy zine featuring interviews with the likes of Julian Clary and Quentin Crisp.

Dishwasher (1992-98, 2007) documented the musings of Dishwasher Pete (aka Pete Jordan) on 'one man's quest to wash dishes in all fifty states'. In this issue he 'washed dishes at sea' while on an oil rig off Louisiana. *Temp Slave* (1993-2000s), by Jeff Kelly, was a zine about working as a temporary employee. *Answer Me!* (1991-94) by Jim Goad took a 'misanthropic' look at the darker side of fandom, with ratings of serial killers.

Two examples provided a new look at consumerism. *Beer Frame: The Journal of Inconspicuous Consumption* (1993–) by Paul Lukas, critiqued the absurdity of everyday commodities, including such products as toothpick dispensers and EZ Squirt Blastin' Green Ketchup. Lukas asks: 'What is inconspicuous consumption? It's about deconstructing the details of consumer culture – details that are either so weird or obscure that we'd never see them, or so ubiquitous that we've essentially *stopped* seeing them.'[14] Al Hoff's *Thrift Score* (1994–c. 2000) was about thrift shopping and finding ways of saving money. With tips on bargain-hunting, Hoff emphasizes that thrift shopping is about 'you' and what you want to buy.[15] Any critique of consumerism, Duncombe reminds us, must also include a critique of 'how culture and products will be produced and consumed'.[16]

Anti-capitalism also incorporated critiques of work culture. Jeff Kelly's *Temp Slave* (1993–2000s) provided 'a voice for disgruntled temporary workers'. Kelly's first issue was prompted by his experience as a temporary worker for an insurance company that reneged on a promise for full-time employment in its mailroom. With access to a photocopier and paper, Kelly printed off 25 copies with his editorial rant – 'temp work is a losing proposition' – and distributed it to colleagues during his mail round. He explains, 'The first issue is very rough…I was just *mad*, so making the zine was a blast.'[17] *Dishwasher* (1992–98, 2007), produced by Dishwasher Pete (aka Pete Jordan), was a document of 'one man's quest to wash dishes in all fifty states'. Yet, more than a perzine or travel zine, *Dishwasher* also commented on the life of an itinerant worker 'accepting lower pay for less responsibility and more anonymity'.[18] His travels took him across thirty-three states over a ten-year period, during which he had eighty-eight different dish jobs and in the end produced fifteen zines.

And finally, *Guinea Pig Zero* (1996–2001) was defined by its producer, Robert P. Helms, as 'an occupational jobzine for people who are used as medical or pharmaceutical research subjects'.[19] The commentary provided by its producer (also involved as a human research subject) questioned bio-ethics, investigated medical and scientific research facilities, and wrote about the experiences of the guinea pig 'field reporters'. The fanzine's impact was summed up by Carl Elliott, a philosopher and bio-ethicist, as: 'In its small way, *Guinea Pig Zero* was revolutionary. Before *Guinea Pig Zero,* nobody had really even thought about research subjects as a kind of community.'[20] Fanzines, as informative and thought-provoking publications, also served to shape the values of the groups out of which the zines emerged.

Mainstreaming DIY

The 1980s and 1990s was an exciting period for zines, and it is important to note that alongside these newer varients (rave zines, consumer zines) older genres continued to thrive. For example, it is probably true that there were more indie rock zines being produced in this period than ever before or since. The same holds true for the football and sports zines.

But it was the newer genres that piqued the interest of the mainstream, and as we have seen, co-option by the mainstream culture industry was commonplace. Sometimes this was greeted with horror, though on other occasions it was embraced as part of a natural evolution. As fanzines and their producers became absorbed into consumer culture and the mainstream – whether through book deals, or by appearing on television and radio – questions around 'selling out' were debated. For example, *Holiday in the Sun* (1998–99) was a Canadian metazine that included interviews with the star zinesters of the day. Its ironic tag line stated: 'INSIDE: a zinester who writes ads for cigarettes, another who is a demographic informer, another who writes for *Fortune* and another who writes novels for Rupert Murdoch.'[21]

This comment on zinesters in the mainstream was undoubtedly a sign of the times. However, the fanzine world is infinitely malleable, and even as the perception of zines becoming anaesthetized by the mainstream was taking shape, so a DIY reaction was also happening – the subject of our next chapter.

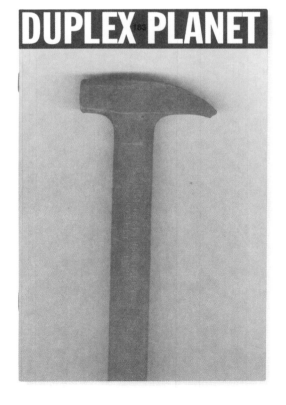

CGBC (1990s) defied categorization, arguing
for a publication of 'high quality' without
being 'stuck with a fan-zine classification'.
Cometbus (1983–) by Aaron Cometbus is a
perzine about the author's travels and punk
locale, and is made more distinctive through
the obsessive handwritten text. *Beer Frame*
(1993–) is by Paul Lukas and looks at the world
of consumer products. David Greenberger's
Duplex Planet (1979–) takes a humorous look
at people in nursing homes.

Boing Boing (1988–) by Mark Frauenfelder and Carla Sinclair is a quarterly 'neurozine' that looks at gadgets and popular culture. *Plotz Notes* (1995–2002) was an East Village Jewish pop culture zine looking at the humorous side of daily life. *Crap Hound* (1994–) is a seminal clip art zine with themed issues (e.g. Death, Telephones, Scissors) by Sean Tejaratchi. *Tiki News* (1995–) by Otto von Stroheim is devoted to the world of Polynesian-themed 'Tiki' culture.

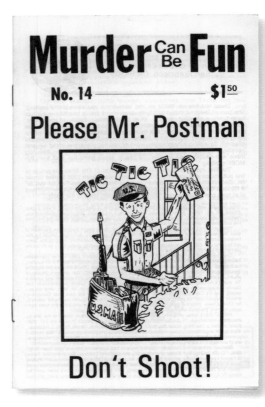

Zinesters' greatest source of information and visuals was used and out-of-print books and magazines. *Murder Can Be Fun* (1986-2007) was irregularly produced by John Marr in San Francisco as a 'death-and-disaster journal', with each themed issue covering subjects from post office shootings and 'the art of murder' to zoo deaths and 'naughty children'. The first issue was 16 unbound photocopied pages; by issue 17 it had gone to 48 pages of 600dpi laser printing. *Mystery Date* (1994-98) by Lynn Peril drew inspiration from the 1965 edition of the Mystery Date board game and from 1950s economics textbooks and etiquette and dating manuals. Source material also came from Bunny Yeager's *Model Diet* book, giving each issue a classic 1950s retro feel. *Teen Fag Magazine* (1993-n.d.) was a sporadically published queerzine that looked at gay rights and issues, including here 'bath houses for me', 'pro-life queers' and an essay on 'bad bad homos' such as serial killer Jeffrey Dahmer. *Teenage Gang Debs* (1988-c. 1993) was by brother and sister zinesters Don and Erin Smith and took as its starting point a nostalgic view of 1970s and early 1980s American TV popular culture, with *The Brady Bunch* among other obsessions.

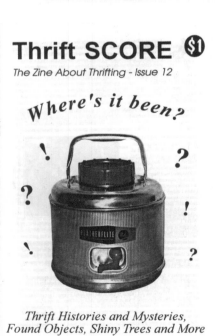

Many fashion and anti-fashion zines of the 1980s-90s that had begun in the underground became key players within the mainstream fashion industry. *Thrift Score* (1994-c. 2000) was produced by Al Hoff (aka 'girl reporter') out of Pittsburgh for those who knew 'why it's cool to thrift'. The zine featured information on places for thrift shopping, the 'weirdest things ever thrifted', and a column 'My most unforgettable thrift store'. On the cover of the zine, Hoff would often add sample fabrics – in the case of issue 3, a 'genuine swatch of retro-denim' – to help her readers identify their thrift purchases. *Details* (1982–), founded by Annie Flanders and then sold to Condé Nast, chronicled New York's downtown scene. The early issues were produced with a DIY fanzine aesthetic, born out of financial need. Flanders says, 'We really thought we were doing a magazine for ourselves and 100 other people.' *Cheap Date* (1997–) was a charity-shop-inspired fanzine by Kira Jolliffe, later with Bay Garnett (2002). Its strap line, 'antidotal antifashion for thinking thrifters', summed up the 1990s desire for economical fashion solutions combined with an increasingly hip approach to fashion styling and reporting (celebrity journalists included Anita Pallenberg, Poppy de Villeneuve and Sophie Dahl). Terry Jones, founder of *i-D* (1980–), revolutionized the way in which street fashion could be a hip and much sought-after commodity. The early issues (printed at Better Badges) capitalized on the rapid absorption of the 1970s punk aesthetic.

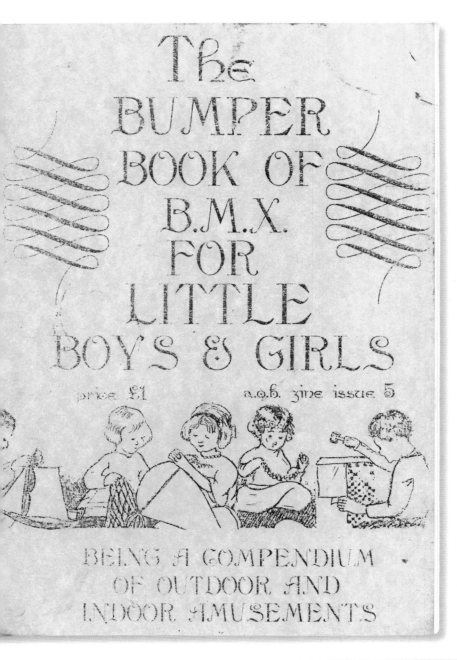

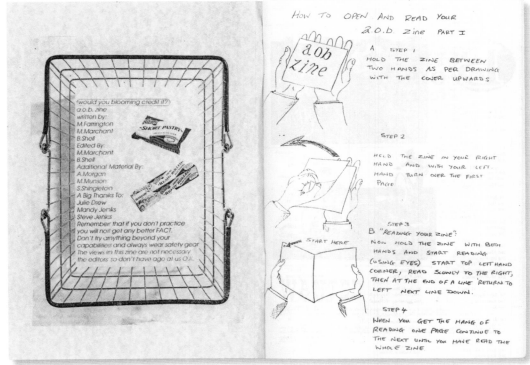

Sports zines flourished during this period. *A.O.B. Zine* (mid-1990s, cover and inside spread) was a dirt-bike sports zine. *Skatedork* (1998–) is a zine about skateboarding focusing on the 'personal side'. This tradition continued into the 2000s, with *Oscar's Eye* (2000s), combining skateboarding and 1980s thrash music, and *Sauce* (2000s), a free skateboarding zine out of Portland, Oregon. The Glasgow-based Celtic football fanzine, *Not The View* (1987–) was produced by fans to 'give the ordinary Celtic fans a voice and a place to air their views'. *Johnny Miller 96 Not Out* (1989–) is recognized for its 'notable addition to the cricketing press because of its satire'.

ISSUE ONE £1 / €1.50 / TRADE

OSCAR'S EYE

ENCYCLOPEDIA TOMMY COMSTOCK SKATEBOARDING

RANTS, RAMBLES AND REVIEWS

SAUCE

#007 FREE

SKATE ROCK
OLLIE, OLLIE OXEN FREE
PHOTO MISSIONS
PIPE DREAMS

THE VIEW

Celtic Fanzine No.34 50p

OLD FIRM STUNNER!

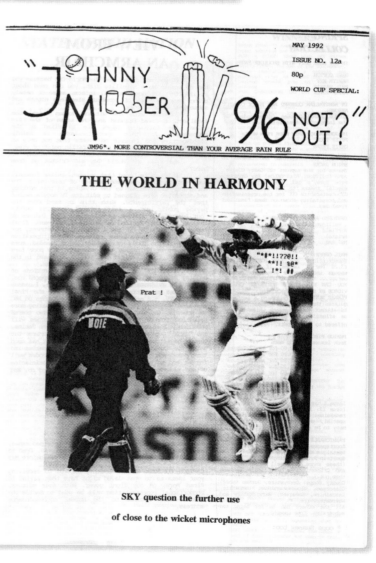

MAY 1992
ISSUE NO. 12a
80p
WORLD CUP SPECIAL:

"Johnny Miller 96 NOT OUT?"

JM96*. MORE CONTROVERSIAL THAN YOUR AVERAGE RAIN RULE

THE WORLD IN HARMONY

SKY question the further use
of close to the wicket microphones

blow football

'MOYNIHAN'S GONE!'

ISSUE FOUR: FIFTY PENCE

When Saturday Comes no.7

35p

MERGERS: No Victory Yet

The fiasco at Fulham and the continuing uncertainty over the future of Wimbledon and Crystal Palace have brought into the open many of the realities of football in the 1980s which are too often kept hidden below the surface. As we go to press, the final outcome of both these situations is still far from clear, but even at this distance the lessons to be learnt are pretty obvious. Some people have more to learn than others.

The League

Although the Football League for once didn't try to pass the buck, they are far from blameless in the merger affairs. In fact, their whole structure was called into question.

The decisions of the League Management Committee mainly effect the clubs, obviously. The clubs are run by their Chairman and Directors. The League Management Committee is composed entirely of Chairmen and Directors. They are defendants, judge and jury. In this case, two members of the Management Committee, Ken Bates and Ron Noades, had a direct interest in the outcome of the merger proposals. In Bates' case his interest was a personal financial one, as well as a professional one, since he owns 20% of Marler's shares. (His protestations about Marler's valuation of Stamford Bridge which pushed their shares up substantially should also be seen in this context — he would stand to gain a lot of money by selling those shares). Noades would be helping to decide on a merger proposition which he himself may even have helped to initiate, and which is scarcely of minimal significance to his club!

This is at the root of the League's lack of will in previous dealings with the Bulstrodes of this world. They all talk the same language, they understand each other. The League already has what sound like fairly watertight rules on ownership of clubs, e.g. *"Except with the prior written consent of the management committee, no club may, either directly or indirectly, have any power whatsoever to influence the management or administration of another club."* (Rule 80, Clause 4). David Bulstrode had had no communication whatsoever with the League when the story first broke.

The problem is with the will to enforce the rules. Bulstrode's influence (owner of two clubs, in effect, and one other ground) is grossly in breach of the League's rules, in spirit anyway, even if he can get round them technically. So is Robert Maxwell's, with his son in charge at Derby. So is Terry "I wouldn't mind owning four of five clubs" Ramsden's. So was Anton Johnson's before the law (not the League) caught up with him. Even more of a challenge to their authority is the fact that these people can float their barmy ideas for mergers (don't forget Thames Valley Royals) with some expectation that the League will actually let them do it? If the League isn't able to control absolutely the names and grounds of the teams which they allow to take part in their competitions, just what *do* they control?

One of the reasons why Fulham are in financial difficulty (apart from the fact that Ernie Clay pocketed a reported £6 Million personally, when Bulstrode bought him out), is the new set of rules brought in this season which direct more TV, sponsorship and gate money from the small clubs to the larger ones (see issue 2). So when the League talk about their burning desire to save clubs like Fulham, it would be naive in the extreme to take them at face value. They are committed to a policy of so-called 'natural' wastage, whereby no club that goes out of business will be replaced in the League. The fact that they were shamed into action on this occasion doesn't guarantee by any means that the same will apply in the future.

The Council

In Fulham's case, much has been made (particularly by Brian Glanville, who described Ernie Clay as "a hero of our times") of the original decision by Hammersmith and Fulham Council to refuse permission for partial redevelopment at Craven Cottage, which prompted Clay to sell out. While this kind of scheme now looks to be about the best that Fulham can hope for, the desecration of two sides of their ground was hardly an attractive option at the time. In the recent furore, the Council have, so far, done the football club proud and should be applauded for their resolve. The previous (Tory) council to some extent created this whole situation by giving Marler outline planning permission to redevelop Stamford Bridge. If the present council had been as pliable, there would now be no future for either Chelsea or Fulham, or QPR for that matter. In Merton, too, the Council have made noises suggesting that their priority is to keep Wimbledon at Plough Lane, although as yet (at the time of writing) their commitment has not been as public. Fortunately in Wimbledon's case there is the added safeguard that the ground is officially designated for recreational purposes only.

The Property Men

Blaming Bulstrode and the rest is pointless. All we can expect from these people is lies deviousness, trickery and financial manipulation. And that's exactly what we got.

The Supporters

The fans' reaction on the whole, was positive, coherent, peaceful and passionate, and this is what got the press on our side. But where no independent supporters groups existed, (i.e. Q.P.R., where the Official Supporters Club *supported* the merger) they had to be quickly set up. The strong organisation of the Football Supporters Association in London was a great help in co-ordinating these actions, but in addition, supporters have to learn from this that every club needs an *independent* Supporters Club which has the authority to speak for a majority of the fans. Fulham were in just such a position, and this helped them to get the lion's share of the coverage.

The whole merger business should now be seen not as a victory or a defeat, but as an *opportunity* for fans in the capital (and elsewhere of course) to get together and organise, not against each other, but against their common enemies, such as Bulstrode, Clay, Hammam, Noades etc. It's now or never.

(continued back page)

INSIDE

More Merger Mania

Hibs Still on the Fringe

Bristol: Rovers Return?

Jimmy Hill "Not power-crazy" Shock!

Dixon For Arsenal? Juventus? Barnet?

PLUS: Forest ...

Reading... Germany

The Shankill Skinhead

Number 8
50p

mufc

SOMEONE LIKES US

NO BALL GAMES

FEB 1991 £1

GOOD MAN
JON HEADS FOR SUCCESS

Blow Football (1989-n.d.) included witty articles on refereeing mistakes and clueless officials. The well-known *When Saturday Comes* (1986-) features contributions from both professional writers and fans. *The Shankill Skinhead* (1990s) was a short-lived Manchester United zine. *Someone Likes Us* (1990s) was a Millwall Football Club zine. *Through the Wind & Rain* (1989-) is a Liverpool Football Club zine that covered the 1989 Hillsborough disaster with sensitivity. *Hail Mary!* (1990s) was packed with information on the American Football and National Football Leagues. *NBA Update* (1991-n.d.) followed the National Basketball Association team results. *Murtaugh* (1990s) was a baseball zine. *Waiting for the Great Leap Forward* (1989-) was a Motherwell Club zine with 1970s comic strips rewritten to reflect the Scottish Football League.

Andy Paton   Steve Kirk

No.8   *the " my left foot " cup special*   50p

Severely Twisted! (1990s) was a queerzine that provided commentary on the cult Australian TV series *Prisoner: Cell Block H*. *Holiday in the Sun* (1998–99) questioned the 'selling out' of fanzine producers and promised to 'demystify the process' of moving into the mainstream. *Question Everything Challenge Everything* (1996–2001) included articles on 'detecting bigots' and animal rights. *U.K. Resist* (1990s) was a mix of political rants and music. *Hoax!* (1991–93) was a satirical zine whose editor remarked that it was also the 'result of [his] first tentative steps into prankdom' – hence the cover with a picture of a 'Yippy'.

Other agit-prop zines flourished. *Ker Boom*
(1994) was an anti-capitalist fanzine that
condemned the 'police state' and included the
cult favourite comic strip 'Young Arnie' by
Simon Gane. *Protest Magazine* (1990s) was a
direct action and animal rights zine – 'the
vandalism of the ALF [Animal Liberation Front]
does not meet with the approval of the public,
but it does liberate the animals from their
prison of torture' – which also contained
poetry and vegan recipes. *Nil by Mouth*
(1990s) was an artzine and provided a forum
for illustrators and collage artists to make
political commentary on broader social issues.

CROPHEAD PRODUCTIONS 1985 PRESENTS

COMBAT ZONE
-INTERNATIONAL-

Nº1

ULSTER

A B H

offensive weapon

ØPPRESSED

INFA-RIOT

SKIN

ZINE

The second wave of the skinhead movement in the 1980s soon went international. It became associated both with the 'oi' music scene and with far right politics, though there were significant numbers of skinhead anti-fascists. *Combat Zone* (1980s) featured German, Italian and French bands as well as UK neo-fascists Skrewdriver. It was notable for its quality photos of skinhead fashion. This issue of *Skins* (1980s) covered a skinhead wedding, an interview with band Combat 84 and a 'Skin Girl Pin Up'. *Boredom Images* (1990s) was a minizine focusing on the history of skinhead fashion and literature. *Nosebleed* (1990s) billed itself as 'the independent voice of rock against fascism' and emanated from Dublin. *Strong & Proud* (1990s), from Spain, was a more sophisticated desktop-published zine, and included a photo report on scooter rallies in Portugal and Sweden. *Revenge* (1990s) was a transatlantic 'split zine' incorporating *Skinhead Liberation Organization* and *Unite for Unity* from the United States, and preached an anti-racist message.

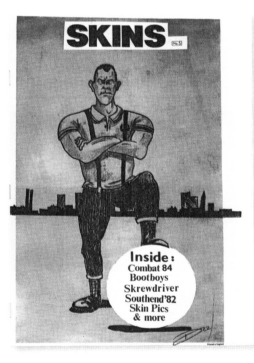

Go Go (1985–n.d.), produced by Jackie Toby
and Bernie Taylor, was billed as a 'monthly'
UK modzine with a focus on 1960s fashion,
music and scooter runs. Interviews with
bands included The Combine, Mood Six
and Paul Weller, alongside album and gig
reviews. Graphically, the zine's front
covers were particularly notable, with a
bold 1960s-inspired typographic logo and
photographic images of 1960s fashion models
reflecting both the Chelsea Girl and the
Mary Quant influence. A full feature story on
Quant appeared in issue 12. The zine offered
a more mellow and more female-friendly take
on the mod revival than its punk-influenced
predecessors in 1979.

EPTEMBER 85

No 6

0p

TV Personalities, the Prisoners, Kick, 5.30, news, clubs, Dreamworld, Mod Aid, gigs....and more!

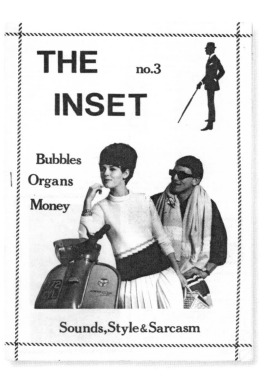

Modzines and more general 1960s-revival zines were a feature of the 1980s. *Smashed Blocked* (1980s) was a modzine produced by Bill Luther, who followed the band Mod Fun on their US tour. This issue of *The New Stylist* (1980s, back cover) was a one-off and focused on a collection of scooter memorabilia, including photos and line drawings of Vespas and Lambrettas. Judy Thomas of *Hip 'n' Groovy* (1986-n.d.) suggested that the mod fanzine scene was diversifying, but 'here, though is a very sixties-orientated zine'. *Real Emotion* (1983-n.d.) was an Irish modzine whose producer, Dev, assured his readership that the he would 'inform all of the Irish Mods who are unaware of the amount of good Mod bands…'. *The Inset* (1980s) was produced by a DJ for 1960s rhythm and soul nights. *Passion, Pride and Honesty* (1980s) was a Chichester-based zine, originally called *Teenage Beat*. *Time Moves Us On* (1985-n.d.) was another Chichester zine, '100% dedicated to mod'.

Mohawk Beaver (1997–) was a lesbian zine produced in Denmark; this issue has interviews with the band Rock Bitch and female entertainer Irma Henriksen. *FF Magazine* (*c.* 1986–90s) was an anarcho-punk queerzine. This issue features comic strips and an interview with comedian and gay icon Sandra Bernhard. *Holy Titclamps* (1989–2003) by Larry Bob was a popular queer punkzine out of Minneapolis then San Francisco. It was produced first as a single broadsheet page then as a 'grab-bag' format. *Kim Wilde Fan Club News* (1981–97) was about a pop star who was an icon in both hetero and gay worlds.

Kim Wilde

Fan Club News

WORLD COPYRIGHT 'BIG M', PRODUCTION L.T.D.........

vol.3 nom.3

1984 PRINTED IN GREAT BRITAIN. PUBLISHED BY THE KIM WILDE FAN CLUB....................

50 ¢

SUBTERRANEAN POP

Subterranean Pop (later *Sub Pop*) (1980–, covers and inside spreads), produced by Bruce Pavitt in Olympia, Washington, was dedicated to emerging indie rock bands in the US Northwest (later labelled 'grunge' by the rock press). Pavitt produced his first issue while still a student at Evergreen College in Olympia, and in issue 3 stated that '…we have to decentralize our society and encourage local art and things and music'. In 1986 he took himself at his word and with partner Jonathan Poneman set up indie record label Sub Pop, famous for signing Mudhoney, Nirvana and Sonic Youth. The label is largely regarded as having changed the path of rock music.

*ACE OF HEARTS	Box 579, Kenmore St., Boston MA 02215
*AMBITION	Box 3584, Washington D.C. 20007
*ARMAGEDDON	c/o 2775 E. Bankers Industrial Dr. Atlanta GA 30360
*BAD TRIP	11020 Ventura Blvd. Suite 218 Studio City CA 91604
*DB	432 Moreland Ave. N.E. Atlanta GA 30307
*EAT	400 Essex St. Salem MA 01970
*ENGRAM	P.O. Box 2305 Seattle WA 98101
*FETISH: import	
*FRIENDS	319 E. Broadway Vancouver B.C. Canada
*FRONTIER	P.O. Box 22 Sun Valley CA 91352
*HUNKY RECORDS	Box 1287 Milwaukee WI 53201
*HYRAX	P.O. Box 274 Old Chelsea Stn. NY NY 10011
*LAFMS	c/o Box 2853 Pasadena CA 91105
*LUST/UNLUST	P.O. Box 3208 Grand Central Stn. NY NY 10163
*MUTE: import	
*MYSTERY TOAST	Box 195 Saratoga Springs NY 12866
*99	99 MacDougal St. NY NY 10012
*OIL TASTERS	Box 92823 Milwaukee WI 53202
*ON/GO-GO	P.O. Box 8333 Philadelphia PA 19101
*PARK AVENUE	P.O. Box 14947 Portland OR 97214
*POSH BOY	P.O. Box 38861 Los Angeles CA 90038
*QUINTESSENCE	1869 W. 4th Ave. Vancouver B.C. Canada
*RED	810 Longfield Rd. Philadelphia PA 19118
*ROLLIN ROCK	6918 Peach Ave. Van Nuys CA 91406
*SHAKE	186 5th Ave. NY NY 10010
*UPSETTER	Box 2511 LA CA 90028
*SST	P.O. Box 1 Lawndale CA 90260
*STIFF: import	
*SUBURBAN INDUSTRIAL	1218 Loma Vista Long Beach CA 90813
*TRAP	Box 42465 Portland OR 97242
*TWIN TONE	445 Oliver Ave. So. Minneapolis MN 55405
*UPSETTER	Box 2511 L.A. CA 90028
*WHIZ EAGLE RECORDS	308 S.W. Washington Portland OR 97???

Hi there —

My name is Bruce and we have to decentralize our society and encourage <u>Local</u> art and things and music. SUB/POP can be an outlet for this kind of subversive entertainment perspective but only if you help me by writing <u>local</u> gossip and sending it in right away to me with money and photos of you and your friends playing rock star. Send it in and I will print it. O.K.

x Bruce

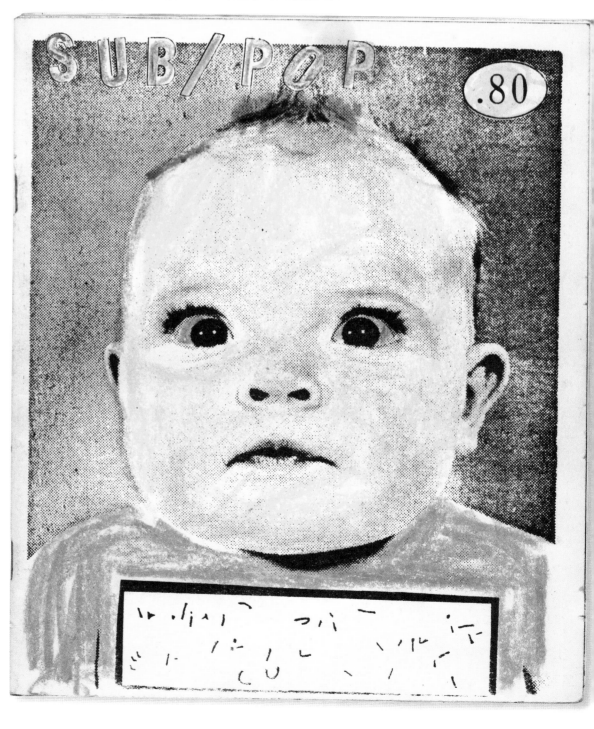

OIL WELL DERRICK

OIL WELL DERRICK

S U B

P O P

S I X

Probably anyone reading this would agree with me when I say Ronald Reagan is not a good American. He allows large corporations to run rampant over our environment, huge tax breaks for the rich while stabbing the poor in the back with cuts in social services, and then spends $55 million to kill teenage girls in El Salvador.

So what are you doing about it? Dressing like an idiot and buying records by four people who get up on stage and sweat a lot. If all an alternative scene does is let you forget about the real world for a couple hours a week, than it's no better than T.V., AM radio or Harlequine romances. The time has passed where we can afford to provide a place and a means for people to forget. We must rid ourselves of the things that hold us back from being truly alternative. One of those things is alcohol. It is provided for us by a leach-like industry that makes a few people (filthy) rich while numbing and anesthetizing the rest. When bands play in bars, not only do they segregate the scene by discriminating against their younger fans, but they teach their younger fans that it is cool to go to bars and get drunk, and thus support Reagan's best friends. Alcohol is just one way they use to oppress the populace, to funnel your hard-earned money back into the hands of the few. What we need is a network of all-ages performance halls where music can be experienced free of all that corporate bullshit, where the audience isn't segregated by age, and where the state liquor board (Police) would have no business interfering.

So. Don't just sit around picking your nose. If you're a musician, when you've got the audience's attention, use it to do something other than getting a hard on. If you edit a fanzine or do a radio show, you have a perfect opportunity to educate people about their government as well as their music. Don't think you can't make a difference, because you do. **CALVIN**

Howdy neighbor. Put down that gun and pick up this magazine.

SUB/POP IS AMERICAN. WE ALTERNATE BETWEEN A C-60 CASSETTE AND A PUBLICATION. WE ARE INTERESTED IN A DE-CENTRALIZED NETWORK OF REGIONAL AND LOCAL BUMS WHO REFUSE TO GET AN HONEST JOB. SEND US YOUR INDEPENDENT RECORDS, TAPES AND MAGAZINES. WRITE: SUB/POP C/O LOST MUSIC NET-WORK, BOX 2391, OLYMPIA, WA 98507.

GRAPHICS, COORDINATION. . . . BRUCE PAVITT
FRIENDS AND NEIGHBORS. . . . CALVIN JOHNSON, JAN LOFT-NESS, TUCKER PETERTIL, GARY MAY

FINALLY PRINTED IN FEB. 1982

1981? Simple enough . . . Britain gave us New Romantic white/electro/disco/funk and America gave us . . . what? Hardcore.

While art bands continued to take their orders from the U.K., aggressive muscleheads from around the country formed bands, started labels and bull-dozed an anti-authority network that is digging its way into every suburban high school in the U.S. Punk-thrash is now faster, louder and more American than ever.

Surprise. Today's Hardcore teenage army is the most dominant, the most obvious scene in the American music underground. Hardcore is intense, honest American music; burning red, white and blue images confronting specific American problems. Anthems like "Justice For All," "Six Pack," and "Guns or Ballots," band names like the Dead Kennedys, The Minutemen, and yes, even Jody Foster's Army. Does this sound British? No!

Things are bad. America is falling apart; the economy is collapsing; Reagan is a puppet of the rich and the Pentagon is going to blow life as we know it into fragments. We must react. American culture desperately needs to confront American problems.

Hardcore America is organized. L.A. puts out a new compilation every time I open the mailbox. Posh Boy, Happy Squid, New Alliance, Bemisbrain, SST—all working on organizing teenage revolt. D.C.'s Dischords—savage and defiant. Incredible. Chicago's Autumn records has released the first regional compilation to emerge from Chicago-Hardcore. Touch and Go fanzine just released a compilation of Mich/Ohio bands—more youth riots. Noise fanzine (Ohio) is collaborating with Reno, Nevada, and putting out a great-looking trans-regional cassette. Teenage America in action!

Of course, any strongly defined movement is going to be guilty of bigotry, and Hardcore is no exception. Bands are either Hardcore or they suck. How depressing. Gang mentality is no substitute for independence. Like Black Flag says: "Think for yourself."

I like Hardcore. I like the rush and I like the attitude. Fuck Authority. I hate war and I hate big business and I'm glad that other people feel the same way. Isn't it great that not all teenagers are sucking bongs on the way to play Pac-Man at some sick zoo of a shopping mall? RISE ABOVE. **BRUCE**

More *Sub Pop* (see previous page). The cover
to issue 6 explains how the zine alternates
'between a C-60 cassette and a publication',
and solicits demo tapes from new bands (*Sub
Pop* no. 5 Cassette, 1982, sold 2,000 copies).
Pavitt was inspired in this strategy by two
radio DJs in Melbourne, Australia, who had
founded a cassette fanzine titled *Fast Forward*
(1980). The *Sub Pop* Cassettes are now extremely
collectible. Other zine covers featured the
remarkable cartoon artistry of Charles Burns,
a cult figure for his contributions to *Raw*
magazine, who offered a vision of alienation
via his use of heavy blacks and retro imagery.
The other cartoonist closely associated with
Sub Pop was humorist Peter Bagge.

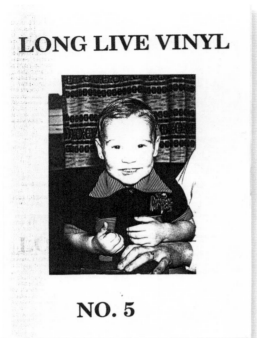

LONG LIVE VINYL

NO. 5

Big Muff 3½

50p

Hole

AC Temple

Ween

The Primitives

Whipped Cream

Rebel Sound

VOLUME ONE NUMBER 3

JAWBOX

RADICTS

HELMET

NAKED RAYGUN

BLASTER!

...RIDES AGAIN

2

A HOUSE
SHONEN KNIFE
DRIVE
WHITE TOWN
NED'S KROSS
TONY HARCOCK
THE FINNISH SCENE
YOUNG FRESH FELLOWS
R AMERICAN COUSINS

every keen
otorcyclist

117

MINUS ZERO RECORDS
071-229-5424
£1

lesson

8

'chummy but earnest'
Includes archive Tape feature...

A range of 1990s music zines. *Long Live Vinyl* (1990s) was a collection of band interviews and album reviews out of Nottingham. *Big Muff* (1990s) was an indie music zine produced in London, in this issue featuring an interview with Courtney Love and her band Hole. *Rebel Sound* (1990s) was a punk rock zine whose producer wrote: 'I love doing the zine and I'm thrilled at the fact that I've received so much positive support.' *117* (1990s) became known for its regular feature 'The A–Z of Psych (and other great sounds)', which reviewed records from the 1960s–70s. The format of *Blaster!* (1990s) was designed around the inclusion of a 7 inch vinyl single.

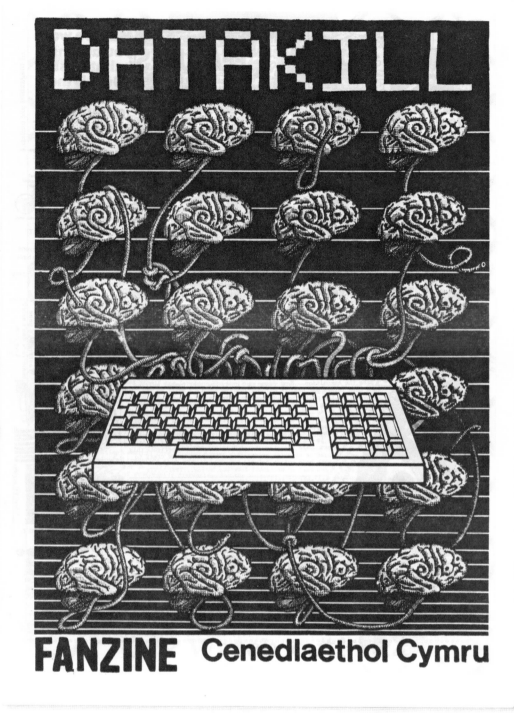

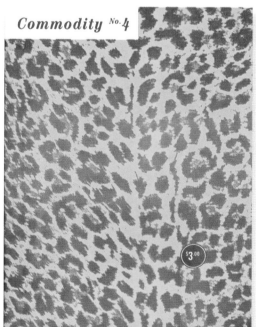

Lesser-known 1980s-90s music zines are seen on this page. *Då* (1990s) was a Swedish zine printed on yellow stock and using quality photographs. *Calling Dr Crankin* (1989-n.d.) declared itself to be 'the fanzine which offers the discarded, forgotten, overlooked, or just plain neglected, the chance to even the musical score'. *Datakill* (1989-n.d.) was an indie music zine with a Welsh slant produced by *Hoax*'s editor Johnny Datakill. *Lil' Rhino Gazette* (1990s) was a Fort Worth quarterly 'zine of miscellaneous cultural debris' featuring local talent. *Commodity* (1994-n.d.) was a self-consciously 'designed' music zine by Josh Hooten (later an art director for *Punk Planet*) and Tony Leon.

Boy's Own (1987-92) was a football and acid house zine produced by DJs leading the London scene. Its distinctive logo and series of covers were by illustrator Dave Little. *Beach Boys Stomp* (c. 1980s-) is a long-running zine dedicated to the discography and gigs of the California band. *Teenage Depression* (1976-80s) bridged punk and mainstream rock-and-roll fanzines, focusing on a range of bands. This issue featured boogie rock outfit Status Quo. *The Farm Fanzine* (early 1990s) provided a mix of stories about the band as well as commentary on 1990s 'Scally' (Liverpudlian) culture. *Moonlight Drive* (1980s) was a rock zine with almost an academic approach to the subject.

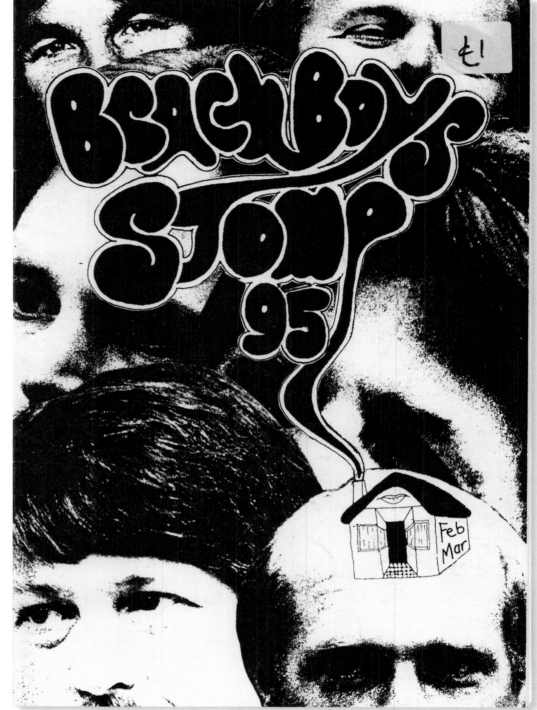

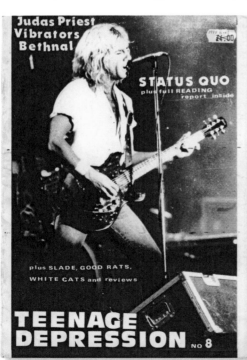

T Mershi Duween Zappa Fanzine (1990s) was a text-heavy Frank Zappa zine out of Sheffield that prided itself on extensive bootleg reviews. *Boomshackalacka* (1990s) specialized in reggae music but also announced that it was 'now a sound system' playing for dances which 'have been showcases of unity and good vibes'. *Morri'Zine* (c. 1989–c.1994) was a quarterly dedicated to reporting on the music of Morrissey and the Smiths. *Pick of the Bunch* (1970s–) is 'Scotland's longest living hotchpotch zine', mixing music with perzine-style reflections. *Omaha Rainbow* (1973–n.d.) in its 1980s incarnation provided a mainstream rock-orientated alternative to the prevailing punk zine aesthetic. *Rockrgrl* (1995–2005) was devoted to women in rock, regardless of category. *Offering* (1990s) was a Carpenters zine.

femme flicke

ISSUE 4

$2.00

The Real World

Heavenly Creatures

Rebecca Spinones on music videos

Four Free Ways to Get your Film SEEN

Women in the Director's Chair

ThE so-CaLled rEAl WorlD

I was never a fan of the New York or Los Angeles Real Worlds. But for the past year, everytime I flick on MTV, if I catch a glimpse of Rachel, Cory, Pedro, Judd, Puck, Mohammad, or Jo, from the Real World, San Francisco, I find it virtually painful to change the channel. I'm addicted to the Real World!!

It' weird because usually for me it's hard to get emotionally involved in fictional TV drama, like 90210. (Don't get me wrong, I watch it almost every

week, but I don't really relate to the characters or storylines—although I have to admit Donna's attempted-rape scene had me in tears this spring).

But the Real World is like watching actual people...sometimes like watching myself. I feel for the "characters."

God, that scares me: that there's not a clear line between

reality and TV. That makes me feel creepy. But somehow, I still can't stop watching.

I think part of the reason might be that I know (well, at least I'm pretty sure) that what happens on the show is real. No one wrote a script for them. Sure, the producers clearly chose people with personalities that might clash, and therefore cause good

drama. But the people still have actual emotions and personalities.

Now lest you think I'm totally hyping up the "realness" of the show, let me tell you, I'm quite aware that the editors are very selective about what they show—the final product is by no means a fair, or fully balanced representation of the housemates' daily lives. We never get to see any of the "characters" talk about the fact that they are the Real World, that they are going to be on TV every week, and what that means about how they live their lives and (inter)act in front of the camera.

I mean, they must explain why they are constantly being videotaped when they're going on job interviews, or going into a restaurant. I've never even seen a stander-by make a face or ask a question. What else aren't we getting to see?

We never get the family or friends responses to being on the show. Everyone just acts like there's no camera. That's not real. I mean, I can see the characters getting used to the camera eventually, but not outsiders like friends (like Rachel's giddy friends from Arizona), business aquintences (like when Judd goes to LA to pitch his cartoons), and family members.

Granted, the shows are all taped before they begin airing, so obviously there's not going to be a high recognition factor— people saying "hey, you're Rachel from the Real World"—or a high family response factor— like "Pedro, what do you mean you're engaged to Sean?"

In one of the first episodes Puck (what a confused mess of an

egomaniac he is!!) "discusses" (I use that term lightly when it comes to Puck) 90210 with the other housemates, and he accuses them of being "psycho" for actually caring about Brandon Walsh. The thing is, I agree with him. That's sick when people get all worked up about a character on a show and talk about them like they're real, isn't it? But what about if I think I care about the Real World cast? Am I fucked? To me, are they people, or are they characters, no different from Brandon Walsh? I don't know them...and somehow I'm not sure if they fit in the "real person" catagory or the TV character catagory.

... is a

gilligan's IsLanD

RIp OfF

THEME '70 FANZINE

No. 2

£1:50

BRUCE LEE

TOUGH GUYS

ISAAC HAYES

CLAUDIA JENNINGS

BLAXPLOITATION!

EXPLOITATION

The consumer world of pop culture and television features in these examples. *The TV Collector* (1982-99) was an unashamedly nostalgic bi-monthly publication for collectors of television films, videotapes and memorabilia. *No Remakes* (1990s) has a cover featuring the characters Starsky and Hutch but is in fact a music zine – each issue gloried in seeing 'who'll be waving goodbye to their career'. *TV Times* (n.d.) was a Situationist-inspired 'literate and graphic destruction of TV culture', containing pithy phrases such as 'We apologise for the loss of meaning. Please do not adjust your life'. *Totting Times* (1999-2000, renamed *Rag 'n' Bone* 2000-02) was produced by fans of the popular British TV sitcom *Steptoe and Son*. *Femme Flicke* (1990s, cover and inside spread) by Tina Spangler featured work by indie women filmmakers, as well as 'how-to' advice and DIY film resources. The spread ruminates on the ethics of the MTV reality show *Real World*. *Theme '70 Fanzine* (1994-n.d.) took a wry look at blaxploitation, kung fu films and ex-*Playboy* Playmate starlets.

Fish Piss (1996–) is an irregular bilingual
Canadian zine by Louis Rastelli, combining
comic strips and drawings with fiction and
poetry. *Pop!* (n.d.) was a 'free' perzine which
folded out to a larger sheet photocopied on
both sides with musings about Joe Pop's life
and popular culture. *Chicken Is Good Food*
(late 1990s) was a visually playful music
and popular culture zine with 1950s retro
illustrations and articles. *The White Dot*
(1996–2000) was an acerbic 'newsletter for
television-free households'. *Nancy's Magazine*
(1983–), produced by librarian and writer Nancy
Bonnell-Kangas, provides insights into daily
life: for example how to plant and cultivate
seeds. *Chip's Closet Cleaner* (1989–) is about
'pop culture, humour, triva and fun'. *Giant
Robot* (1994–) is a bi-monthly glossy magazine
that began as a small punkzine, featuring
Asian pop culture and Asian-American
alternative culture. *Robot Power* (2000) was
a short-lived smaller 'zine-within-a-magazine'
insert featuring Chris Ware and Daniel Clowes.
Oriental Whatever (1995, 1998–) is an Asian-
American-orientated zine that went from 100
to 1,500 copies distributed internationally.

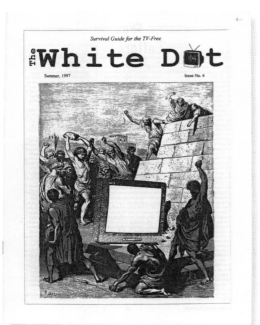

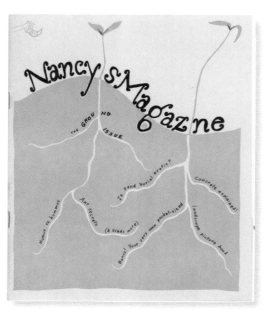

Pop Culture ▼ Humor ▼ Trivia ▼ Fun

Chip's Closet Cleaner

Number 11 — Four Bucks

Really Weird Sex!

◆

Almost Dirty Words!

◆

My Girlfriend **Wears My Favorite** Tees!

◆

Unseen Spinal Tap!

◆

Scary **Products!**

◆

8-Track **Madness!**

◆

4,487 Rippin' Book and Zine Reviews!*

◆

...And Much More Than You Can Chew **in One** Bite!

*give or take a few

Horror film zines emerged around the same
time as early science fiction fanzines.
and in the 1990s enjoyed a short boom in
production. An early predecessor was *Gothique*
(1960s). dedicated to the Hammer Films actor
Christopher Lee. who portrayed some of the
all-time great horror characters. *Vincent
Price File* (1996) by London-based Simon Flynn
was a genuine 'fan zine' with tribute pieces
about the horror film actor. who died in 1993.
Psychotronic Video (1980-2006) was a fanzine
that featured articles on the film genre of
the same name.

The other zines on this spread exemplify a selection of genres: music, art and popular culture. *Ain't Bin to No Art School* (n.d.) was an art zine by Michael J. Weller that comprised single tear-out sheets of magazine adverts, comic-book pages and newspaper television schedules and also featured his own page of 'Xerox poemik' collages. *Lip Service* (1980s) was a crossover zine combining music and popular culture in the tradition of punk. The cover pays homage to Lady Diana and the Royal Wedding. *Zine Zone* (1990s) was a free monthly culture zine whose editor suggests that 'our speciality is to identify new trends'.

MaximumRocknRoll began as a punk-rock radio show in 1977, then became a print zine in 1982 with music reviews from zine writers such as Jen Angel, Jack Rabid and Matt Wobensmith. *Punk Planet* (1994–2007), a 'designed' publication, focused on the culture of punk and was notable for its extensive record reviews. *Profane Existence* (1989–98, 2000–08) was a zine and record label run by an anarcho-punk collective out of Minneapolis. *Revolting* (1993–n.d.) was a political zine with a punk attitude. H.A.G.L. (c. 1984–) provided coverage of punk music in the north-eastern United Kingdom.

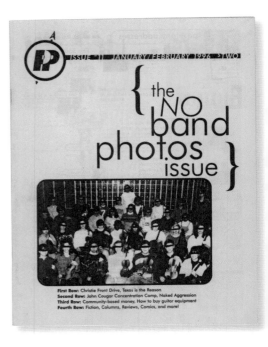

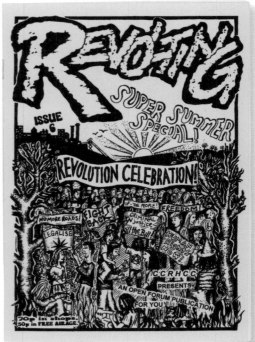

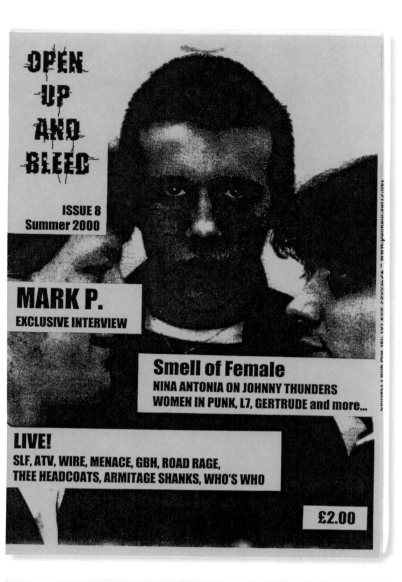

Open Up and Bleed (c. 1998-) is a punk and garage fan's zine inviting readers to contribute actively to revisiting the 1970s scene: 'let us know about your wildest anecdotes and how you made history queuing, boozing, puking, squatting, shagging…' The producers pay homage to 'the genius of Mark P.' (of *Sniffin' Glue*) and the history of punk music, fashion and popular culture in general. *Ruptured Ambitions* (c. 1989-c. 2008) was a Devon-based fanzine that prided itself for reporting on lesser-known local bands. *Your Flesh* (1981-) reports on the Minneapolis punk-rock scene as well as 'alternative/outlaw art, politically incorrect and irreverent social humor and skateboarding'. The cover art became notable, with contributions from Lee Ellingson (this issue), Ron Clark and Jeff Gaither.

THE DEFINITIVE GUIDE TO THE ZINE REVOLUTION

FACTSHEET5

Comics
Music
Food
Sex
Art
Stuff
Kooks
Politics
Literature

#48 $3.95

Metazines and zine catalogues flourished during the 1980s-90s. *Factsheet Five* (1982-98) was the most important of the genre, founded by Mike Gunderloy (with subsequent editors including Cari Goldberg Janice, Jacob Rabinowitz, Hudson Luce, R. Seth Friedman and Jerod Pore) and providing comprehensive zine reviews that were often more entertaining that the zines themselves. It became a focal point for the burgeoning international zine communities and created a prototype zine taxonomy. *All Genre* (1990s) was bi-monthly and 'dedicated to the freer dissemination of music and information of all styles and genres'. *Amok* (late 1980s) was a series of 'dispatch sourcebooks' produced by Ken Swezey and Adam Parfrey (an influential underground publisher) with a contents list including 'exotica', 'sleaze', 'sensory deprivation', and 'mayhem'. *Action Resource Guide Cata-zine* (c. 1991-95) was devoted to 'grassroots, political actions' and included 'a prisoner and zinester network contact list', as well as the usual listings. This issue incorporated *Prisoner's Speak* [sic] which was 'a collection of words and images from incarcerated prisoners'.

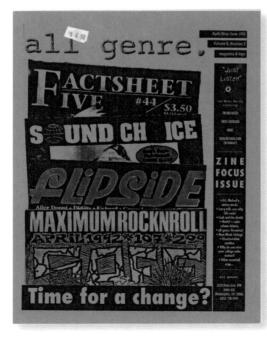

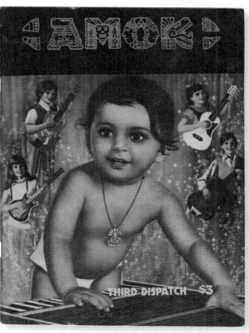

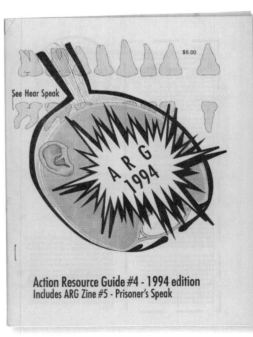

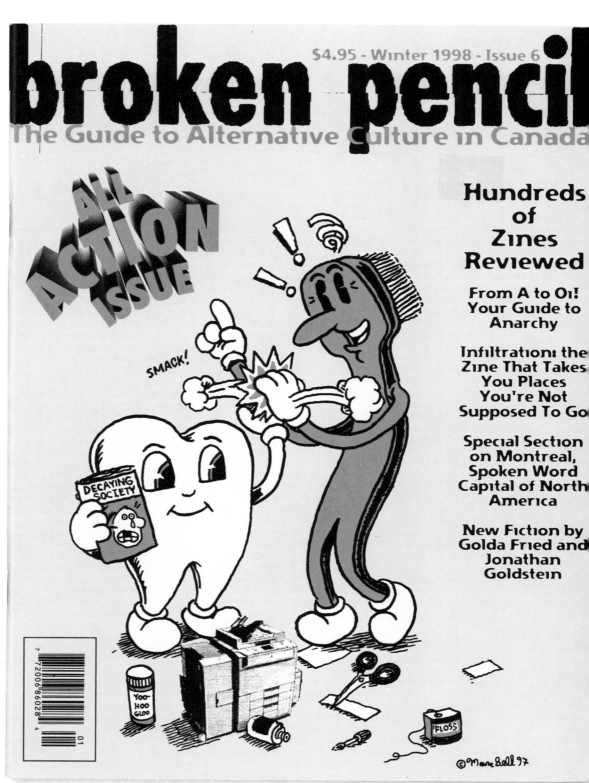

Bypass (early 1990s) was a UK-based review magazine for 'zine producers, self-publishers, small press organizations, pamphleteers and outside agitators'. It was relaunched in 2007 online. *Book Your Own Fuckin' Life* (1992–) is a DIY resource guide published by *MaximumRocknRoll* and the Amoeba Collective, notable for its international reach. *Broken Pencil* (1995–), out of Canada, reviews alternative publications in print and online and has taken over where *Factsheet Five* left off. *The Zine* (1990s) was the most concerted attempt in the United Kingdom to produce a mainstream version of a fanzine complete with free classified ads and zine reviews.

CHAPTER FOUR

GIRL POWER AND
PERSONAL POLITICS
1990–1997

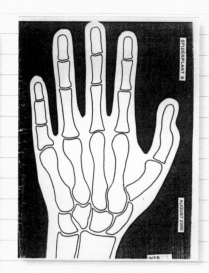

Bikini Kill was 'more than just a band – it's a revolution', and the fanzine *Bikini Kill* (early 1990s) demonstrates band member Tobi Vail's commitment to the rise of a new feminism as seen through the riot grrrl movement. The band's singer, Kathleen Hanna, produced *April Fool's Day* (1995), in which she confessed she was an alcoholic: 1 April is when she decided to stop drinking. In the perzine *Spiderplant* (2000) the producer remarks: 'I first wrote my first fanzine at 15.'

After the high point of punk, the 1990s was a prolific period for fanzines that were politically motivated. The rise of the music-inspired riot grrrl movement revitalized small press publishing through a slew of new fanzines, including most famously, in the United States, *Bikini Kill* (Tobi Vail, Kathi Wilcox and Kathleen Hanna, early 1990s), *Riot Grrrl* (Molly Neuman, Allison Wolfe, 1991–n.d.) and *Girl Germs* (Molly Neuman and Allison Wolfe, 1990–92). These and others helped to galvanize a new generation of feminists to continue questioning, as their 1970s counterparts had done before them, notions of gender identity, sexuality and representation, queer politics, multiculturalism and equality with their male counterparts in the music industry (and elsewhere).

From Punk to Grrrl Revolution?

The riot grrrl movement came to public consciousness in 1991 at the International Pop Underground Convention held in Olympia, Washington – a six-day festival organized by Calvin Johnson (founder of the K Records label) and Bruce Pavitt (producer of *Sub Pop* fanzine, who had created a new form of fanzine, with two issues released as compilation cassettes). The first evening of the festival was aptly titled 'Love Rock Revolution Girl Style Now', and featured all-women bands such as 7 Year Bitch, Jean Smith and Bratmobile. These women ascended the stage in a collective act of defiance against the dominant male music industry, especially that represented by punk. As one promotional flyer promised: 'There will be lots of time to talk with other women about how we fit or don't fit in the punk community.'

The mainstream press made much of this connection early on with punk,[1] while acknowledging that many of the riot grrrls were too young to have experienced punk in its first incarnation. The most explicit connection between punk and riot grrrl was through a shared notion of DIY.[2] Punk's promotion of the philosophy that 'anyone can do it' had prompted young women to pick up their guitars and to rediscover earlier bands, such as the Raincoats – an all-female punk band and precursor to riot grrrl notable for addressing issues of gender and image. In the fanzine *Mental Children* (1980), one interviewer comments that 'the Raincoats are out on their own, proving that girls can produce vital new music, owing nothing to anyone else but themselves'. Gina, a member of the band, remarked that 'punk wasn't the final push for me, it was the initial push'.[3] By 1993 riot grrrl surfaced in the United Kingdom with bands such as Linus, Mambo Taxi, Skinned Teen, the Voodoo Queens and Huggy Bear, whose 1993 track 'Our Troubled Youth' was described as one of the best documentations of youthful British angst since punk's famous Clash album *London Calling*. The difference, however, was that riot grrrl advocated a female exclusivity, which was not always present in the manifestos of earlier female punk bands. These later bands were pioneers of a 'Girl Now Revolution', often meaning an aggressive display of female sexuality reminiscent of first-wave feminism. Fanzines became an integral part of the movement.

Personal is Political

Whereas punk fanzines took an authorial position that reflected predominantly male concerns, featuring groups consisting of 'four guys with guitars' and variously defined interests in anarchist politics, riot grrrl zine texts often adopted a women's autobiographical approach (such as diaries and storytelling narratives) reflecting personal opinions and aspirations that were by their very nature a critique of the punk zines that had come before. Sleater-Kinney band member Corin Tucker, who was also the producer of an early American-based riot grrrl zine, *Channel Seven* (early 1990s), summed up her feelings by stating: 'I choose to write about my life for myself and because I think there is something to be learned from most people's personal experiences.'[4]

The importance of the fanzine as a space for a women-only discourse was underscored by the first line of the 'Riot Grrrl Manifesto', written in 1991, which appeared in the second issue of the zine *Bikini Kill*: 'BECAUSE us girls crave records and books and fanzines that speak to US that WE feel included in and can understand in our own ways.' Riot grrrl bands often criticized the motives of the mainstream music

The handmade is showcased in these three early riot grrrl zines. Producers Rachel and Sarah announce on the cover of *Kitten Carousell* (early 1990s) that this is the 'special nail varnish issue'. *Bombshell* (early 1990s), out of Merseyside, uses stars as part of the handwritten title. Karren Ablaze was one of the early promoters of women in music through her fanzine *Ablaze!* (1987–93) and in this issue she experiments by attaching the table of contents to the cover.

press, in which they were often misrepresented. Corin Tucker reflects that the entire movement was trivialized by the mainstream press as 'being a fashion statement'.[5] Huggy Bear famously practised a media blackout, giving interviews only to fanzine producers. Fanzines provided a forum in which riot grrrls could critique and reject mainstream media, but also importantly represented an uncensored arena for reaching out and sharing experiences with other young women.

The personal is also reinforced through the visual identity of each individual riot grrrl fanzine. These fanzines took the graphic language of punk – photo-booth images, hand-drawn comic strips, collage illustrations and cut-and-paste ransom-note lettering – and added a set of feminist-inspired characteristics, each producer introducing her own unique DIY style. Producers appropriated techniques to add a 'sweetness' or visual associations of femininity. *Kitten Carousell* (early 1990s) used hand-painted nail varnish for the title of an issue whose main feature was about experiments on animals by the cosmetic industry. *Rebel Grrrl Punk* (1997–2000) adorned its covers with hand-drawn stars and hearts surrounding photographs of feminist icons such as Courtney Love. The visual thus sanctioned the ethos that riot grrrls were both empowered to be feminists and had the choice to be feminine.

Riot grrrl fanzines can be paradoxical and often iconic. Graphic devices that are considered 'feminine' are pitted against those that are found to be 'masculine'. Take, for example, the adoption of the Japanese-produced 'Hello Kitty' as a third-wave feminist icon. This cute illustration, created in 1974 by the designer Ikuko Shimiz, provided riot grrrls with a symbol of femininity and at the same time of commodity fetishism. Within the context of riot grrrl fanzines, Hello Kitty is a tool of cultural subversion signalling the desire to protest against, but equally to reclaim, the term 'girly'. Hello Kitty is re-contextualized as simultaneously feminine and radical by means of a post-punk fanzine aesthetic of high-contrast photocopied imagery, degradation of tone into unreadable areas of text, and collage-like layering of cut-out texts.

Borrowing from the Mainstream

Such an approach continues through the way in which the format of the riot grrrl fanzine draws from the conventions of mainstream women's magazines. First, riot grrrl zines draw upon mainstream media imagery, much of it literally cut up from newspapers and magazines. Secondly, riot grrrl fanzines often replicate the content format used by mainstream girls' magazines, such as review columns, readers' pages and feature stories. Yet, unlike the readers of girls' magazines, the riot grrrl producers are in a proactive position of empowerment. They operate outside mainstream fashion and lifestyle consumer culture, often in direct opposition. Lucy Sweet, writing in her fanzine *Chica* (2001–c. 2004, UK), announces that 'there's something about the superficiality of a woman's magazine I really enjoy. But boy, oh boy, they are just so frustratingly predictable.'[6] *Chica*'s layout conforms to the conventional divisions of a mainstream magazine with 'The Features', 'Regulars', 'Editor's Letter', 'Letters Page', 'Horoscopes', and 'Stars Letters'. Its strength, however, is in its ironic intent (such as in spoof columns like 'Slut in the City'), where Sweet draws inspiration from 'having a bit of old-fashioned fun' in writing and the cut-and-paste imagery from 1980s *Jackie* annuals (*Jackie* was a best-selling mainstream girls' periodical in the United Kingdom, subsequently subjected to trenchant feminist criticism). Sweet acknowledges that 'it's got a kind of knockabout, cartoony feel to it, and it's very rude, with an anti-celebrity slant and lots of crumpet and swearing. It's definitely no *Glamour* and it doesn't fit into your handbag.'[7] Fanzines thus actively engage with popular cultural texts in much the same way that punk did thirty years earlier.

These fanzines never forgot their second-wave feminist predecessors. Riot grrrl zines form part of an established feminist publishing history with forerunners such as *Spare Rib* (1972–93) and *Shocking Pink* (c. 1982, 1987–92) in the United Kingdom and *Ms. Magazine* (1972–) in the United States that were forums for raising such issues as equal pay, child care, health care and anti-ageism. *Spare Rib* emerged out of Britain's counter-cultural underground in 1972,

The tension between being a feminist and at the same time 'feminine' resonates in the use of visual imagery in many riot grrrl fanzines. *Starlet* (1994) is a 'tiny little fanzine' (in a mini format), with Marilyn Monroe as this issue's cover icon, yet inside, articles on weight problems among young women feature. *Twinkle Eye Fizzy* (n.d.) combines pink copy-paper with photo-collages of young women, and cites Drew Barrymore as a feminist icon. The zine-style programme for *Le Tigre and Las Sin Fronteras* (2000) promotes 'a feminist cabaret' at the Solar Culture club, starring Le Tigre (Kathleen Hanna's band post-Bikini Kill) plus opening act Las Sin Fronteras.

Botramaid

£1

FANZINE WITH MANNERS

SPACE

MEKONS

CATATONIA

SHED SEVEN

Record reviews: Bikini Kill, Shed Seven, Ash, Mekons, Terrorvision, Ride, Sleater-Kinney, The make-up

Also: quiz, cartoons etc ....

Botramaid (late 1990s) by Gail Douglas and Lorraine Douglas was an entertaining mix of music, cartoons and cut-out paper dolls. In the United States, Sabrina Margarita Sandata founded the feminist/queerzine *Bamboo Girl* (1995–), challenging stereotypes from a Filipina/Asian point of view. The Pretty Ugly Collective in Australia produced *Pretty Ugly* (2002–) in the hope of 'inspiring young women to write zines'. It asked whether 'the riot grrrl movement has had its day' and wondered what happens to girls when they become women.

pretty ugly

issue #2

BAMBOO GIRL

The riot grrrl ethos continued to evolve via a series of festivals. The *Ladyfest Glasgow* programme (2001) documented the first European Ladyfest, where bands such as Katastropy Wife and local Scottish indie group BIS took the stage. *UK Ladyfest Artwork 2001-2008* (2008) was a collection of posters, programmes and flyers from 18 festivals complied by Heather Crabtree and Melanie Maddison, to demonstrate the diversity of approaches to the visual identity of riot grrrl.

becoming a vehicle for the women's liberation movement. This second-wave feminist magazine saw its founders, including Marsha Rowe and Rosie Boycott, focus on the 'personal being political' by covering such topics as sexuality, lesbianism, masturbation, women in industry and equal working conditions. *Shocking Pink* announced its remit was to 'counter the propaganda of magazines like *Jackie*' and to celebrate women's sexuality – whether straight or lesbian.[8] The graphic language of each publication built upon a distinctive DIY aesthetic where handwritten texts and stark black-and-white photographs featured within a layout more post-punk than glossy women's magazine.

Perhaps the most significant aspect of the graphic language employed by riot grrrl fanzine producers is the use of the three 'r's in the revamped word 'girl', in an attempt not only to reclaim the term but to reinforce it through embellishment. The world 'girl' is invested 'with a new set of connotations', which now may be read as an 'angry feminist who relished engaging in activity'.[9]

Historians have recorded that the term 'riot' originally derived from a passing comment, 'We need a girl riot, too', in reference to 1991 riots in Mount Pleasant, Washington, DC, sparked by a shooting amid racial tensions.[10] The term 'riot grrrl' is also reported to have derived from Bratmobile drummer Tobi Vail, who wrote about 'grrrls' in the fanzine *Jigsaw* (1988–). Whatever its origin, the term graphically comes to life if 'riot grrrl' is visualized and read as an aggressive-sounding 'growl'. The multiple 'r's have a strong impact. The word is simultaneously read and heard. Writing is treated as 'visual text' – the way in which the forms are drawn facilitates communication of the riot grrrl message. Equally, 'grrrl' as a word is symbolic and is interpreted by different fanzine readers and producers to mean different things, thereby catering for (and representing) the range of voices and audiences riot grrrl embraces.

Girls Grow Up

In 2000, riot grrrl supporters organized the first Ladyfest convention in Olympia, Washington. Ladyfest was given its name as a way to

reclaim the word 'lady'. Allison Wolfe of Bratmobile remembers that founder Kathleen Hanna remarked, 'We will have to find a new word when we get older and become ladies.'[11] Although riot grrrl was initially seen as a response against the patriarchical attitude of the mainstream music industry, it was symptomatic of attempts to empower women more generally. Ladyfest Glasgow (2001), the first European festival following the Olympia event, similarly aimed to reject the conventional role models offered by the dominant cultural industries.[12] Lee Beattie, one of the Glasgow organizers, explains: 'The whole ethos surrounding Ladyfest was to take the ideas away and make them relevant where you live… Ladyfest does inspire you to start changing things yourself, no matter what the scale or size.'[13] Ladyfest provided opportunities for fanzine producers to sell and exchange their zines. At the same time, spoken-word artists and, in this case, menstrual activist Chella Quint, of the fanzine *Adventures in Menstruating* (2005–, UK), had a stage on which to share their fanzine stories verbally through readings. Since Glasgow, these primarily women-only festivals organized by volunteers have taken place all over the world, showcasing bands and female acts as well as 'creating a space to explore ideas, network, meet', and through such efforts strengthening the riot grrrl community.[14]

The idea of community is explored in the following chapter in relation to the way in which digital technologies and the Internet have provided fanzine producers with new opportunities to disseminate zines on a global scale. It raises the question of the status of the print fanzine and where its future might reside. For riot grrrl, however, the signs are that print zines will continue to flourish. The format of the printed fanzine as a tactile and immediate form of communication reinforces the personalized nature of riot grrrl narratives. The riot grrrl fanzine is an intimate experience of reading, in the negotiating of public and private spaces, but also in the building of a social relationship between producer and reader.[15] This also explains the continued popularity of the Ladyfest events; at the time of going to press, Ladyfest is set to celebrate its tenth anniversary as a 'global DIY movement'.[16]

Punk-style cut-outs and collage mix with ubiquitous signifiers such as stars, hearts and feminist icons in this spread of 1990s zines. *Bikini Kill* (early 1990s) is focused on the eponymous band (quote: 'three of my best friends are in Bikini Kill and we made this fanzine together… and we all play music together…'). *Leeds & Bradford Riot Grrrl!* (1993) gave a localized spin on the movement: the interior spread below is a manifesto for activism. *Dancing Chicks* (1999) makes the point that fanzines are more than just writing about 'cool bands' and reflects on how zines have affected the writer's life in a positive way.

BIKINIKILL #2
GirlPower

LEEDS & BRADFORD
RIOT GRRRL!
80p

♡ OUR HERSTORY
♡ GRRRLZINE INFO
♡ USING THE *G WORD*
♡ HOW TO HANDLE HECKLERS
♡ PRACTICAL PUBLISHING TIPS
♡ WHAT THE NME WOULDN'T PRINT
♡ HOW TO START A RECORD LABEL ♡

more'n you can guess

ACTION IS SIMPLE

You don't have to lead big marches to be politically active you don't have to carry every sorrow of the world on your shoulders but you can make a difference. Here are some easy ideas for direct action in your own neighbourhood.

1) Defacing hoardings, write something succinct and vitriolic with your trusty cfc free spray paint. What is really good at the moment thanks to the recession is that there are quite a few posterless hoardings so go for it, it is loads of fun. But only go around in small groups max 3 people you don't want a criminal record. Make a collage of posters stick paper flowers on whatever you like really.

2) Fly posting, if you can get your hands on a photocopier for free print a load of posters saying whatever is pissing you off at the time and post them around your neighbourhood on streetlamps and the places where posters go up for bands and shit in town.

3) Ripping down sexist posters, gives great satisfaction. I did this with some friends in Sheffield cos the Roxy were advertising a strip night with posters of girls with their tits and arses hangin out.

4) Going to shit sexist movies like Body of Evidence and laughing very loudly at all the stupid cliches in it and making comments like" Why the fuck is Madonna wearing bucket knickers?" or "Oh what a surprise she had to die in the end, oh great a bit of witch drowning oh terrific." In a really sarcastic voice so that the rest of the audience can't swallow the Holliwood myth and let themselves be duped into thinking it was good. It's a dirty job but someone has got to do it.

5) Going into public libraries and ordering feminist books pariculary ones with stuff about the goddess and serious radical arguments in them. This has two effects as the governement is trying to shut down libraries because not enough people are using them. It does not occur to them that most libraries are not designed to be comfortable congenial places where you can hang out and expand your mind in relaxed peace. Also you are expanding the availability of feminist literature to those who can not afford to buy them. You could combine this with a poster campaign.

6) Hassling your MP write letters and make appointments to see him or her they usually have things called surgeries (mmmm lovely name) so you can go and hassle them about something you care about that he/she can change but you need to have done some research and perhaps have a bit more support from other people but that is what Riot Grrrl is for.

OK so there are some ideas for you to activate on the cheap they can be a lot of fun, it is fun and silliness that will win the day as we oppose the stuffed shirt regime of oppression. May comedy terrorism win our freedom nothing hurt except male anal retentive pride.

love Elizia!

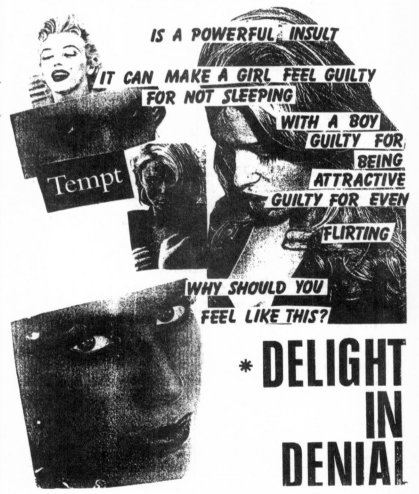

PRICK TEASE!
IS A POWERFUL INSULT
IT CAN MAKE A GIRL FEEL GUILTY FOR NOT SLEEPING
WITH A BOY GUILTY FOR BEING ATTRACTIVE GUILTY FOR EVEN FLIRTING
Tempt
WHY SHOULD YOU FEEL LIKE THIS?
*DELIGHT IN DENIAL

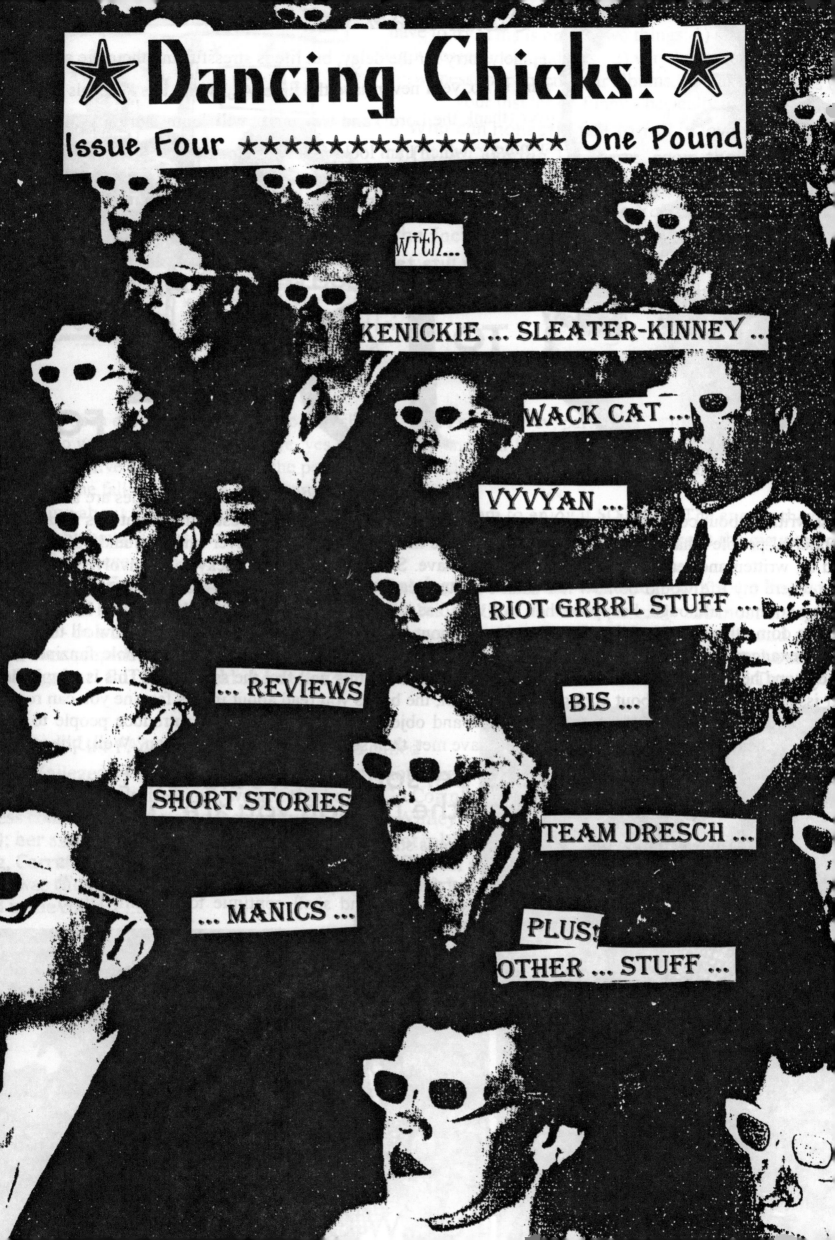

★Dancing Chicks!★

Issue Four ★★★★★★★★★★★★★★★ One Pound

with...

KENICKIE ... SLEATER-KINNEY ...

WACK CAT ...

VYVYAN ...

RIOT GRRRL STUFF ...

... REVIEWS

BIS ...

SHORT STORIES

TEAM DRESCH ...

... MANICS ...

PLUS!
OTHER ... STUFF ...

Riot Girl London

* newsletter *

January 2001

WHO ARE WE?

Riot Girl London is a group dedicated to spreading a girl-positive message and encourages girls to form bands, start zines and stop pandering to the stereotypes that society throws at us. We are not anti-men, we simply feel that there is an imbalance in this world and we would like to change that. Every month or so we meet up, but a lot of RGL is based on the internet. We are putting out this newsletter to involve more people who do not have regular access to the net and to try to get some non-internet action going.

INTERNET

Our website is updated all the time and now features a copy of our flier, a guestbook, mailing list, poll and some great links (not to mention even more info & news). You can also email us (and we'll even reply sometime soonish - whoohoo!). Its all at:

http://gurlpages.com/riotgirl.london

email us at: riotgrrrl@protest.co.uk

SPREADING THE WORD

Currently we try and spread the word about Riot Girl London by posting on websites & mailing lists, but most importantly by giving out fliers. We have a set 'manifesto' that is on the fliers & website, but people are free to change it & design their own leaflets. If you would like some fliers to hand out, email us and we'll send you some, or make some yourself. We are also looking into making RGL badges & stickers, but aren't sure exactly how to do that, or how to afford it! If you can help, let us know. ☺

ZINE

We are currently putting together a zine and need articles & artwork from all you willing contributors. We want to make sure it represents the views of as many London girls as possible. There isnt a deadline yet as such, but we are hoping to get it done pretty quickly - maybe out by March? Anything to do with your feminism/beliefs, relevant London stuff, rants, etc is welcome. You can email any questions & zine stuff to us. Thanks!

GIRL GIG

We have an ambitious plan to put on an all girl bands gig this summer. If you could help with ideas/money/bands please do!!!

CONTACT

As this is supposed to help non-net people, we know it sucks that we don't have a 'snail mail' address. When we have some funds a P.O box addy will be arranged. Til then, off to the cyber café!

Don't expect a newsletter every month because we'll probably be working on these projects for a while. When we have more stuff to tell you about or things to beg for, we'll do a new one. Please keep in touch with us, ok?!

☆ feel free to copy this and pass on ☆

THE Jigs@w
numbere 5½

jigsaw

number five

space time donuts

girl

Veronica

germs No. 3

channel seven

price: just 1.50

heavens to betsy lyrics inside!

Riot Girl London Newsletter (2001) is a call for zine contributors in an effort to 'get some non-internet action going'. The examples on this page include several very early American fanzines that were still very much in a punk mode. *Jigsaw* (1988–) was put together by Tobi Vail, later of *Bikini Kill*, and initiated many of the visual and textual characteristics of the emerging scene. *Girl Germs* (1990–92), with its unapologetically homoerotic cover, was another pioneering zine, created by Allison Wolfe and Molly Neuman of Bratmobile fame. *Riot Grrrl…Believe in Me!* (1991) was a 'call' for fanzines and tapes to distribute through Riot Grrrl records and press. *Channel Seven* (early 1990s) was created by Corin Tucker from the band Heavens to Betsy, and Erika Reinstein.

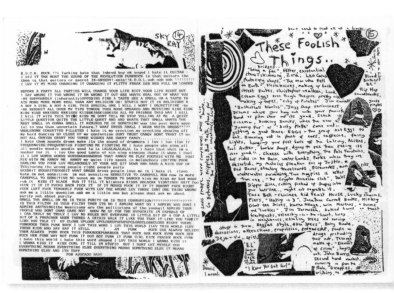

Humour always played a big part in getting the message across. *Reggae Chicken* (c. 1993, cover and inside spreads) was an early zine for Huggy Bear fans full of small point-size typeset words, cut-out type and handwritten texts, repeated punctuation marks, hand-drawn hearts and stars, and photo-collaged images. The feminism was angry but tongue-in-cheek ('dying to pee then peeing is sooo good!'). *Drop Babies* (1993, cover and inside spreads) by Elizabeth and Layla includes 'hunky' male pin-ups and various 'domestic bliss' scenes from British Ladybird children's early-reader books.

These British zines depict the history of the movement through the efforts of Cazz Blase. *Vaginal Teeth* (1998) references a 1970s *Ms. Magazine* cover which itself was a parody of the 'feminist icon' Wonder Woman. This one-off zine features reflections on the first Leeds Riot Grrrl meeting. *Aggamengmong Moggie* (1993-99) was a long-running perzine (29 issues) by Blase notable for the honesty with which she shared intimate details of her youth. She exhorts feminists 'to challenge the things that aren't right', while exploring the issue of alienation ('I don't fit in here, I don't fit in there and nobody seems to care').

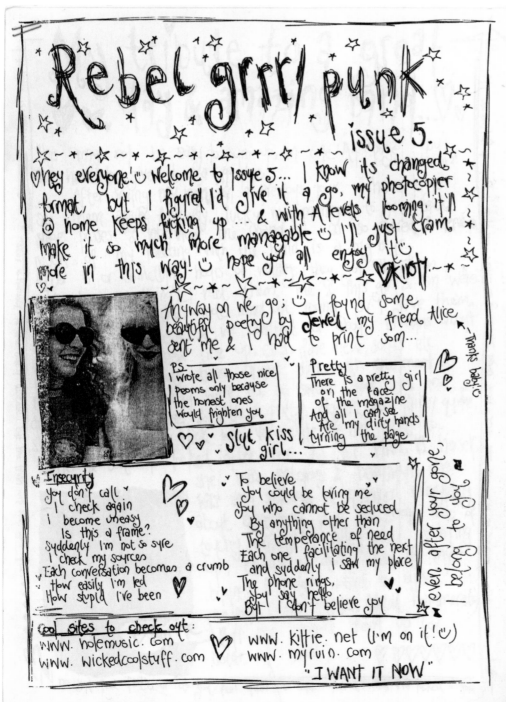

Visual references to feminism continued to be developed in different ways as a second generation of riot grrrl fanzines emerged in the late 1990s. *Rebel Grrrl Punk* (1997–2000) by Kirsty took the opposite path to punk shock tactics (such as bad language and aggressive typographic forms) by employing hand-rendered hearts and stars and images of 'feminine', feminist icons such as Courtney Love. Sophy, producer of *Sista Yes!* (1997–99) cites 1970s feminist zines as an influence, and acknowledges a debt to musician Patti Smith. This issue is safety-pinned together, and has a cover featuring a remarkable hand-drawn illustration of the band L7.

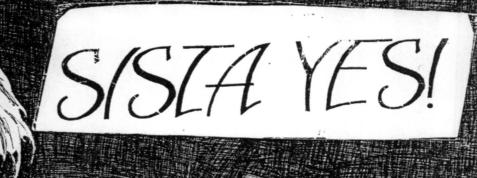

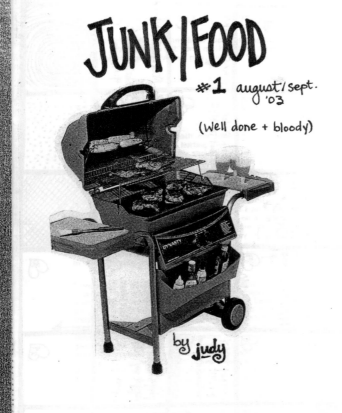

60P

JUNK/FOOD

#1 august/sept. '03

(Well done + bloody)

by judy

EAKFAST CEREAL TO THE FROSTING CONCOCTION. CAUSE ICING IS FIVE HUNDRED TIMES TASTIER THAN BORING OLD MILK. AND IT'S NOT LIKE I'M GOING TO LET ALL THOSE CALORIES DIGEST, ANY-WAY.

YEARS FROM NOW I CAN SEE MYSELF BAKING COOKIES, PERHAPS, FOR MY DAUGHTERS GRADE SCHOOL CLASS, ON HER BIRTHDAY, MAYBE. I WONDER WHETHER THE USE OF THIS RECIPE WILL STILL TRIGGER TEMPTATION TO DEVOUR IT ALL OR IF I'LL BE FAR ENOUGH REMOVED FROM BULIMIA THAT JUNK-FOODS WILL NO LONGER MOVE ME.

hello kitty

I KNOW. LIKE ANY COMPULSIVE DISORDER OR CHARACTER FLAW OF THE ADDICTIVE SORT, THIS PROBLEM OF MINE IS NOT EVER GOING TO GO AWAY COMPLETELY.

DEEP DOWN I KNOW THAT IF/WHEN I AM SERIOUS ABOUT RECOVERING I'LL ALWAYS + FOREVER HAVE TO BE ON GAURD AND READY FOR THE FOODS + FEELING THAT CAN KICK-START A BINGE.

IT IS SO FUCKING HARD FOR ME TO IMAGINE BEING FREE OF BINGEING/PURGING. SOMETIMES I WISH I COULD BE AN ALCOHOLIC OR DRUG USER, IF I'M GOING TO HAVE A HABIT AT ALL. IF MY "JUNK" WAS DRINK OR DRUGS, RECOVERY WOULD REASONABLY REQUIRE NEVER HAVING IN MY HOME SUCH SUBSTANCES THAT ARE TEMPTING. WITH FOOD IT'S NOT AN OPTION. EVERYDAY I'LL BE AROUND MY DEAREST + MOST DANGEROUS LOVE. I WILL HAVE TO SIT DOWN TO DINNER WITH MY ENEMY EVERY SINGLE EVENING.

---

ode to lexapro

My heart is cracking inside my ribs and terrifying realizations hit me harder and faster than I can keep up with. I am feeling worse tonight than I have any of these last nine months I've spent with my head in the toilet and my feet on the scale. Absolutely everything has fallen apart. My universe has been upended. It's the only way I can describe "recovery".

The antidepressant medications I take seem to be working. I've taken them for two weeks, which is the minimum time they require to begin activating changes in the brain's serotonin. Already I have noticed that I am less preoccupied with food, not as critical of my body as usual. I haven't been picking fights with my boyfriend, like I used to. I don't feel I get nearly as angry these days. When pissed off about something, I have been able to acknowledge the issue and pretty much drop it, without overaction or hostility. Overall, I just plain feel better.

It is shocking and I'm not sure I know how to handle it. Depression has been a part of my life as long as I can remember. When I was eight and nine years old I had begun thinking about and planning suicide, I started purging in the 6th grade. Maybe self-injury and despair are not a healthy way to live, but that is all that I have known. And now it all seems to be gone, or well on it's way out.

My heart is breaking and, according the the abusive way I've come to cope with myself, the only thing I know to do is go throw up or cut myself. But I don't really want to, and that is confusing. When things get all fucked up, when I normally do that is run for a razorblade and a half-gallon of icecream. Everything IS absolutely fucked up. But I am not hungry, and I don't feel like cutting. What the fuck is this shit? What can I do now? I don't know what to do. What the hell do normal healthy people DO?

I guess I will just keep crying. And I guess afterwards I will stop. And I guess that is all there is to it. I hate this, I feel so fucked up right now.

Being sick is to what I am accustomed. It is not the safest way to go through life, but I know how it is done as a bulimic. I understand how to deal with feeling like shit. My self-identity has been dispelled and dismissed. Now what am I? I have no idea what to do with myself now that I have a brain that processes thoughts healthfuly.

It is like a fog has been lifted, and I do not know where I am. I am utterly lost and alone.

Every one of my desires was an illusion. All of my energy has been invested in a denial. I have believed myself to be a monster, having never really been who I am. The things I have done to protect myself having been destroying me.

It is a betrayal of my self to admit these things.

Who knew feeling better would feel so fucked up.

TO?
YOU RISE ANOREXHEA, ANAEMIA, LIVER
IMPAIRMENT, KIDNY AND GALL STONES,
VITAMIN AND MINERAL IMBALANCES GUT
AND ELEVATE BLOOD FAT...'
WHAT MORE REASON DO YOU NEED TO KICK
THAT FOXY 'DIET' IN FOR GOOD?

WHEN I OPENED YOUR L LETTER IT MADE
ME CRY. YOU SAID WE'D BE STRONG
TOGETHER THAT YOU FELL BETTER AND HOW
MUCH HOPE I HAD GIVEN YOU. HOW CAN
I FIND THE WORDS TO TELL YOU THAT FOR
THE PAST MONTH I'VE FALLEN BACK INTO
MY DIET COKE AND BLACK COFFEE DIET.
FEEL SO WEAK AND SUCHA FAILURE. NO
MATTER HOW MUCH I ENGROSS MYSELF IN
FIGHTING TALK ITS STILL THERE. I'VE
TRIED SO HARD NOT TO CARE BUT I DO.
I KICKED THE SCALES TODAY BECAUSE I
GAINED 4 POUNDS. BUT I DON'T WANT
YOU TO FALL BACKWORDS TOO BECAUSE I
ADORE YOU SO MUCH. IM TRYING SO HARD
TO BEAT THIS, TO BECOME STRONG AND
GET BETTER. ITS THE HARDEST BATTLE
IM EVER LIKELY TO FACE BECOMES IF
COMMON SENSE IS AGAINST ME AND IM NOT
ALLOWED TO BELIEVE WHAT I SEE STARING
AT ME IN THE MIRROR.

FOOD IS MY ENEMY- ANN RHODES
FOOD IS MY ENEMY IT CAUSES SO MUCH
PAIN. MY BRAIN KNOWS THE TRUTH. I
CANNOT ALLOW FOOD TO ENTER WITHIN
MYSELF. IN NEED TO BE MY THIN, SO
THAT I CAN VANISH FROM THE
FACE OF THE WORLD. WHY SHOULD LIVE
REVOLVE AROUND MEALS? IN MY HOUSE
IT CERTAINLY
DOES AND SO I REBEL
AGAINST THIS
INJUSTICE.
WELL THIS
IS HOW I FEEL! *tomorrow my*
I AM 21 YEARS *life will be*
OLD AND HAVE *transformed*
FOUGHT THE URGE
FOR FOOD,
COMMONLY KNOWN AS
AN EATING DISORDER
FOR NEARLY 10
YEARS. LIKE MANY
PEOPLE IT STARTED
WITH TAUNTS FROM
BULLIES. I WAS
FAT AND I KNEW
IT. I WAS DIAGNOSED
WITH TENDANCIES
TOWARDS BOTH

there is HOPE

A ZINE FOR THOSE WITH EATING DISORDERS WHO WANT TO STOP THE RIDE

Toast and jam

BY RACHEL KAYE

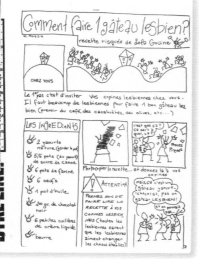

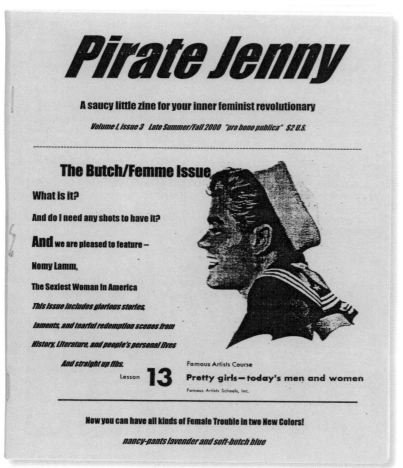

Sexuality and body image were growing concerns in the movement. *Junk Food* (2003, cover and inside spread) by Judy is a confessional perzine that looks at her relationship with food: Hello Kitty is subverted, summing up the producer's feelings with the caption 'Hello Sicky'. Rachel Kaye's *Toast and Jam* (1997-98, cover and inside spread) is a self-help zine for those with eating disorders 'who want the ride to stop'. *Il Pleut des Gouines!* (2005-, cover and inside spread) is a French Canadian bilingual comiczine (translated as 'It's Raining Dykes!'), with tips on how to make a lesbian cake. *Pirate Jenny* (2000-n.d.), from California, included a 'Butch/Femme' issue and took an almost academic approach (interviews with Susan Faludi and Jennifer Baumgardner).

Covers and interior spreads from the long-running transatlantic (Chicago and London) riot grrrl perzine *Radium Dial* (1994–). It was produced by Ilona Jasiewicz (who now works in mainstream publishing and who was actively involved in Ladyfest London), and was notable for its use of found magazine photography, including cover images of men (for example Harvey Milk). The blocky lines of text overlaid on colour photocopies provide an almost formal layout, far removed from the punk aesthetic (although the rock-and-roll content was a constant). Like many zine producers, Jasiewicz ended up writing a blog, also called 'Radium Dial'.

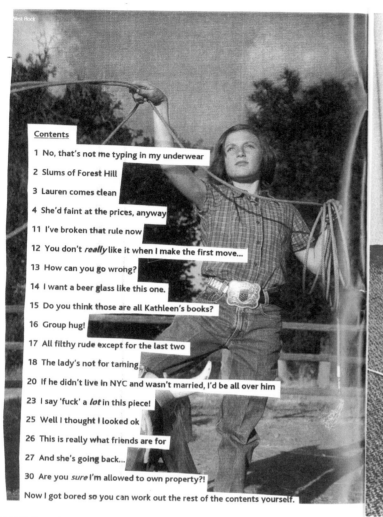

Contents

Now I got bored so you can work out the rest of the contents yourself.

Well, it's been a long time. (*Been a long time, been a long time, been a long lonely lonely lonely lonely...*) Sorry. I'm a bit drunk and am writing this editorial at work. Yes, drunk at the office. Whoo-eey! Hey, there was a party in the Sales department with snacks and booze, and those are two things I cannot say no to. Since the last issue of Radium Dial, things have been keeping on keeping on. Home-life is happy; work is, miraculously, still rockin'. Love life? Don't even *talk* to me. Well, lets just say that if there's one lesson I learnt in 2002 (and that's being optimistic), it's that my relationships are less cut and dried than I previously thought. I've spent the last six months e-flirting with a girl I like, a guy who lives in NYC and is married, and someone who I don't even know if I *am* flirting with. And it's all ok. I don't need it defined and in a little box marked "We Are Dating" or "Unrequited Love" or "Lesbotronic", even. (But that's a pretty great word.) So I think in 2003 I'm going to take things as they come. Not read too much into catching someone's eye or an unreturned email. Just go with it, and if something happens, great, and if not, that's ok too.

Jesus God. Really shouldn't write editorials while tipsy. Will I ever learn?!

Ilona xxx

No skills

---

good thing s.

stroking peoples hair
coffee
lying in bed all day reading
telling teachers to fuck off
whispering "bollocks"/"that dress makes you look fat" into the ears of BA fashion students
cats and some dogs

bad things

fuckers who mosh with lit cigarettes
patent leather airwalks.first appeared around april fools day, funnily enough.
people who disrespect the zine.its not a beer mat,you you cunts.
italian tourists with EF rucksacks.
people who stop suddenly when youre walking behind them.
all the blokes at Blow Up who dance with their elbows stiking out.and they have very sharp elbows.
serpents

17

Ivy's guide to underwear

As Cynthia HEimel stated in "Sex tips for girls",clothes serve the purpose of keeping you warm (aswell as telling everyone your tastes in music,your occupation, wealth etc.).underwear is purely about sex.well it should be anyway.Why is black such a popular colour choice for bras? it shows through almost everything. why is white worn by so many women? it gets dirty and goes grey after a couple of washes.why dont we all buy flesh coloured support bras,like our mums do?

i think its because girls thiks about sex...ooh..85% of the time.(or is it just me?) and wearing satin push-up bras/pink lace bodies/black lycra knickers makes us feel frisky,confident,witty,empowered,

Dont tell me thats rubbish; doyou wear your 50p knickers and a thermal vest to a party? ripped pants and an elastic racer-back sports bra on a hot date? didnt think so.also,dont worry about being a traitor to the feminist movement or somthing,theres nothing wrong with being a sex goddess (or feeling like one) why shouldent you take advantage of your sexuality to get what you want

but anyway,this is supposed to be a guide.so heres my rule:just wear what makes you feel beautiful,mysterious,clever,cunning,cocky,like a cheeky minx.but please make sure its underwired and preferably in a totally impractical colour.lilac,powder-blue,shocking pink, black ,and red are all quite suitable.but i will leave the topic of colour with the undisputed Queen of Undergarments,Dianne Brill...

Pick a color and check what it means. Then make it happen, you boudoir bombshell!

THE U-WORLD COLOR KEY:

White: Innocence. Purity. Trust. Bride.

Black: Sublimely horny. Wanting and willing. Hungry, seducing, commanding. Ready (right now!). Experienced. Strong.

Red: Speedy. Insatiable, accessible, in demand. Beautiful for the skin. Playmate. Cliché-risque. The other first option along with black or white. When a babe wears red, she *means* it.

Fuchsia: Hot bordello babe. Easy, fast. Almost real.

Pink: Playful. Almost innocence. The naughty-but-nice coquette. In deeper shades, especially with any black trimmings, it means subliminal "female triangle."

Nude: Practical. Measured self-denial.

Beige: Subtle to the point of boring. Non-threatening.

Fluorescents: Fashionable fun. Not serious. Not sexy . . . except under black light, then *incredible!*

Blue: Little boy blue is cool but gentle. Naivete . . . but only pretending. Navy blue is novel—so intriguing but only from time to time—and watch out, it could be chic-cold-fish like grey.

Peach: Always the bridesmaid, never the bride.

Yellow: Remember—don't you dare.

18

Riot grrrl was not without its left-field faction, which took the form of 'radical cheerleading' – protest and performance-based activism that began in Florida in 1997 and spread to major American, Canadian and European cities. Cheerleaders used fanzines as an outlet for disseminating their 'cheers'. The front cover of the *Radical Cheerleader Handbook* (2000), with its multicoloured tampon, is gleefully explicit. The *Ladyfest Cheerbook* (2001), published on the occasion of Ladyfest 2001 by the Haymarket Hussies, defines radical cheerleading as 'doing the splits with middle fingers extended'. *Shag Stamp* (c. 1994/5–c. 1999) is a perzine by Jane Graham that highlights burlesque striptease and comedy performances.

Radical Cheerleading equals protest plus performance..It's doing the splits with middle fingers extended..We think protesting shouldn't have to be boring..

We're the Haymarket Hussies, a Radical Cheerleading squad based in Chicago. We adopted our squad name in honor and memory of the Haymarket Martyrs - 8 Chicago anarchists who were framed for a bomb explosion which injured and killed a number of Chicago police officers during a labor rally in 1886. Ultimately convicted and wrongfully executed for the crime, the Martyrs are a reminder to us of the capacity for bravery in the fight against a system which places profits ahead of human needs.

SHAG STAMP

N06 1996

'Revolution girl style now', from Bikini Kill's
1991 song, became the battle cry for grrrlzines
during this period. *Hysteria Action Forum*
(1994) was notable for its illustrational style.
An anti-copyright stencil book, *Revolutionary
Women* (2005), pays tribute to Harriet Tubman
and Angela Davis among others. *Rote Zora* (1984)
featured interviews from members of the German
Women's Armed Struggle Group. *Bark + Grass*
(early 1990s) focuses on cooking a 'revolution
supper' and features recipes free from animal
products. Patty Hearst features on the cover
of *Drum Core* (1993) — a zine about drumming.
What's This Generation Coming To? (1992) is an
early riot grrrl-inspired 'angry zine'.

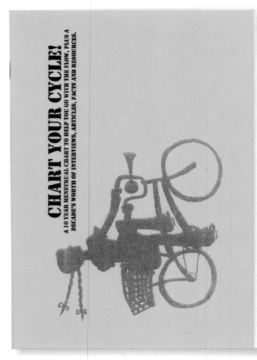

Menstruation has long been a feminist issue, but the riot grrrl movement gave it an angry and often hilarious spin. *Heavy Flow* (1995–9) by Saskia Hollins includes poems, fiction, comics and interviews with women about when they first heard about monthly cycles. *Chart Your Cycle* (2005) was a companion zine by Chella Quint to *Adventures in Menstruating* (opposite page). *Red Alert* (1999), out of Montreal, is part of the 'menstrual product activism movement' and contains articles and cartoons that look at some of the pragmatics of menstruation. This issue is bound together by a thin red string.

The menstruating theme also made its way into live performance. *Period; A Menstru-Rama!!* (2001), produced by the Las Sin Fronteras riot grrrl collective (based in Tucson, Arizona), used the fanzine format to document workshops. These events were a combination of art, performance and discussions. Chella Quint, who also produced *Chart Your Cycle* (opposite page), uses the fanzine *Adventures in Menstruating* (2005–) as a text for her comedic spoken-word performances. The interior pages draw on visual material from American and British sanitary-product adverts from the 1930s and 1940s.

Flash, Public Image, The Gang of Four. They were even flown in to Manchester especially to play at the opening of the Factory's Hacienda club.

ESG have to be one of the most sampled groups of all time. Their tracks have been sampled by the likes of Public Enemy, Big Daddy Kane, 3rd Bass, LL Cool J, Marley Marl, Doug E. Fresh and loads more I'll bet. Unfortunately in the early eighties the laws on sampling were unclear. The girls didn't get what was owed to them and as a result they have spent most of the last ten years trying to get the money they deserve. They even released a single in 1993 as a ironic look at their situation called 'Sample credits don't pay our bills'.

Unfortunately Liquid Liquid were sampled by Grandmaster Flash for his hit single 'White Lines'. Liquid Liquid were on the same label in America, 99 Records, as ESG were. The record company was run by Ed, their manager and the label took the situation to court, and in the process lost all their money. The label came to a close and so did ESG's career for a while.
In 1991 they released an album on the independent Pow Wow label. This featured 'Erase You'. They continued to play live through the nineties and released other music. Sadly these releases didn't get as much attention as their early eighties music did. Today ESG features two of Renee's daughters, Chistelle and Nicole on bass and guitar. They played in the UK last year to great reviews. I would have loved to have seen them of course but they played London and you know the rest!
ESG are one of the most influential acts of all time. They made amazing, unique music that stands up today as truly diverse and original. But more than that they made and make music that totally rocks! And yeah, they were women too!

¡women rock!

affair; whether Adele knew or not, Rosenman was justifiably incensed and after speaking his mind to Jimmy the next morning, the two were to stay out of contact for over a year. Jimmy had a strong self-destructive streak, especially tragic given his need for companionship. He became increasingly narcissistic, taking hundreds of photos of himself and trying to get Kazan to say which he preferred.

As soon as filming ended Kazan wanted Jimmy off the lot – he was simply far too disruptive. Apart from his usual antics, he had bought a new, larger, noisier motorcycle, a Triumph 500. It proved quite difficult to find a landlord or landlady who would take Jimmy, given his nocturnal habits,

You're like the best song I never heard. My

Boys that I would like to put in my pocket: David Bowie (in the thin white duke period), Tobey Maguire, Christian Bale, Jonathan Rhys-Meyers, Alec Empire, Terry Hall, Bryan Ferry (in his youth), Iggy Pop (for the shock value), Phil Daniels (in the film Breaking Glass made in the early 80's. The mass inspiration for the band.)

Girls that rool the skool: Lili Taylor (she played Valerie Solanas in Who shot Andy Warhol? the film, I had a HUGE obsession with this.), Patti Smith, all of The Go-Go's especially the drummer, Janis Joplin, Eve, Dusty Siobhan Fahey, Sarah, Andi, Siouxsie Sioux, Ricki Lake (for being in Hairspray),

Sweet ladies can be lovers as well as everything else.

I hold you in my skin is dancin you shout. Wh with electric s strings around

Oh. It rumbles in the distance. This hypnotising rhythm. I can't explain it but it's like the best rock 'n' roll. The best Zep riff. The best punk yell. It's like metal crashing against metal. It's like drums in the distance. It's like agonising feedback, slowly crushing my skin. It's like pretty guitars that make my tongue fizz like sherbert. It's like that Roxy vibrato. It's like shivering melodies tickling my back. You make me smile.

ELECTRA #4

Interviews with Chicks On Speed, Sarah Dougher, Manda-Rin and Catherine Redfern. Also: Feminist Fury, Lady Vibes, Women's Musical History, Men and Feminism, Le Tigre, Bratmobile, Electrelane and Valerie Live, Why Feminism Still Has Work To Do, Zine & Music Reviews and More!

KITTY MAGIK

NUMBER FIVE

Molly Neuman of **Bratmobile**

Tracy Wilson of **Scissorettes**

Lisa Carver of **Rollerderby** & **Suckdog**

BRASSY

R&B singer **Kelly Price**

STS of **The Haggard** & **Cadallaca**

A series of music zines connected both by their producers and by the desire to raise awareness about women in the indie music industry. *Electra* (2002, cover and inside spread) contains interviews with female bands including Chicks on Speed and BIS. Marisa of *Kitty Magik* (1996–) drew upon a growing network of women zine producers including Lisa Carver (*Rollerderby*) and Molly Neuman (*Girl Germs*). *Rollerderby* (1990s) ran for 25 issues over ten years and covered such issues as masturbation and incest. *Popgirls* (1998–n.d., cover and inside spread) is based on the producer's experiences as a member of BIS.

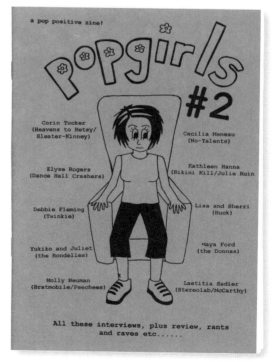

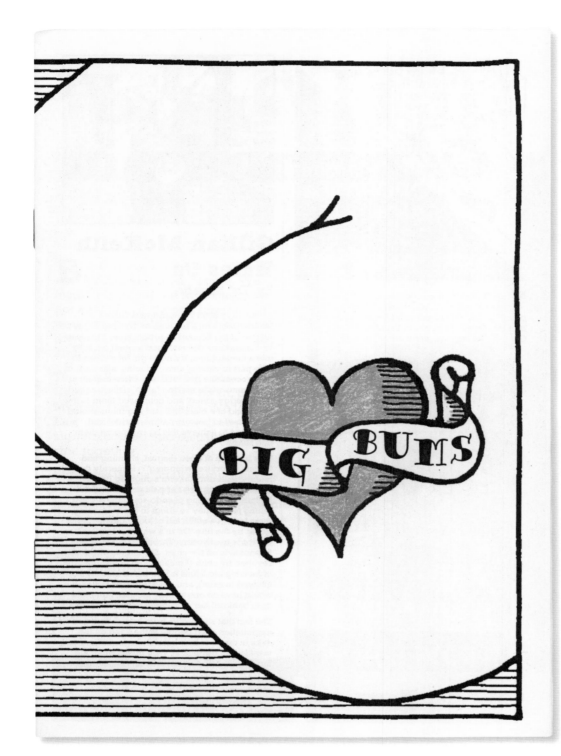

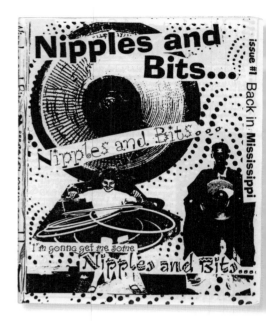

'Fat is a feminist issue'... *Big Bums* (1998) was a one-off zine suggesting 'positive fattributes'. *Nipples and Bits* (n.d.) talks about the producer's experience of sexual harassment. *Bust* (1993-) is a tribute to women who have broken the 'moldy mold of female stereotypes'. *Punktum* (2002, cover and inside spread) by Rachel House was a one-off zine reflecting on her enrolment at art school. Queerzine *Unskinny Bop* (2003-) began its life at Ladyfest London, and 'aimed to honor the work of fat people in popular music'. *Unskinny* (1990s) took an amusing angle on gluttony.

ISSUE #3 CONTENTS

the next

Unskinny Bop

Nov 27 2004 see website for details

www.unskinnybop.co.uk

FAT

Welcome, Boppers, to the third Unskinny Bop zine. It's over a year since our first effort, which set out our manifesto and pledge to offer an authentic and sincere alternative to the 'fashion show' mode of nightclubbing still unfortunately prevalent in this city. First, a history lesson for all you newcomers.

Unskinny Bop started at Ladyfest London 2002. It was a one-off disco which aimed to honour the work of fat people in popular music. We got a shout out from Amy Lamé on the radio, there was a Top 10 Podge Pop countdown (starring the likes of Aretha, PM Dawn, Missy Elliott, The Pixies, and of course Mr. Elvis Presley), we gave out free badges in four designs, and all in all it was a massive success.

BUT YOU KNOW IT

The hunt was on to find a permanent venue for our disco machine, which by now was acquiring disciples of a non Unskinny nature. We were offered guest spots at gigs and clubs by friends made at Ladyfest, playing at after-shows for The Gossip, Gravy Train and later Le Tigre. We put on our first gig at the Betsey Trotwood, a sell-out show starring Lesbo Pig, Valerie and The Blue Minkies, and then celebrated Christmas with the help of fabulous dance troupe The Actionettes.

In March 2004 we finally found our perfect venue and went bi-monthly at the Pleasure Unit in Bethnal Green. We love this place. It's a straight pub with a gay history, pints, seats, a big dancefloor and modish leanings, which means the mix of people is always eclectic and eschews the monotony of fashion clubs with generic dress codes.

X FAT!SO?

for people who don't apologize for their size

issue #4   spare tires $3.50

GIRL CULT
GIRLKULTURZINE
Volume 3, Issue 1

No ogling, please, we're 'ladies'

$£2

Body image, sexuality and stereotypes feature in this series of zines. *Fat!So?* (1994-n.d.) by Marilyn Wann is a humorous look at being overweight. *Girl Cult Girlkulturezine* (late 1990s) included comic strips by Rachel House. *For Your Own Good* (2004), produced by Kate, responded to criticisms from her own mother about her weight, and includes a collection of stories from women about body image. *GirlFrenzy* (1991-n.d.) by artist Erica Smith pays tribute to the US proto-riot grrrl 1970s band the Shaggs in this 'Fat Lib' issue. Seven issues of *Fat Girl* (1996-n.d.) were produced by a collective of 'fat dykes'.

For   Your
Own   Good:

a zine about   mothers,
daughters and
body image

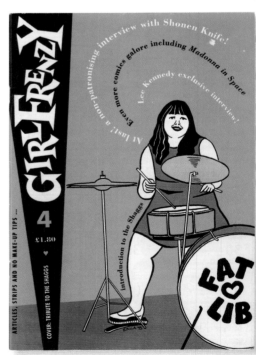

GIRL FRENZY
4
£1.80

FAT ♡ LIB

FaT  GiRL

$5

#5 **A Zine for Fat Dykes and the Women Who Want Them**

LEGENDS

POLITICS

ADVICE

SMUT

ART

PROZAC

20 mg

LOTS O' FUN ! ! !

vist our web site:

http://www.fatgirl.com/fatgirl

Women from different ethnic and national backgrounds were also celebrated. *Catch that Beat!* (1999–2000s, cover and inside spread) was a Tokyo-based riot grrrl zine produced by Yayoi, who published reviews of music gigs and of other 1990s zines. It was printed on yellow copy-paper and shared a similar graphic aesthetic to its Western grrrl counterparts, using a visual language of hand-drawn hearts and stars and stencil letterforms. *Asian Girls Are Rad* (1994–n.d.) was produced in Austin, Texas as an account of the producer's friendships with Asian women and fascination with Japanese popular culture.

G I R L Y #6

TRANS-
GENDER
'ZINE

ready for your close-up?

OCT '96

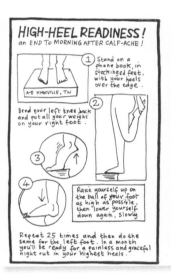

HIGH-HEEL READINESS!
an END TO MORNING AFTER CALF-ACHE!

① Stand on a phone book, in stockinged feet, with your heels over the edge.

A-E KNOXVILLE, TN

② Bend your left knee back and put all your weight on your right FOOT.

③

④ Raise yourself up on the ball of your foot as high as possible, then 'lower' yourself down again, slowly

Repeat 25 times and then do the same for the left foot. In a month you'll be ready for a painless and graceful night out in your highest heels.

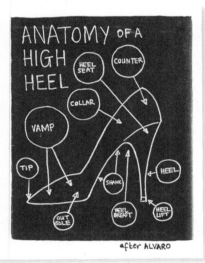

ANATOMY OF A HIGH HEEL

HEEL SEAT   COUNTER
COLLAR
VAMP
TIP   HEEL
SHANK
OUT SOLE   HEEL BREAST   HEEL LIFT

after ALVARO

SKY HIGH HEELS

GIRLY transgender zine

FREE!   issue 7

Girly Transgender Zine (1995–c.1999) was produced by Mona Compleine (aka Simon Murphy), a longtime contributor to the fanzine and music communities, who had a unique perspective on London's trash drag culture. Each issue of the quarterly zine was produced on a different-coloured stock and used a format that dispensed with staples by folding down a larger piece of paper. This made it cheaper to produce and as a result it was given away for free. Mona also produced *Sky High Heels* (n.d., cover and inside spread) as a minizine, which celebrated the wonders of the high-heeled shoe.

Pink for a little girl… or a riot grrrl. *Amp Minizine* (1998–c. 2007, covers and inside spread), an award-winning fanzine, was established as a print minizine and e-zine by the music and lifestyle journalist Miss Amp (aka Anne-Marie Payne). *Red Hanky Panky/Hormone Frenzy* (1995–2000) was produced by comic artist Rachel House and sets out to explore 'nonstop queer punk girl boy kung fu action'. *The Pamzine* (2000–c. 2008) was produced by the band Pam Savage as a 'propaganda machine' for their music. *Honeypears* (2000s) by Heather Middleton provided interviews with such bands as Le Tigre together with articles on reading and making comics. The cover of *Vacuum Boots* (2000), an indie musiczine by Miss Rachel and Angel, features an image of Twiggy.

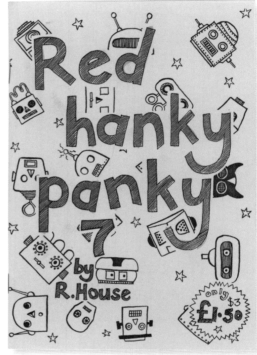

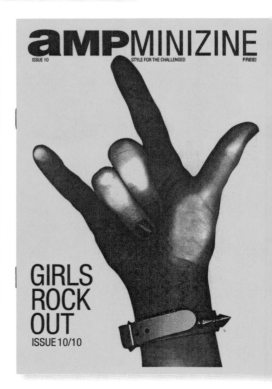

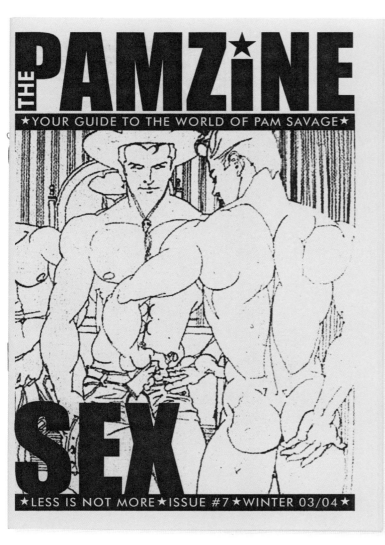

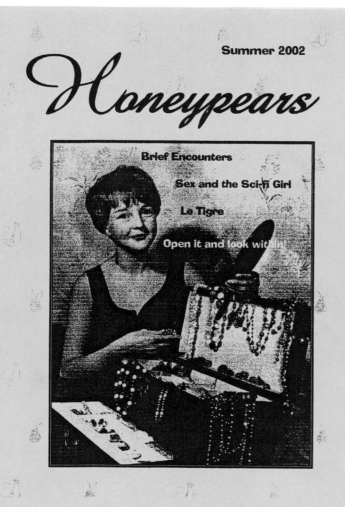

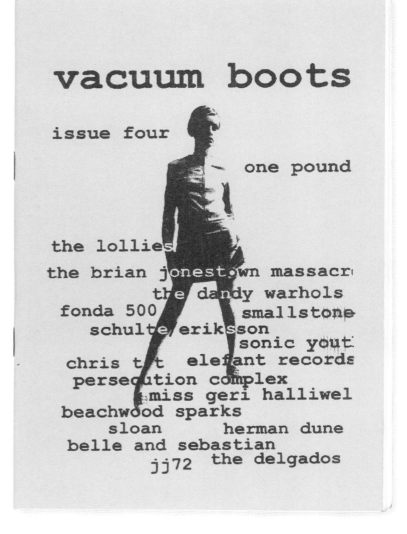

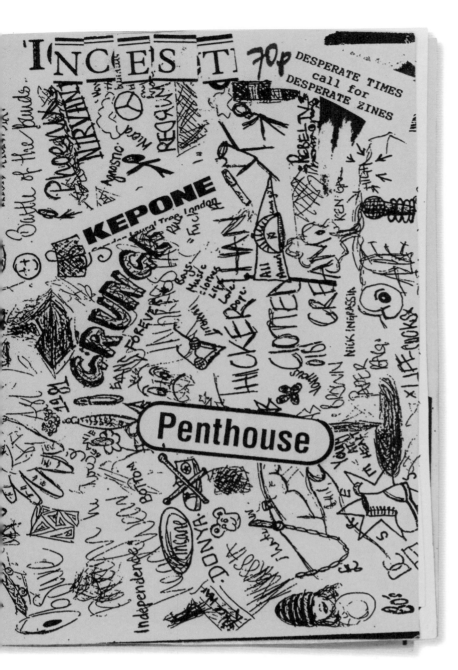

Riot grrl was about independence and gaining confidence where the 'personal is political'. The provocatively titled *Incest* (1990s, covers and inside spread) was a 50-page minizine whose scrawled drawings and frenzied layout photocopied on to coloured paper provided the backdrop, in the issues shown here, for essays on the band Mudhoney, cartoon strips, plus an editorial about 'a writers revolution'.

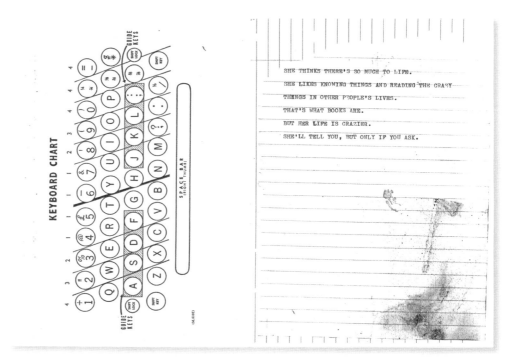

SHE THINKS THERE'S SO MUCH TO LIFE.

SHE LIKES KNOWING THINGS AND READING THE CRAZY

THINGS IN OTHER PEOPLE'S LIVES.

THAT'S WHAT BOOKS ARE.

BUT HER LIFE IS CRAZIER.

SHE'LL TELL YOU, BUT ONLY IF YOU ASK.

pink lemonade no.3

Notes & Errata (c. 2008, cover and inside spread) by Susy Pow!, from Australia, was a perzine whose producer's life story was expressed through notes, poems and random illustrated thoughts. The art/ perzine *Pink Lemonade* (2000) featured an interview with Kathleen Hanna (of the band Le Tigre) and reviewed books about women's history. It advertised for artists, filmmakers, photographers and other writers to get in touch. *Gun Wounds Again?* (1997), produced by Emily Sessions, is a personal collection of poems.

slampt

under ground

organisation

PO BOX 54
HEATON
NEWCASTLE
UPON
TYNE
NE6 5YW
U.K.

1

catalogue May 1997

May 1997

Greetings our pals and supporters.
This being our Slampt-o-logue thing, we'll tell you
what's occuring in the Slampt axis of the thing..
Okay so – first up the Red Monkey band is touring
Holland, Switzerland, Germany, and France for 2½
weeks starting the 21st May. Also we are moving at
the end of June, so for a while in late Spring /early
Summer we expect a small amount of confusion because
of this. Please be a little patient and understanding
with us. We will be giving mail order top priority
and will sort it out as soon as is possible.
As regards our new releases, the Wimpshake L.P. is
finally out now. Yay! In the works are Fast Connection #4 and a Kodiak 7". Red Monkey have recorded
their 2nd 7" which will come out on Troubleman unlimited
and is entitled "The Time is Right". We at Slampt is
angling to get a whole bunch of these singles available
over here via our mail order if not anywhere else, so
don't panic if you want it badly. Probable not too
distant future releases are a Small Black Pig 7", a Red
Monkey L.P., the Troubleman/Slampt split compilation !.
L.P. and an Accessory Girl 7" (maybe? sigh, they're
just so damn busy with that Tunic band).

I am learning to drive (which I must say is shocking
to even me) ! And Marc E. Cha Cha cut my hair on 13th
April. which meant I grew it for an entire year, al-
theguh I've still not received the £1.79 i had riding
on the matter. On the Slampt turntable at present are
Digital Hardcore records, Crass, The Warmers, Dawson,
Lee Perry, Wandering Lucy, Excuse 1 7, but what do
you care?
Please send us any cool vegan recipes you may've
encountered. Love from Rachel xxxxx

Distribution was key in creating a female network of zine producers and readers. *Slampt Underground Organisation* (1992-mid-2000s) ran a record label and published a distro (distribution) catalogue for zines and indie records. *Riot Grrrl Press Catalogue* (early 1990s) was created to promote the riot grrrl network. *Word Is Born* (2004) was a university dissertation about riot grrrl by Julia Downes, subsequently produced in zine form. *Barnard Zine Library Zine* (2005-6) was an introduction to the zines held in the Barnard College collection. *Riot Grrrl* (2005) was a thesis by Yuka Ogaki. *I'm Not Waiting* (2004) by zinester Melanie Maddison is adapted from her Master's thesis.

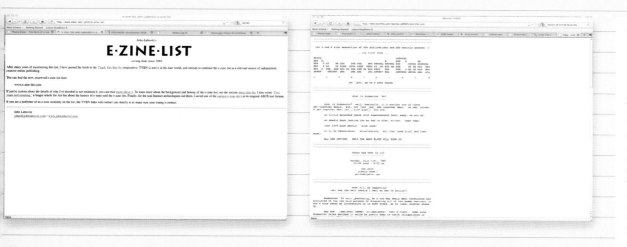

It is hard to imagine the world without the internet. For many people, hardly a day goes by without logging on and off, looking at websites for news, checking out Facebook and MySpace profiles or tweeting messages to an ever-expanding group of Twitter followers. Social networking is now part of the new media landscape, comprising a vast net of personal pages where friends and family meet within virtual communities and where new digital relationships are formed. In the twenty-first century, the concept of an information economy is a commonplace.

While a paradigm shift is taking place in mainstream publishing (printed newspapers under threat, literary publishing in decline), surely this brings good news for the self-publishing community. Much in the same way as early Gutenberg printing presses sparked off a literacy revolution as books reached a wider audience, online publishing services have provided cheaper forms of printing and distribution. This has changed business models. 'Print on demand', for example, uses online technology to print copies of books at the time of ordering, which for small press publishers suggests certain economic advantages (such as not having to pay for storage and maintaining back catalogues). Other services have also altered the way we think about independent (and amateur) self-publishing. Self-publishing website Lulu allows authors to retain direct control of both design and production, prompting comparisons with the DIY ethos witnessed in early fanzines. The digital medium is immediate, inexpensive and widely available. Publishing forms are evolving quickly and this has an impact on the culture of fanzines – both on- and offline, underground and overground.

This chapter explores the way in which fan cultures embrace the realm of online publishing though e-zines – a shortened version of the term 'electronic fanzine' (the original meaning of which was applied to non-mainstream online self-publishing, but which has increasingly been applied to more mainstream outputs). Questions that might be asked include: how has the web enhanced a fan community? What has the web brought to fanzine production? And in what way has online fan publishing altered the writing and design of zines?

A Brief History of Electronic Media

Early e-zine producers were known as 'adopters', and as *E-Zine List* (1993–c. 2005) editor John Labovitz reflected, they became the 'experimenters who took the net for what it was, and imagined its possible futures, without trying to bend it to fit the constraints of traditional media like newspapers or printed magazines'.[1] It was indeed this DIY spirit that prompted the migration of print fanzines on to the web, with production of early e-zines that took advantage of ASCII (American Standard Code for Information Exchange, used on Bulletin Board Systems) characters. In the late 1970s, artists and designers adopted ASCII for their e-zines, responding to its unique characteristics in order to create an early computer art language. For example, e-zine text headlines were created using words, spacing and repeated punctuation characters, developing a vocabulary of shapes and visual images.[2] Three distinctive styles have been identified by computer historians: *Oldskool*, *Newskool* and *Block*. Oldskool uses slashes and lines and emerged out of 'text art created on the Commodore 64 to decorate the File Listings on "Release" Floppy disks'; Newskool uses symbols and punctuation marks to create images; Block is a more sophisticated format used in the first instance by IBM with a series of extended characters to create a 'block-like' image.[3] Some of the earlier science fiction e-zines such as *Dummer Con* (1995–n.d.) used these techniques (in this case, Newskool, to create its distinctive title image).

E-zine subjects followed along similar genre headings as their print counterparts. Subjects such as music and science fiction remained common, but added to this list was a new subgenre of technology-inspired productions. One such subgenre emerged out of 'hacking' (illegally cracking computer programs) – and the phenomenon of 'phreaking' (cracking phone lines to obtain 'free' long-distance calls), which flourished during the 1980s, 'illegally' intervening into Usenet newsgroups and email. Examples include the long-running *The Hacker Quarterly 2600* (1984–) and the self-proclaimed underground zine

The Zine (2004–n.d.) by Mr Maul (a text-based ASCII zine) focuses on 'phreaking'. In this issue he transcribes the conversation he had with an operator to dial a toll-free number. ChipRowe.com (1995–) was produced by Chip Rowe, a journalist, who emerged as one of the highest-profile zine producers working in the 1990s. The e-zine collected his previously published work from Playboy, Spy and his own photocopied fanzine Chip's Closet Cleaner (1989–late 1990s).

Phrack (1984–), where, even today, editors request the text to be submitted in 'ASCII 7bit with lines no longer than 75-columns long'.[4]

By 1992, it was evident that a specialist e-zine community was emerging. Factsheet Five's Jerod Pore recognized this and set up the zine newsgroup alt.zines, providing an online discussion group with 'tips on how to make zines, discussions of the culture of zines, news about zines (e.g. who is being censored and why), specific zines and related stuff'.[5] Other e-zine newsgroups were also established, for example: alt.pup (for 1930s zine enthusiasts) and alt.zines.samizdat (for underground Russian periodicals). John Labovitz, mentioned above, was another important figure. By 1995, his E-Zine List was reviewing 600 e-zines, confirming the fact that this new form had arrived.

Despite the technological characteristics of this new medium, Labovitz's definition of e-zines showed that they remained remarkably true to the original form: 'Zines are generally produced by one person or a small group of people, done often for fun, and tend to be irreverent… they are not targeted towards a mass audience, and are generally not produced to make a profit.' The difference, he argues, is in the mode of distribution, since e-zines are 'distributed partially or solely on electronic networks like the Internet'.[6] As technology moved forward, so too did the way in which zinesters used the medium. Although, as cultural historian Stephen Duncombe has pointed out, computers had been a tool in the zinesters' armoury since the 1980s (with desktop publishing coming in around 1984),[7] it was only with the coming of a new browser called Netscape Navigator in 1994 that information on the Web became more accessible, thus prompting a new generation of web-based e-zines.

Pixel Perfect

'ISN'T A ZINE JUST A PAPER BLOG? No way! Zines are totally different, [not least] because they are physical objects that exist and take up space IRL [In Real Life]. You can't hold your blog together with tape and staples; and you can't hold your zine together with css and html.'[8]

What has the Web brought to the fanzine concept? Zine scholars have highlighted the fine line between defining zines 'proper' and other forms of 'personal publishing' found on the internet.[9] Chris Atton argues that the 'e-zine appears less distinct, its culture more amorphous', while Duncombe's point is that the internet has made 'communication too easy and that the deviant socialization process of the underground might be lost as a consequence'.[10] Zine producer Pagan Kennedy, creator of the early 1990s zine Pagan's Head, remarked in an interview with Wired magazine: 'I think the zine classification just doesn't work in the online world. The savviest online zines probably will stop calling themselves zines altogether.'[11] Despite such reservations, and recognizing the inevitability that definitions will be questioned, the way in which zinesters have come to make the medium their own is worth exploring.

Many contemporary zines have both a Web and a print presence, yet the intent of the online mode does vary (including promotional, informational or interactive). One example of the use of the Web as a 'static' promotional arena is the quarterly zine The Flaneur (2009–). This 'lo-fi, arty, indie publication' reports an interest in publishing 'great art, short fiction, humour and reviews'. The producer of this zine uses social networking sites such as Facebook, Twitter and We Make Zines (an online zine community) to advertise for contributors, and as a means to promote the print zine (twenty pages, small-format, self-printed, black-and-white) to a broader readership. The site does not ask for the viewer to interact with the information in developing a dialogue with its producer other than to hit the 'buy now' button.

On the other hand, some zinesters, such as Tony Drayton (Ripped & Torn and Kill Your Pet Puppy), have used the full potential of a website as an archival resource for their print zines (photographic and articles), in Drayton's case also listing current events and maintaining a blog with readers' comments. The format is less static and provides functions that design into the site a means of interaction between members of a community: in this case, punk music enthusiasts. Other interactive forms of online zine networking have become popular: ZineWiki

Mystery Date Online (2001–) continues what began in the print zine as producer Lynn Peril's obsession with used books. *Duplex Planet* (c. 2000s), David Greenberger's online site, began as a print zine in 1979, about his conversations with the elderly in nursing homes. *A Little Poetry* (1996) showcased contemporary poets' works and resources in this journal-like format. *Blind, Stupid and Desperate* (late 1990s–2006) was a typical football e-zine. *Jersey Beat* (n.d.) began as a print zine (c. 1987) and covers punk and the alternative music scene primarily in the Tri-State area around New York.

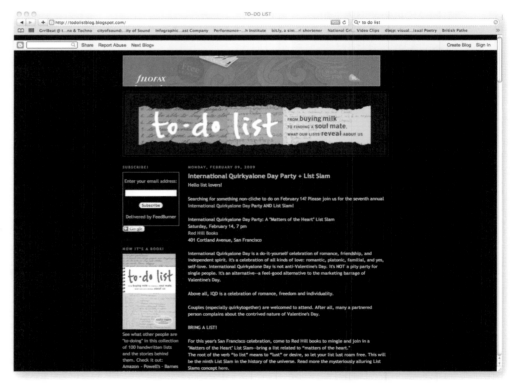

Producers use the Web in different ways:
for example, blogs may be personal diaries
or promotional sites. *The Flaneur* (2009–)
is an independent quarterly journal that
carries art, fiction, journalism and cartoons
and which uses its website for selling
subscriptions to the print version. *Stolen
Sharpie* (2008–) is a blog by Alex Wrekk,
author of the resources zine *Stolen Sharpie
Revolution* and an organizer of the Portland
Zine Symposium. *To-Do List* (c. 2000–) is
produced by Sasha Cagen (who coined the
zine-speak term 'quirkyalone') and uses the
lists as a way of exploring the mundanity
of everyday life.

A meta approach to zines provides an entertaining overview as well as linking producers together. *Broken Pencil* (1995–) is a quarterly Canadian print and online metazine reviewing fanzines, and related subjects. It was founded by Hal Niezviecki with current editor Lindsay Gibb, and continues to foster zine culture and the indie culture scene. *Irish Books and Zines* (2008–) is a blog founded to provide a space for digitizing Irish zines and other related ephemera 'in high quality pdfs'.

(2006–) is a user-generated open source wiki site, while *Zine Library* (n.d.–), an 'open publishing' site, allows users to upload and download pdf files of printed radical zines as well as broadcasting the latest indie news. Such sites point to an increase in the user's ability to exert greater control over what text is read, together with an awareness of who the readership is and potentially how far the limits of free speech might stretch.

Another way in which e-zines mimic print zines is in their inclusion of comic strips. However, once again the potential for a new kind of aesthetic exists. American comics theorist Scott McCloud has pointed out that on the web a comic strip can exist on 'an infinite canvas' (endless horizontal or vertical scrolling, click-through navigation, etc.). Having said this, it is true that few zines have utilized this potential to date, and prefer to reproduce short strips that have the familiarity of the old-style print scene.[12]

Librarian Jenna Freedman in her online essay 'Zines Are Not Blogs: A Not Unbiased Analysis' suggests that one of the shared aspects of blogs and print is 'motivation'. That is, both have the 'desire to express rather than to profit as a motivation'.[13] This is readily evident in the act of blogging.[14] Blog writing is diary-like in tone, with brief, descriptive entries regarding a specific activity, observation or event that has happened in the writer's life. The template is predetermined for most blog sites and relies on the blogger writing a couple of paragraphs for each entry; entries normally run in a linear sequence and in reverse chronological order (last entry appears first when scrolling down the screen 'page'). The analogy with more traditional print perzines is clear, though purists always defend the design and materiality aspects of printed zines. E-zine websites, on the other hand, are intertextual in that they allow for a greater flexibility to move in between texts or through links to external sites.

There is immediacy inherent in the technology, for example, for updating entries and providing feedback to original postings. Comment boxes also provide and record the dialogue between content and response or author and reader (or a 'nanoaudience' – the name given to small audiences that follow a blog). For the producers of printed fanzines, on the other hand, receiving feedback is often much slower, especially when zines are published on an irregular basis. The so-called 'sociology' of zine reading is altered, therefore: a fact underlined by the ease and speed with which a blog can be accessed versus the old-style method of sending off for something in the post. A different sort of connection between reader and producer now exists.

E-zines are often produced from a menu of templates with predetermined grids and typefaces. Another kind of zine aesthetic has emerged. Attempts at replicating the attributes of print zines successfully online do exist: Laura Oldfield Ford, for example, uses print-based illustrative collages on her home page for *Savage Messiah* (2005–), as do the producers of *Our Hero* (2000–02) with their website using typewriter and handwritten texts, crossings-out, collaged images, and so on to get across the fanzine concept. But in general e-zines are at their best when they play to the strengths of the computer.

E-Dreamers versus Print Purists

In writing about comic e-zine fandom, Matthew J. Smith comments that 'the potential for community, facilitated in publications like e-zines' will continue to develop, as do the possibilities of increased online interaction.[15] This is undoubtedly true, especially with the advance of ever-more portable computer devices. However, it also worth noting that anti-e-zine sentiment exists. Back in 1997–98 the producer of the print musiczine *Make Room* made his case clear by publishing the top ten reasons why paper zines are better than the Web versions. Among these: 'no annoying link bullshit, you just turn the page'; 'everyone knows only GEEKS surf the net'; and 'you look cooler carrying this around'. Today, those arguments still hold true for the print purists, who argue that you can't have a zine fair in cyberspace. E-zines have facilitated some of the best work in the field: but the death of print is evidently greatly exaggerated.

Digizine (1995) was an interactive music and entertainment magazine brought out as a CD-ROM. It was created by Timothy Zuellig and published by Bob Ahrens. When it hit mainstream newsstands, the first two issues sold out with reportedly 60,000 for the first issue and 90,000 for the second. Interviews with alternative rock bands such as Nine Inch Nails and Jesus Lizard were interspersed with comments from technology guru Howard Rheingold and comics by American artist Heather McAdams. Five years earlier, advances in desktop computer technology prompted 'cyberslacker' Jaime Levy to publish the artzine *Cyber Rag* (1990–92) as a HyperCard floppy disk. The first multimedia issue (1990) emerged out of Levy's Master's thesis, and contained 'bizarre pictures, sound, animation and words'. *Cyber Rag*'s three issues were followed by *Electronic Hollywood*, in which the producer shared her experiences in Los Angeles.

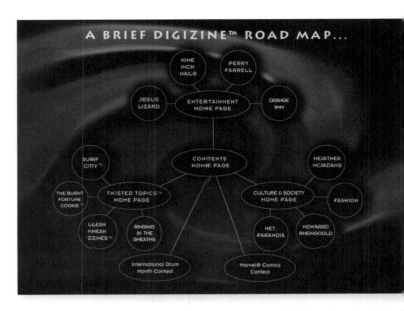

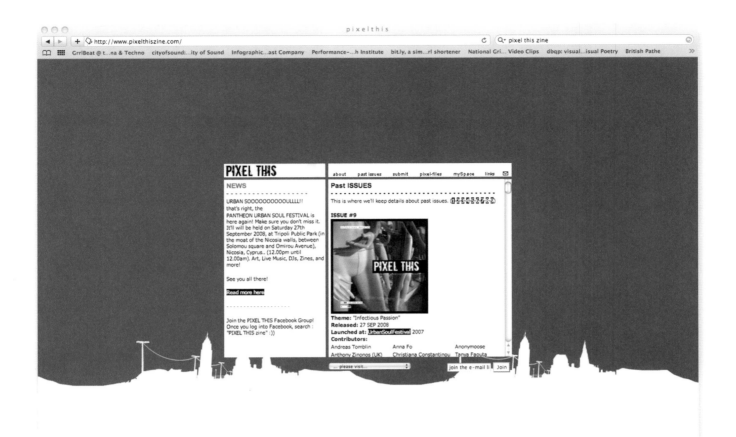

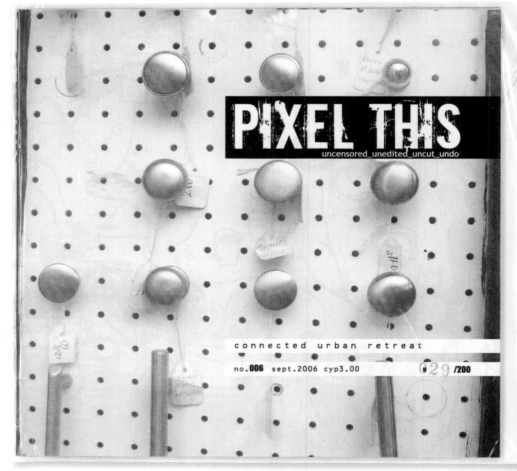

Pixel This (2003-c. 2009) was produced out of Nicosia, Cyprus, and styled itself as a forum for both local and international artists, writers, poets, photographers and others. While the website provided a immediate venue for feedback, the print issues were steadfastly DIY in the old sense: formatted as a square (20 x 20cm, 8 x 8in) and inserted into a plastic bag sealed with a sticker on the back. Each issue had a theme and a print edition of 200. New issues tended to be launched at club events, dance festivals and the like.

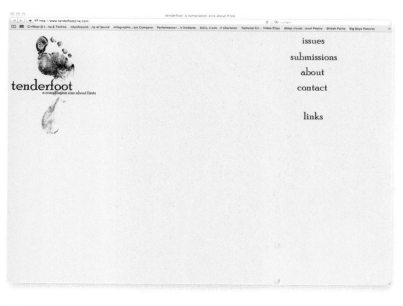

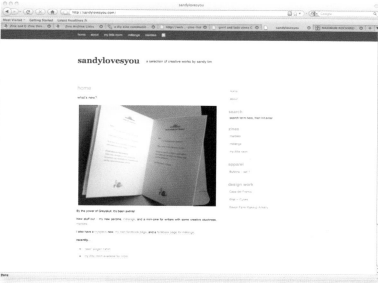

Produced by Jenna Weiss, *Tenderfoot*
(*c*. late 2000s) used an online format
for notification of the sporadically
published compilation zine of the same
name: it collected stories and comix about
'firsts'. *Sandylovesyou* (n.d.) is created by
Sandy Lim, a web designer and creator of
Mélange (2010) from Western Australia, as
a showcase for her art, design and writing.
10 Things Zine (*c*. 2007) is the blog version
of the print zine *10 Things Jesus Wants You
to Know* (1991-99), the largest-circulation
fanzine in the northwestern United States.
Produced by Dan Halligan, it provided news
and information about the independent
Seattle music scene.

the **Black Cloud**

clips from a doomed journalism career #1

Punk continues to influence both online and print fanzines. *The Black Cloud* (2007–), by ex-punk Bret, presents 'clips from a doomed journalism career', exploring the idea of using previously published work reprinted in an amateur format. *Punks Is Hippies* (September 2007–) is a blog dedicated to archiving punk fanzines that relies on contributors to post images. The spontaneity of *Kissoff*'s (1997–2009) print-version punk graphics is replicated on the website, with gritty photocopied black-and-white drawings. *The ChickenFishSpeaks* is an online archive for *Mutant Renegade Zine* (1990–2000), a music fanzine with reviews, interviews, games, videos and photos from various gigs.

Loserdom, (n.d.) by Anto and Eugene (the
Loser brothers) from Dublin, provides a
selection of articles and cartoons from
the print version of the same name (1996–).
It also provides a selling point for both the
zines and merchandising (such as T-shirts).
The illustrational content has always been
outstanding: especially the screen-printed
covers, which reproduce well on the Web.
Topics have included punk, cycling and anti-
war politics. The producers also run a zine
distro point at events such as the Dublin
Anarchist Bookfair.

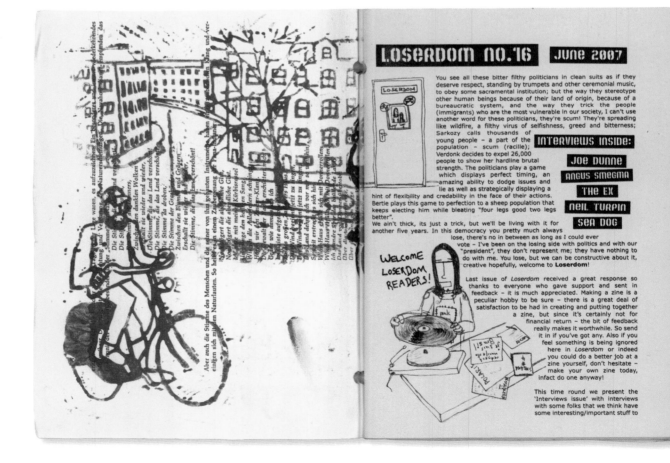

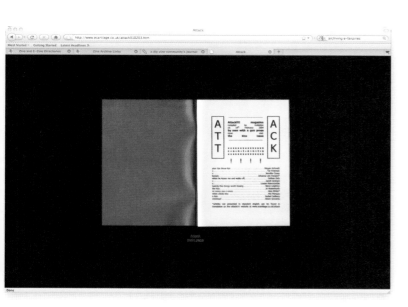

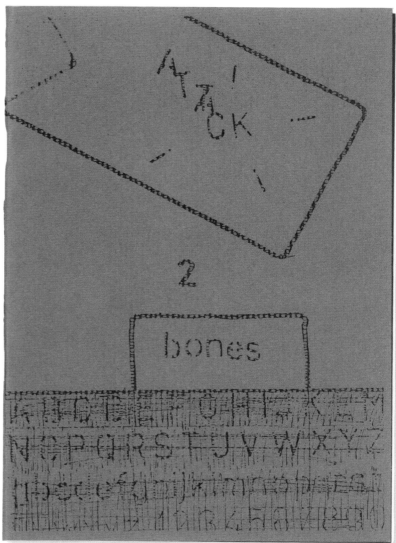

Attack! (2001-) was 'curated' by Wes White
- initially a numbered edition of 150 print
zines, showcasing collections of original
artwork by writers, artists and musicians.
White expanded his idea to include a DVD
encompassing live shows. The accompanying
website *Cartilage* (n.d.) contains scans of
sold-out issues, a blog and links to the work
of contributors. *Kill Your Pet Puppy* (1979-83)
was a British punkzine produced by Tony
Drayton (of *Ripped & Torn* fame) and is now an
online web resource and archive for his zine.
The background pattern is constructed out
of images of the original print zine. *Woofah*
(2007-) is a sporadically produced independent
music fanzine covering reggae, grime and
dubstep with both online and print versions.

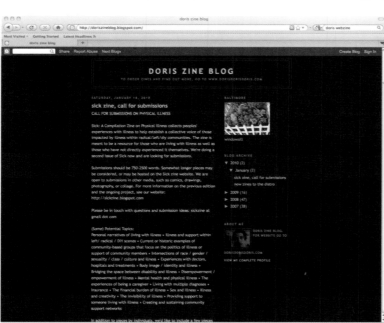

Doris Zine Blog (2007–) operates as a showcase forum for a riot grrrl distro, run by Cindy Crabb ('Doris'). The blog is a continuation of the printed perzine, but radically different in its design, being subject to a pre-existing grid template. Examples of covers from the print version indicate an appealing illustrational style that is difficult to replicate with any warmth online.

More web/print crossovers. Artist Laura Oldfield Ford's provocative zine *Savage Messiah* (2005-) reports on her psychogeographical wanderings through London using cut-and-paste, photocollage, drawing and writing. Her commentary is on the gritty realities of urban spaces, reflecting the early anarcho-punk art of the 1970s and paying homage to the graphics of Crass member Gee Vaucher in particular. A less refined fanzine aesthetic is at play in the music/queerzine *Ricochet! Ricochet!* (2005-) by Paffy (Patrick) and Colly (Colette), which has an art-band orientation.

One of the advantages of having a musiczine on the Web is that songs and videos can be sampled. *Supersweet* (2004–) began as a print-based Thai fanzine, emerging out of the indie disco scene of Bangkok and London and morphing into an online presence; 1,500 copies of the photocopied zine were distributed, but the website provided a much broader platform. Having gone digital, experimentation with sound could begin (e.g. the 'Contact us' link is accompanied by the sound of an old-fashioned telephone ring). By contrast, *Morgenmuffel* (c. 1997–) is an autobiographical comiczine drawn by artist Isy that sticks closely to its print roots. The first issue was produced in Germany, and it was not until the second issue and a move to Brighton, UK, that its producer began to use the zine as a forum for drawing comics about her own life and activities, which included direct action and grassroots organizing. The website provides followers with downloadable pdfs of early issues of the print zine.

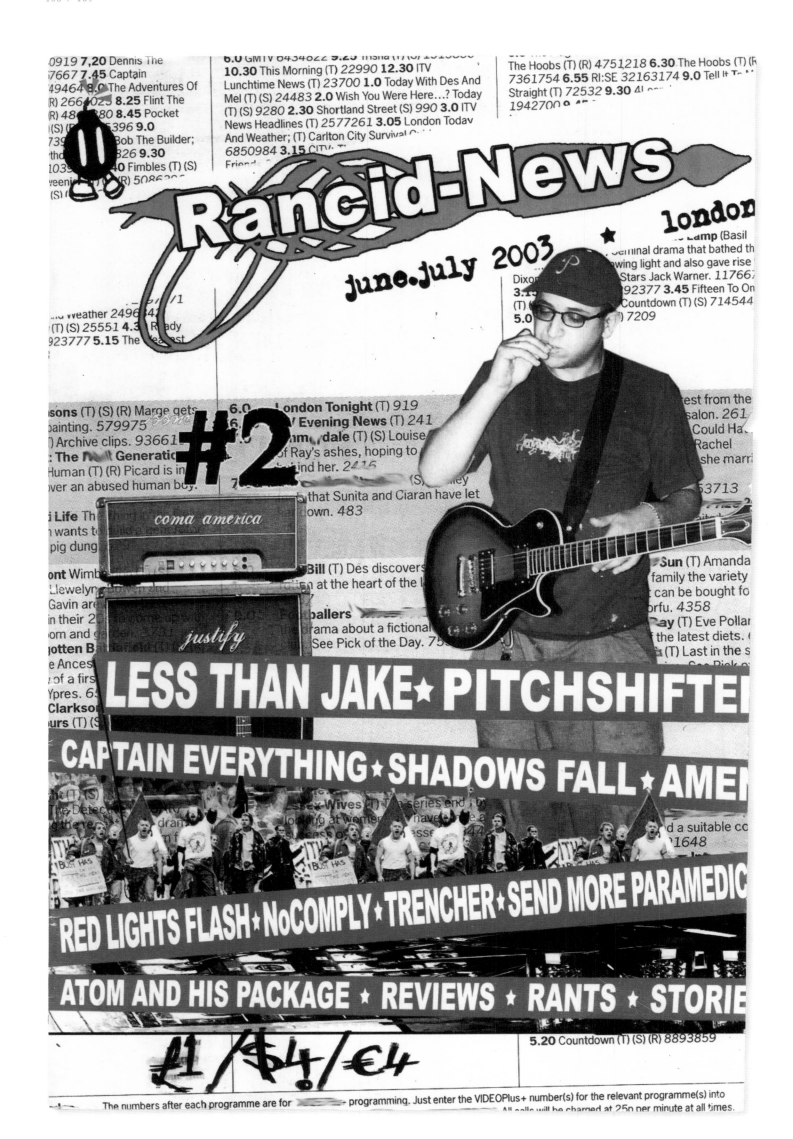

Rancid-News

london

june.july 2003

#2

coma america

justify

LESS THAN JAKE ★ PITCHSHIFTE

CAPTAIN EVERYTHING ★ SHADOWS FALL ★ AME

RED LIGHTS FLASH ★ NoCOMPLY ★ TRENCHER ★ SEND MORE PARAMEDIC

ATOM AND HIS PACKAGE ★ REVIEWS ★ RANTS ★ STORIE

£1 / $4 / €4

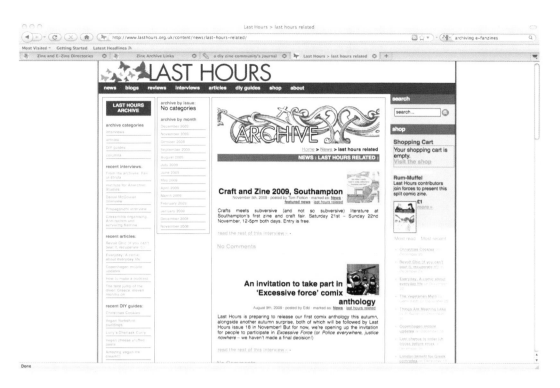

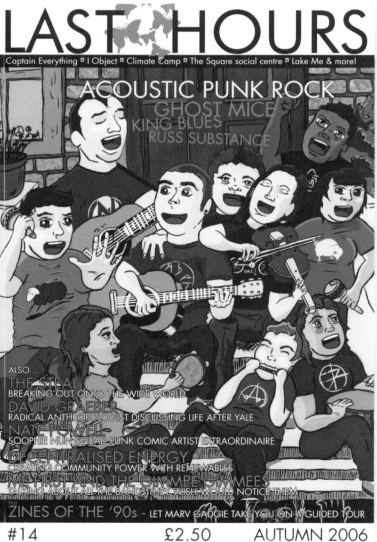

Political zine agitation has found a sympathetic home on the Web. *Rancid-News* (2003–05), produced by Edd Baldry, was a print punkzine that ran for nine issues until issue 10, when its name was changed to *Last Hours* (2005–08). It moved beyond a conventional music review zine and found itself putting out themed issues and devoting more space to political news and articles on such matters as veganism – something that gave the website a more serious aura than others in the genre. Regular contributors included Isy from *Morgenmuffel* and Alex Wrekk from *Stolen Sharpie*, organizer of the Portland Zine Symposium.

Everyday life is a common theme for both print perzines and online versions. *When Language Runs Dry* (2008–), by Claire Barrera and Meredith Butner, is a health-related zine for 'people with chronic pain'. *Karen* (2004–), by Karen Lubbock, states, '… fashion is Lesley and her mannequin Mandy, beauty is a washing line, health is Pat's and Carol's bunions. Art is a visit to the local tattoo parlour, and gardening is a mole that needs catching in the garden.'

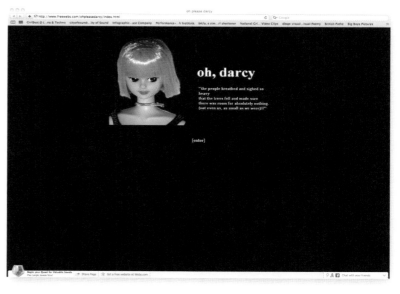

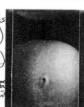

Autobiography is another staple of the perzine. *PonyBoy Press* (1994–) is a blog that operates as a perzine and a point of sale for the writer's zines and craft objects. The co-producer of *The Donner Party* (n.d.) used her website *Oh, Darcy* (n.d.) to promote the fanzine and showcase her poetry. Ayun Halliday's website promotes her print zine **East Village Inky** (1998–). *Ghost Pine Fanzine* (c. 1996–) is an autobiographical zine by Canadian writer Jeff Miller, and this site contains extracts from some of his short stories.

The hand lettering and pink background are as distinctive of *Fever Zine* (*c.* late 2000s) on the web as it is for its print version. Originally a photocopied creation by music journalist Alex Zamora and graphic designer Simon Whybray, it provides a showcase for 'hip' writers, illustrators and photographers, including Tim Murray, Andy Council and Paula Kopecna. The online zine links to social networking sites (the creators are active tweeters) and to interviews with the zine's contributors on YouTube. *Fever Zine* has been featured in British design magazine *Grafik*.

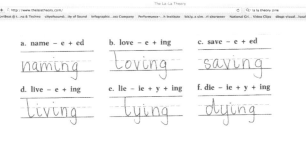

Disparate enthusiasms characterize
the web zine community. The website for the
irregularly produced website *Breakfast* (n.d.)
– 'the zine about your favourite meal' – by
Vincent Voelz is a companion site and sample
archive for the paper zine. The politically
orientated *Clamor* (1999-2006) was founded by
Jen Angel and Jason Kucsma as a 'DIY guide
to everyday revolution'. *The La-La Theory*
(c. 2007-) is a zine about language by Katie
Haegele, a linguist and professional writer.
Her website and blog promote the literary
zine as well as her writing for the
Philadelphia Inquirer.

More diversity on the web. *Hack this Zine*
(2004-) is a collective of 'artists, crackers,
hackers and anarchists' who work with
open source and tech activism. The zine
is available as a pdf to download from the
website. Tomas writes *Rad Dad* (2005-), a blog
zine about parenting, with its origins in a
print zine notable for its letterpress covers.
It won the 2009 'Best Zine' award from the *Utne
Reader*. The website for the *SocialDesignZine*
(2003-09) was maintained by the Italian
Association for Visual Communication Design
and focused on social responsibility. *She Must
Be Having a Bad Day* (2008-) by Dana Raidt, is
a web and print zine for female food service
professionals. *Urinal Gum* (2008-) is a comedy/
satire zine aiming to 'enhance others' lives
through drivel'.

Once into the 2000s women and grrrls contributed to feminist debates in a range of formats - from print to Twitter. *Bust* (1993-), by Laurie Henzel and Debbie Stoller, was one of the first to bring riot grrrl to the mainstream, and has maintained its edge in digital form. *Bitch: Feminist Response to Pop Culture* (1996-) was launched in print with 300 copies distributed by hand; the acclaimed website (n.d.-) is now part of Bitchmedia. *Ladyfest London 2008* used their website to announce the event and to provide the zine programme as a downloadable pdf.

ontreal's pansexual *Lickety Split Smut
ine* (2004–) presents work from 'artists,
allen women, playboys, rakes, trollops and
trumpets!' *Ladyfriend* (1999–2007) by Christa
onner originated as a themed print zine.
rrl Zine Network* (2001–) is an established
eminist zine network listing more than 1000
ines. *Grrrlzines A Go-Go* (2002–) facilitates
ine workshops in community venues, especially
r teenage girls. Belgium-based *Scumgrrrls
0% Feminist Energy* (2002–) takes its title
om Valerie Solanas's *Scum Manifesto.*

The Web has provided zinesters with a global audience. In the case of *Sticky Institute* (2001–), an artist-run initiative in Melbourne, Australia, this notion is extended to providing a shop and a non-profit art gallery dedicated to Australian and international zine culture. As a resource, the online *Zineopedia*, produced by Eloise Peace for the Institute, provides a supplementary compendium. The DIY spirit is also kept alive through activities such as the 'Festival of the Photocopier', though the site does receive funding from government arts bodies. Its distinctive illustrations and navigational links make it a focal point for Australian zinesters.

US teen TV series *Our Hero* (2000-02) featured Kale Stiglic, a 17-year-old high-school student who wrote a zine about her life as a teenager, facing such issues as gender identity, drugs and relationships. The series ran for two years, during a period when fanzines and DIY culture had become established currency among North American teenagers. The accompanying *Our Hero* website pays homage to the visual aesthetic of Kale's printed fanzine, using typefaces that replicate typewritten text, cut-out photographs and hand-drawn illustrations. Fans can interact with the site by uploading zines or completing a questionnaire to predict Kale's future.

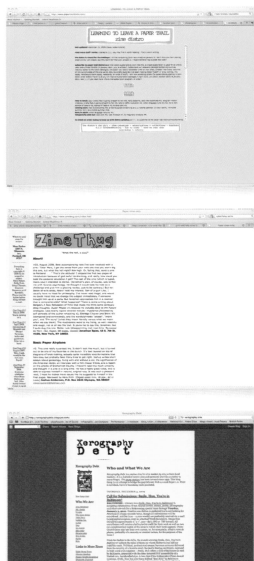

Meta-webzines (zines that review other zines) are a quick and easy way to stay in touch. In the tradition of *Factsheet Five*, *Xerography Debt* (1999–) began as a 16-page production with issues averaging around 50 pages. The expansion of its readership through a website and blog (2008–) guaranteed a greater submission of zines for review, and kept the print version in production. As the editor writes, 'Print is not dead, but it is becoming more pixelated'. The now-defunct website *Learning to Leave a Paper Trail Distro* (2003–10) founded by Ciara Xyerra, was typical of a number of indie distros that rose and fell in the 2000s. Although *Zine Thug* (2003–09), edited by Marc Parker, was published infrequently, it is a useful resource as an archive of reviews.

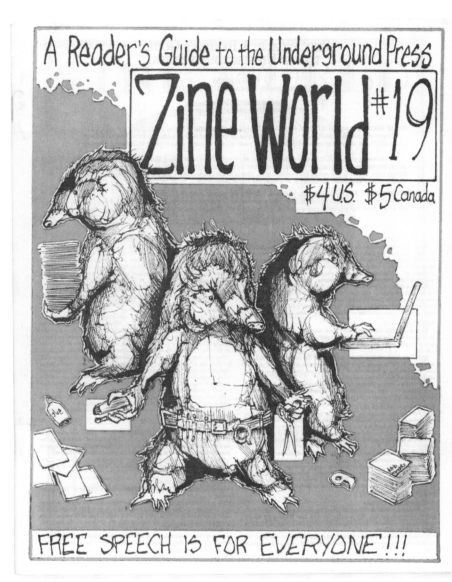

One of the longer-lasting metazines is *Zine World*, which began as a print zine in 1997 and continues today in blog form. Produced by Doug Holland and an all-volunteer staff, it takes a decidedly critical viewpoint. Critics have included Bill Brent (author of *Make a Zine!*), Jeff Somers (science fiction writer) and Karl Wenclas (Underground Literary Alliance). As well as covering zines it includes DVDs, comics, books and other small press/DIY counter-cultural projects. The producers state: 'When publishers are brought up on charges for what they've published, when kids are kicked out of school for creating a zine, we try to spread the word....'

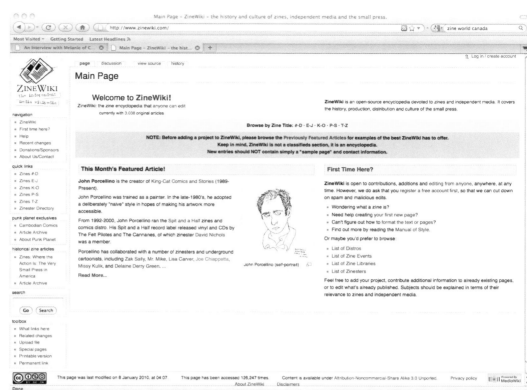

In *Library Bonnet* (c. late 1990s–) Tommy
Kovac and Julie Fredericksen share their
personal experiences as librarians. *FYP
Fanzine* is a Twitter site that accompanies
Five Year Plan (2003–), the fanzine for
Crystal Palace football club. *The Oatcake*
(n.d.–) is a message board for Stoke City
supporters. *ZineWiki* (2006–) is an open
source encyclopaedia devoted to zines and
independent media, created by Alan Lastufka
and Kate Sandler. *Zine Library* (n.d.–) is an
open publishing platform where zinesters can
upload and download copies of fanzines. *80s UK
Zine Archive* (c. 2005–) is an online resource
that collects together 757 zines.

CHAPTER SIX

THE CRAFTING OF CONTEMPORARY FANZINES

Popular culture and music continued to provide a focus for many fanzine producers. *Kurt Cobain Was Lactose Intolerant Conspiracy Zine* (1998) was a riposte to the 1998 documentary film *Kurt and Courtney* and suggested it was milk, not drugs, that killed Cobain. *Publish and Bedazzled* (1995–2004) focused on the career and strange personal life of British comedian Peter Cook. *Pull to Open* (2001–) is a fanzine about the world's longest running science-fiction TV programme, *Doctor Who*.

It is 2006. The place is The Square social centre, a large Victorian squatted building in central London's Russell Square, in which the second annual London Zine Symposium is under way. Tables and stalls cram the lower floors of the house with zines and small press books. The basement has been turned into a screen-printing room, with one corner reserved for an exhibition of zine art. But, in the garden, beyond the pandemonium of zine buying and trading, something else is going on: a group of young men and women are sitting cross-legged in a circle on the grass. They are knitting. Just clicking away quite happily with their knitting needles. I have never seen anything like it before. The fact that it is men and women is even more remarkable: as one organizer of the event observes, it is '… totally punk rock and just goes to show the sexism behind common gendering of hobbies'.[1]

The links between zine culture and craft culture go back to the early 1990s with the emergence of the riot grrrl scene, where such activities as knitting, crocheting, cross-stitching and sewing were reclaimed as part of a third-wave feminist position. Craft moved out of the domestic sphere, where it increasingly came to be seen as a sign of female oppression, and into a more public domain as a form of hipster 'creative expression'. This shift was significant and led the way towards the refashioning of a craft activity into a political statement. 'Craftivism' (a conflation of 'craft' and 'activism') was coined in 2003 by British crafter and artist Betsy Greer to reflect this: she argued that 'by using my own creative drive as a positive force instead of allowing the wheels of consumerism to direct me, everything I did became part of my activism'.[2] For Greer, craftivism was directly related to socially engaged practices aiming to 'disrupt the prevailing codes of mass consumerism'. By embracing the notion of a DIY culture, Greer and others like her (including Debbie Stoller, co-founder of *Bust*, and Julie Jackson of *Subversive Cross Stitch*) opened themselves up to new ways of exploring gender and identity (how feminine and feminist could co-exist), as well as craft practices. The resulting handwork became a visual act of dissent: in the first instance against dominant forms

of capitalism, but also reflecting social, environmental and political concerns. This has been mirrored in other forms of engagement such as 'guerilla gardening' (the cultivation of disused land).

This chapter will look at the way in which fanzines have reflected this phenomenon, and how they comment on economic structures and political activism while also fostering networks of local (and global) communities. Like the knitting circles, zine publishing has the power to inspire social cohesion. For a new generation of DIY crafters, the politics are still very evident, but now there is a more holistic approach to 'making one's life one's own'. This has indicated a new direction for zine culture, in which an emphasis on DIY is found in new contexts.

Crafting Fanzines

It is worth exploring briefly what is meant by the word 'craft' and what this means for contemporary fanzines. American writer Bruce Metcalf has argued that craft has a set of specific characteristics, which he defines as being 'handmade'. Craft, he writes, is 'medium-specific' and is normally 'identified with a material and the technologies invented to manipulate it'. In addition, Metcalf suggests, 'craft is defined by use', in that craft objects have a function (for example jewelry or furniture), but also that 'craft is defined by its past'. Out of these combined characteristics emerges an aesthetic value. In other words, Metcalf proposes that craft's 'aesthetic value must be located in [the] ways craft is intimate, useful and meaningful'.[3]

This idea can be applied to an exploration of fanzines as graphic forms – in particular, the way in which fanzines are intimate graphic objects, holding meaning through their form and content but at the same time functioning to communicate. Zines are defined by their materiality The fact that fanzines are often visually chaotic (the result of experimenting with found materials and lo-fi DIY production and binding methods) and use scale to advantage, through different sizes and formats (from minizines to broadsheets), results in an object that can be unusually tactile. An intimacy derives from the fact that fanzines

By the 2000s men were back on the covers of fanzines. *Squeaky Sneakers* (2008–09) celebrated the 'retrosexual' man by focusing this issue on beards and 'other hairy facial accessories.' *Manzine* (2008–) edited by Kevin Braddock, takes a humorous look at 'the male phenomenon' and consciously lets go of past images of 'new lads' and 'metrosexuals' to focus on 'men'. *The Robert Edmond Grant Fanzine* (2009) celebrates one of the forgotten 'great men of history', a nineteenth-century naturalist.

remain amateur, 'handmade' productions operating outside mainstream publishing conventions and mass-production processes. The hand – the imprint – of the individual producer or maker is readily evident in the fanzine itself. This suggests, then, that the history of the object is bound up not only with the history of fanzines more generally, but also with the history of the individual maker.

In the 2000s, 'tactility' became a trope and was symbolized by the increasing use of letterpress (a relief print process) and screen-printing (a stencil process leaving ink on paper). While production technologies (including duplicators, photocopiers and desktop publishing) have always been important to the zine aesthetic, this seemingly more sophisticated use of printing techniques had the effect of 'slowing things down'. The immediacy offered by earlier cut-and-paste and photocopied zines was replaced by a more intentional and time-based act of making. As a result, the traditional zine aesthetic shifted (the immediacy of punk and riot grrrl zines, in particular) in the 2000s. The chaotic nature and visual intensity of the photocopied pages and covers started to disappear. Zines are now more clearly akin to the handmade aesthetic of many small press artists' books, with their uncluttered design, handmade stock and unconventional forms of binding. It is telling that zines have started to appear as numbered, limited editions, in a nod to recognizing the value of the time and skills of their producers.

An example of this shift is *Ker-Bloom!*, a bi-monthly letterpress zine produced in the United States by Karen Switzer (aka Artnoose . The zine began production in the mid-1990s and recently came off press with issue 82 (2010). It exemplifies the craft of letterpress production (Artnoose owns her own craft card shop), and it is also a poignant perzine. Each issue takes a personal look at a situation or theme, be it the laborious process of moving a print shop, anti-capitalist business practices, forming a band, being an extra in a film, alcoholism, or playground fighting. *Ker-Bloom!* led the way for other recent letterpress productions, such as the one-off art zine *Cheer Up!* (2010) created by

Oliver Mayes in the form of a mailing tube. It included jokes by British comedians Jack Dee and Jimmy Carr rolled up with page excerpts from the *Financial Times* newspaper. The intention was to help take readers' minds off the recession.

Another example is *Zine 2009* (2009), produced by students from the University of Delaware as part of a letterpress workshop held at the London College of Communication (LCC). The zine format was a prompt for students to explore typographic experimentation but also to experience the letterpress medium. This approach was adopted in an earlier LCC public engagement workshop where local crafters were invited to use the desktop letterpress in the design of their individual pages for a community zine titled *The Memory Cloth* (2006). Zine workshops such as this present opportunities to develop a sense of community through the collective act of making.

Crafting Alternative Communities

It is perhaps no surprise therefore that fanzines are part of a growing alternative craft movement that, as Metcalf has proposed, is 'shifting production back into the hands of ordinary people'.[4] Fanzines are contributing to this lifestyle shift through the publishing of 'how-to' zines, which tell readers about how to produce or make things for themselves. These how-to zines fall into two main categories according to content. The first is zines that are writing about how to make zines (the practicalities of folding paper, binding, printing, distribution). For example, *Stolen Sharpie Revolution: A DIY Zine Resource* is a minizine (and blog) by self-confessed 'crafty girl' Alex Wrekk. In it she reflects that she found independent publishing a means by which she could express herself and be empowered by 'looking at things and saying "I can do that"'.[5] She suggests tips such as the value of knowing who your target audience is, carrying around a notebook to record inspirations, what type of glue to use, where to find clip art, thrift stores as a source for material, and consideration of copyright 'if you are going to reprint something from another zine'.[6] The 'how-to' resource also

...other selection of recent lo-fi productions.
...e producer of *Publish and Be Published*
...005), Eddie Wilson, pays homage to the 1970s
...Y ethic in this practical guide on how to
...blish a novel. Another approach to DIY is
...e 'how-to' guide to zine production — as
...emplified by *Zine Libs* (2005), in which the
...ader is asked to fill in the blanks for
...series of stories. *Just Say No Thank You*
...007) is a mini-perzine out of New Zealand,
...oviding a forum for those who want to share
...periences about being 'asexual' and vegan.

Medical references, tenuous or otherwise, continue to be popular. The title of *Nervous System* (2006), by Anthony, can be read as meaning a part of the body, but it also points up a sense of unease regarding certain authoritative elements of society. *BodyTalk*, art-directed by Sarah Handelman, aims to raise health awareness among youth groups in Columbia, Missouri. *Local Anaesthetic!* (2005–), edited by Tom Noonan and Cliff Anderson, is a grassroots monthly nurturing local artistic talent in Geelong, Australia.

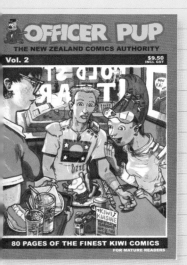

Colour printing became so much cheaper in the 2000s that it was almost ubiquitous. *Officer Pup* (2001–) is a small-format comiczine anthology from New Zealand showcasing Kiwi comics, reviews and news. *You Stink & I Don't* (1995–) revels in satirical and black humour, with plenty of comic strips. *The Squareball* (1989–) is a long-running football zine, which in its 2000s incarnation made the most of colour covers (in this case referencing boys' soccer comics).

covers making paper, using a copier and distribution, including 'building a community by attending zine conferences and events'.[7]

In the second category are the zines that provide lo-fi 'how-to' guides to making your own products or crafts (soap-making, gardening and home composting, jewelry-making, cross-stitching, knitting, sewing…), or advice for healthier living. Raleigh Briggs, for example, publishes a series of pamphlet zines (such as *Nontoxic Housecleaners Zine*, 2007; *Herbal First Aid Zine*, 2006) that endeavour to provide basic advice for such things as making soap at home, or herbal remedies. *Home Composting Made Easy* (1998, reprint 2008), by Forrest and Tricia McDowell, is a zine about 'creating less waste'. *MixTape* (2007–) by Nichola Prested and Justine Telfer, pays homage to the award-winning indie crafting *Croq Zine* (2005–08) and presents a range of 'how-to' tips for crafting, such as the pragmatics of sewing.

The main places where zinesters have traditionally congregated continue to flourish: events such as zine festivals, small press book and comic fairs, independent book stores, and so on. Alternative communities are also established through distribution for both zines and other craft products. This has become evident in the emerging micro-craft economy, where the places for bartering, selling and buying fanzines and DIY 'products' are being complemented by online activity. Zinesters and crafters, for example, use social networking and e-commerce sites such as Etsy (www.etsy.com), which provide inexpensive but far-reaching ways to sell handmade work. While zines may still be found in indie retail outlets (normally indie music or book stores), print distribution also takes place through online distributors ('distros'), such as Microcosm Publishing, Parcel Press and Corn Dog Publishing, to name a few.

At the same time, virtual networks and communities are also thriving (YouTube, MySpace, websites, blogs…) and zines are morphing into new digital formats. Cathy de la Cruz, an artist and crafter, has proposed that 'a podcast today is what a zine was in the nineties'.[8] Zine information as circulated through virtual message boards, Twitter and

Facebook pages is now commonplace: the local is now global and with it has come a renewed commitment to 'political' activism.

It is worth noting the shift in the use of terminology among zinesters, who appear to be moving away from the previously favoured idea of 'networks' to one that is more firmly committed to the development of zine 'communities'. Networks are formed in the way that zinesters are able to reach out to others for the purposes of sharing and exchanging ideas and providing information about their zines and related activities. On the other hand, a much more complex set of relationships is taking place around the notion of communities (for there is no one single community in zine world). The difference is in intent: communities build upon a sense of belonging and shared discourse, whether personal or politically inspired. Communities are also about fostering relationships through participation. This may be between individuals with different authorial positions and voices, as well as between producers and readers: all of them are active participants in a vibrant and thriving zine scene.

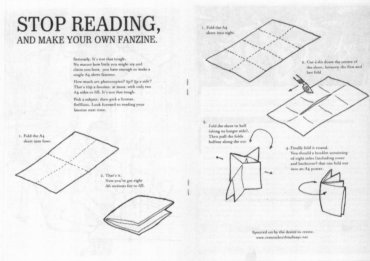

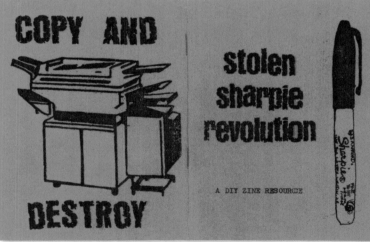

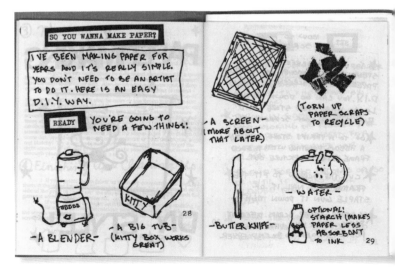

Lo-fi 'how-to' guides did not lose their appeal in the 2000s. *Sweet Shop Syndicate* (2006-, cover and inside spread) is a perzine created by Chris and Rich, who live in two different countries (UK and Austria) and solicit the help of their friends and families as contributors. Among the stories of recent travels and gardening tips is a how-to piece on making your own fanzine. Zine producer Alex Wrekk created the popular resource *Stolen Sharpie Revolution* (c. 2003, front and back cover and inside spread) with tips and advice on making and distributing zines: the interior spread shown here provides information on paper-making. *Zine Making: An Introduction* (2003) was the end publication from a series of workshops for teenagers that took place in Halifax, UK. Its popularity as an accessible resource for other zinesters has meant it is now in its second edition. *MixTape* (2007-, covers and inside spread), by Nichola Prested and Justine Telfer, underlines that the culture of DIY is not limited to making fanzines but extends to the 'making of small things'. The two producers met via their respective blogs and recognized a shared passion for all things handmade. *MixTape* references the indie craft magazine *Croq Zine* (2005-08), and provides practical tips about a range of crafts. With its high-quality illustration, this zine has tapped into the zeitgeist of pop culture: shown here are signature style covers by Australian designer Shannon Lamden (issue 1) and Mandy Sutcliffe (issue 6).

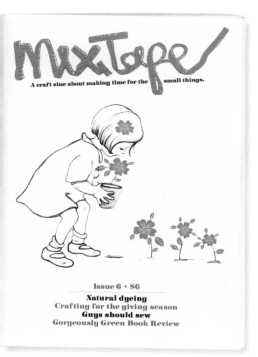

DATES IVE BEEN ON AND NOT BEEN ON

VI

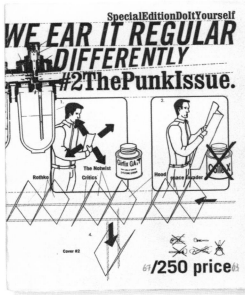

SpecialEditionDoItYourself

WE EAR IT REGULAR DIFFERENTLY

#2ThePunkIssue.

Rothko The Notwist Critics Hood space invader

Cover #2

/250 price

helping you find
the right
jewellry !

YZ

375

3 7 5

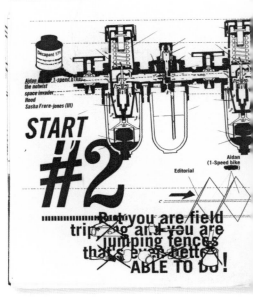

Aidan   1-speed bike
the notwist
space invader
Hood
Sasha Frere-jones (UI)

START
#2

Push you are field
tripping and you are
jumping fences
that's even better
ABLE TO DO !

Editorial

THis is!

(issue Ø½)

Hastily-prepared, very
limited edition ...   50p

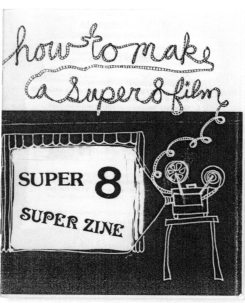

The craft of making has extended into literature, music, filmmaking and cross-stitching, to mention a few. Naturally this has had an effect on the look of zines. *Dates I've Been On and Not Been On* (n.d.), a story about the producer's love life, includes machine-sewn binding. *We Ear It Regular Differently* (n.d., front and back covers) uses folded sheets inserted into a printed cover and sprinkled with gold glitter. Artist Sarah Doyle created *Helping You Find the Right Jewellry!* (mid-2000s), which explores through her drawings a range of accessories. *This Is!* (2002-06), a lively perzine by Helen Wickham, includes hologram food stickers on the front. *How to Make a Super 8 Film* (c. 2006) is the result of a filmmaking workshop taught in junior high schools in Canada. *D90: A Mix-Tape Zine* (2007-08) celebrates the cassette era and asks its readers to 'bring a community together with a tape'. *Hey, Look! It's a Zine about Cross Stitch!* (c. 2010) is a simple 'how-to' guide with amusing patterns.

More inventive designs that riff on the craft explosion. *Ker-Bloom!* (1996–), containing poignant personal stories, is printed on a Vandercook flat-bed press. *The Squares* (c. 2009) is in fact a circular zine that reappropriates the packaging of a Sinitta single (the zine is glued to the vinyl). *In Sickness* (2008) is a colour-photocopied perzine about health obsessions, held together by a rubber band and a paperclip. The award-winning *28 Pages Lovingly Bound with Twine* (2001–) is a perzine from stay-at-home father and artist Christoph Meyer that chronicles the producer's home life. *The Memory Cloth* (2006) is a one-off workshop-based zine. The single-sheet pages of contributions are inserted into a striped paper bag, which is machine-stitched.

CONTRIIBUTIONS BY

SOPHIEE BEARD

RICK MYERS

JOHN MORGAN STUDIO

SUSANNA EDWARDS

RUTH SKYES (REG)

NINA CHAKRABARTI

HOLLY WALES

BEN BRANAGAN

SAM WINSTON

KATE WESTERHOLT

ASTRID AL

JOSEPH YOLK

CHANTAL YOUNG

CHRISSIE MACDONALD

ALEXANDRE BETTLER

DENISE GONZALES CRISP

RACHEL THOMAS

HARRINGTON & SQUIRES

MILENA

SHANE KINGDON

KATHARINA KOALL

CLAUDIA BOLDT

JASON SKOWRONEK

HELEN MCCOOKERYBOOK

CECILIE MAURUD BARSTAD

KRISTJANA WILLIAMS

ELLEN LINDNER

PATRICK LAING

PETE HELLICAR

RACHAEL HOUSE

EDITED & DESIGNED BY

SUZY WOOD

IZZIE KLINGELS

MARTIN MCGRATH

WORKSHOP LOCATION

ECKERSLEY GALLERY

LONDON COLLEGE OF COMMUNICATION

ELEPHANT AND CASTLE

THE MEMORY CLOTH

An Exploration into Craft Memory and Contemporary Design

THIS PUBLICATION CONTAINS CONTRIBUTIONS FROM ARTISTS, DESIGNERS AND WRITERS SUPPLEMENTED WITH PAGES CREATED BY VISITORS TO 'THE MEMORY CLOTH' EXHIBITION HELD ON THE

TWENTY SIXTH

OF JULY TWO THOUSAND AND SIX

INTRODUCTION BY *Angharad Lewis*

Today in the West mass-produced goods, things made by machines and the hands of strangers, fulfill our basic needs. When winter arrives we go to the high street and buy a warm jumper; we shop at the supermarket for pre-prepared food; we live in homes built by others, furnished by production-line furniture. We have progressively lost an appreciation of the craft of making things by hand, especially in daily life.

Revisiting those crafts we're in danger of losing touch with is a way not only to preserve them but also to better understand our relationship to today's world. Craft is about mastering a skill, meeting a need (be it basic or complex), realising an idea in physical form, and the attendant satisfaction of doing so by one's own hand. Craft is also about creating very personal human interaction—skills are passed on from person to person. When I was a child my mother made my summer dresses by hand. Both my grandmothers made many of their children's clothes by hand. They cooked all the family's meals from scratch and baked bread every week. My grandfather crafted furniture for their home. In that sense my family members were being designers and artists every day of their lives. But making things by hand is no longer a necessity—crafts are often relegated to the realm of the hobby; handmade goods have become marginalised and skills practiced less and less are forgotten from one generation to the next. Many artists and designers today, however, are increasingly using their work to question this situation and to revisit those methods in a provocative way. The Memory Cloth fanzine is a collaborative work by such artists and designers. It seeks to explore and preserve the qualities of craft and celebrates its unique synthesis of tradition and invention.

MIX ZINE

♥ A MIX CD & A ZINE! ♥ 50p

ISSUE ONE ★★★★

Dear you
It
mo
I I
cro
litt.....j (
years) with little time
AND..... I I a st
now..... time
its the longest

YOU

1. PIXIES – Debaser

the perky picking of bass strings kicks in, the guitar riff slices across & across, sounding like a siren as we crash into a clarrion call of a song, and I'm back in the dark confines of the student indie night. I'm moshing my socks off, cut loose on 60pence cider. Maybe I'm the only one on the dancefloor, but I feel free and happy as can be. My clonking great sparkly Doctor Marten boots thud as they touch flat on the floor for the merest of seconds before flying up again, and I feel light as anything. I'm in the music. The bass throbs as if it's my own heart. My hair's flicking everywhere, eyes half closed, I can only feel and be the music; only the odd glimpse of disco lights exists in my vision. No one else is here – just me & this corrweating, cutting, biting, blistering electric ecstatic song, and all too soon the thud of its finality closes it.

2. BOUTIQUE: I've told you Before

One of those beautiful moments where you're sorting through old unlabelled C90 casettes. A stream of old Radio One 'Evening Session' songs and in the midst, the grinding grab of a sweet lost indie pop gem tipples over the speakers. My boyfriend & I swapped looks of gleeful nostalgia, shaken up like the dust of some snow globe – a smidgen of memory golden and recovered.

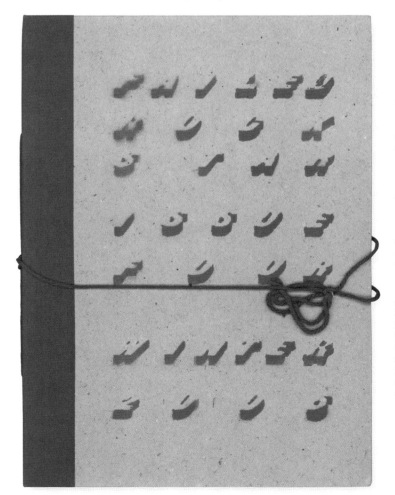

Mix Zine (2009, cover and inside spread) combines a CD with a paper perzine in order to share with the reader sounds selected from obscure musical sources (e.g. 'the perky picking of bass strings' and 'sweeping piano cascade'). Miss Fliss, a music journalist and past editor of *Splinter Magazine*, is the producer of this handcrafted square-format and heavily star-stickered zine. *You* (2001–) is a Melbourne-based fanzine, clearly influenced by art movements such as Fluxus, that comes in the form of a personal letter written by anonymous contributors, folded and sealed in a small bag. Five years of the zine have recently been collected in a book. *Pneumatic Catalog* (n.d., cover and inside spread) contains mail-art-inspired colour-photocopied artworks. The cover of this zine is bespoke and features as part of the inside front cover a pouch in which a smaller perzine, *My Family Album*, is inserted. *By the Time You're Twenty Five* (2008) is an Australian music and perzine by Emma, who takes as her starting point the now disbanded riot grrrrl group Sleater-Kinney. Her hand-drawn cover is created out of a sheet of pink tracing paper and stapled on to the black-and-white photocopied interior, allowing for some intriguing see-through effects. *Failed Rock Star* (2003–) is edited by Rob Phoenix as a portfolio-inspired zine, with single-sheet contributions from 50 artists, writers and designers housed in a screen-printed cloth bag.

Artzines became more evident in the United
Kingdom after the rise of the YBAs (Young
British Artists), both reviewing the
fringe art scene and offering an outlet
for DIY artworks. *Arty* (2001–) consists of
drawings, photographs and reviews by artist-
contributors. *Blitzkrieg Babylon* (2003) is a
limited-edition screen-printed zine that takes
as its starting point an anarchist's view of
the political landscape. *Organ* (1986–)
is an alternative culture, music and artzine,
with a substantial press-run of 20,000 for
this issue. *Plastasine Fantazine* (2008) was a
fanzine edited by artist David Burrows with
participants from an academic conference,
'Art Writing Beyond Criticism' (ICA, London).

Intercity Baby `09

Typical production techniques used in the 2000s included colour photocopying, desktop publishing and screen-printing. *Enough Magazine* (2007–) is an anti-consumerism zine and a mouthpiece for artists and anarchists. *Intercity Baby* (2009–) by Jennifer portrays the train journeys of her 'indie pop comrades' through photographs and writings. *Giant Steps* (2007–, cover and inside spread) is a perzine by Kirke Campbell named after a 1959 track by the jazz saxophonist John Coltrane. One hundred copies of this issue were produced, each with a screen-printed cover and 'tipped-in' mini photozine (pictured).

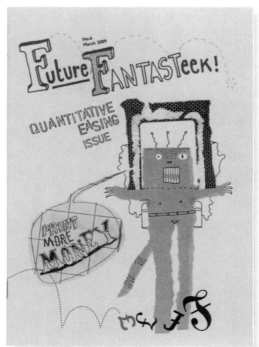

ore sophisticated use of printing methods
such as screen-printing coincides with an
increased use of hand-drawn and illustrated
covers. *Bang!* (n.d 2008) is a substantial
music and club zine produced out of Madrid,
with a striking screen-printed portrait
of a young girl on the cover of this issue.
gly is the New Sexy (2006) is an illustrated
erzine by Bryce Galloway out of New Zealand.
uture Fantasteek! (2006–) is a limited-
dition artzine produced in Brighton by
llustrator Jacky Batey. *Obsession* (c. 2009)
s a collaborative zine curated by Karoline
errie, where artists are invited to draw
ith each having a double-page spread for
heir work. The screen-printed cover artwork
s by illustrator Gemma Carroll. *Rivers Edge*
(2008, cover and inside spread) is a limited-
dition hand-printed zine that explores the
ork of underground artists. This issue also
uestions 'what is a zine' in relationship
o its own publication and its 'intrinsic
IY nature'. *Screw Crash & Explode* (n.d.)
s a stencil-printed artzine that features
utch collaborative artists Monobrain and
arcel Herms. The frenetic nature of each
rinted page is enhanced by the intensity of
ach drawing and the fullness of 'doodles',
plotches and graphic marks.

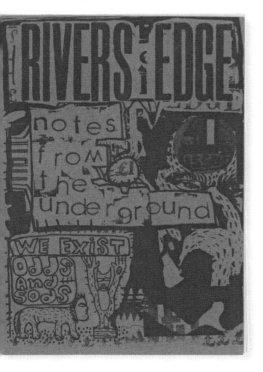

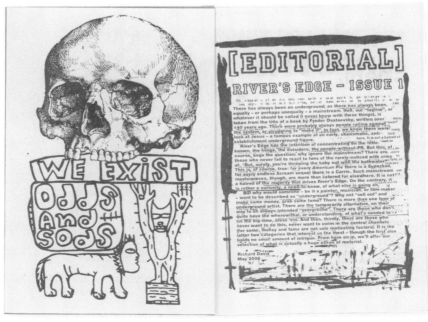

Subject-matter previously considered the domain of mainstream glossy magazines has now entered the purview of fanzines. *Fire & Knives* (2009–) is a relatively up-market quarterly food zine by editor Tim Hayward. It includes contributions from top writers and critics and is designed by Rob Lowe (*Super Mundane*). *Barefoot and in the Kitchen…* (2005–) is a zine about cooking and being vegan by Ashley Rowe, including 'tried and tested' recipes. *Stand Aside* (c. 2000s) takes a look at street fashion in Kilburn, London. This zine was produced as part of a Public Works workshop.

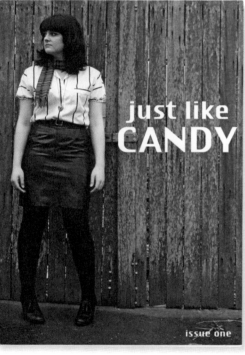

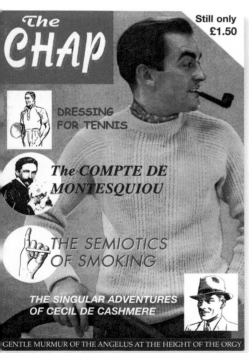

With desktop publishing fanzine style has, in some cases, moved towards that of conventional magazines. *FP: Fashion Projects* (2006–), is a publicly funded fashion zine created to raise awareness of experimental fashion. *Just Like Candy* (2008–) is glossy zine about music, art and film, whose producers 'used InDesign for the first time to create the layout'. *The Chap* (n.d.–) takes an ironic look at masculinity and men's fashion, with for example articles on dressing for tennis and the semiotics of smoking. *Medium Magazine* (2005–) is a quarterly portfolio with contributions from artists and writers including novelist Anthony Gray.

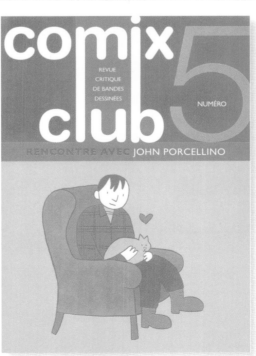

That old staple the comiczine has also moved with the times. *Hey, 4-Eyes!* (c. 2008–) is a limited-edition example allowing various artists to make a spectacle of their spectacles. *Comix Club* (c. 2006–) is a French-language fanzine, with number 5 interviewing American 'ultra-minimalist' artist John Porcellino. *Dame Pipi Comix/DMPP Almanach* (2004–) by Gérald Auclin is notable for its changes in format for each issue. British horror magazine *From the Tomb* (2000–) explores the entertainingly exploitative world of 'pre-Code' horror comics (comics created in the 1940s–50s prior to the establishment of the Comics Code Authority), as well as lesser-known fare in the supernatural horror vein.

Re V'La Cloyis Naody (n.d.) is a French
Canadian comiczine featuring work by Martin
Guimond, whose stylistic approach is part of
a rich tradition of the Quebec underground
scene. Guimond, along with other artists
including Luc Leclerc and Mathieu Massicotte-
Quesnel, came to prominence during the early
1990s with the publication of a series of
bilingual anthologies in fanzine format.

KARINE ALEXANDRINO · A ANTI-DIVA TOMBADA · MOON & BÁ · LIVE FROM NY: CONTINENTAL · ART BRUT · FREAK CINE

2,1

Karine Alexandrino

Por André Mansur

A Antidiva Tombada (E nós precisávamos disso!)

Performática, ela ataca em várias frentes. A cearense Karine Alexandrino é o que se convencionou chamar de artista multimídia. "Quanto mais nuances, códigos e símbolos tiver um trabalho artístico, melhor. Comunica mais", nos conta a própria, em entrevista para a Jukebox. "Tenho uma relação íntima com a body art. Me fotografo, faço meus próprios monólogos e filmes de mim mesma. É exercício diário. Mas asseguro que é natural e não uma simples estratégia". Podem acreditar. Afinal, grande parte desse interesse veio de berço, numa cidadezinha no interior do Ceará chamada Morada Nova, quando a mãe de Karine pagava uma preceptora para dar aulas em casa sobre a história da arte. Aos cinco anos, ela compôs uma música que foi adotada no colégio no qual estudava e, aos oito, já recebia pra cantar nos eventos da cidade. Depois disso, muita coisa aconteceu. Forward.

Com dois discos lançados, Solteira Producta (Gerador Music - 2002) e Querem Acabar Comigo, Roberto (Tratore - 2004), ambos em parcerias com produtor Dustan Gallas, Karine Alexandrino fez valer cada centavo do investimento da mamãe. Com bases programadas (mas nem sempre) e arranjos bem amarrados, as canções trafegam entre Serge Gainsbourg e Yoko Ono embalados a vácuo, numa vã tentativa minha de explanação. Ela mesma já se definiu certa vez como electro-pop-trash-chique. Ou, noutra vez, como neo-tropicalista: "É uma brincadeira meio séria. Nada a ver com batuques e penas na cabeça", pondera. "É o que existia na face íntima do tropicalismo que me inspira muito. Uma proposta de música com liberdade. Tenho o

tropicalismo como legado. Neo-tropicalismo é um nome que os próprios tropicalistas odiariam". Ela tem razão. "Só uso o termo para me comunicar com os universitários", ah, está justificado.

Nas músicas, Karine canta os destemperos da vida em dramatizações invariavelmente passionais. Suas músicas são como polaróides extraídas de filmes do Almodóvar com títulos impagáveis e pra lá de sugestivos como "Diga algo senão pulo", "Amor e glória é só boato" ou "Tenho febre, mas vou buscar nosso dinheiro". Questionada sobre o elemento kitsch presente em seu trabalho, ela rebate: "Kitsch muda de acordo com a moda ou não? Colocar pingüim em geladeira para parecer kitsch, hoje em dia, soa falso. Não é o meu caso. Mas, como faço uma música simples, onde há um certo romantismo na forma, pode-se falar como sendo kitsch. E não pretendo ser uma musicista chata, nem fingir que levo a música a sério, essas baboseiras todas". Justamente daí surge o alarmado papel de antidiva, tão necessário hoje, num mundo infestado de celebridades instantâneas. Karine é sincera e constantemente auto-irônica. Mas ao seu modo, cabe frisar. E como se comporta uma antidiva? "Canta sem frescura, sem pose de blasé. Fica nua se necessário, bate se necessário e se comunica com franqueza com o público. Além de fazer bom uso dos melhores perfumes".

48

49

The pocket-book-size indie music and comiczine *Juke Box* (2006-, cover and inside spread) from Brazil was influenced by the output of comics publisher Fantagraphics. Editor Renato Lima (also an editor at *Mosh!*) brought together comic artists, designers and musicians through the publication to discuss the language of comics. The size of the zine allowed the designers to play with the way in which the reader would engage with the page, mixing the format from portrait to landscape. The launch of each issue centred around a music event located in such cities as Rio de Janeiro and São Paulo. *Cat Quarterly* (1990s) by Annie Lawson is a photocopied small press comiczine in which nuanced humour is presented in stick-figure form. Her work has also appeared in books and in the mainstream press (including the UK paper the *Observer*). *Reality Optional* (2007), created by Andrew Stitt, is a comics perzine responding to a theme of 'Dreams and Nightmares', in which he makes wry comment on the fantasy comics of Neil Gaiman and Dave McKean. The zine was produced for the small press fair 'Caption'. *Tantrum Comics* (2002-n.d.) is the autobiography of professional cartoonist Miriam Engelberg, who, in this issue, reflects on her fears around a breast cancer diagnosis and some of her coping mechanisms, which include watching the TV courtroom show *Judge Judy*.

The zines on this spread are politically
motivated. *Bipedal, By Pedal!* (2008) by Joe
Biel explores the producer's experiences as a
participant in the popular Critical Mass bike
rides protest movement. *Expansion of Life* (n.d.),
out of Japan, is a women's punk and political
zine with articles about 'women changing the
world in the Philippines'. *Whoosh!* (2008–) is
a zine for those passionate about whales and
other 'big animals from the sea'. *Cut and Paint*
(2007–), by Nicolas Lampert, Josh MacPhee and
Colin Matthes, is a DIY stencil template zine,
printed as offset by an anarchist printer in
Portland, Oregon. *How Not To Eat Animals* (n.d.)
is a 44-page vegetarian cookbook designed to
'subvert the dominant meat-eating, animal-
products-in-everything culture'.

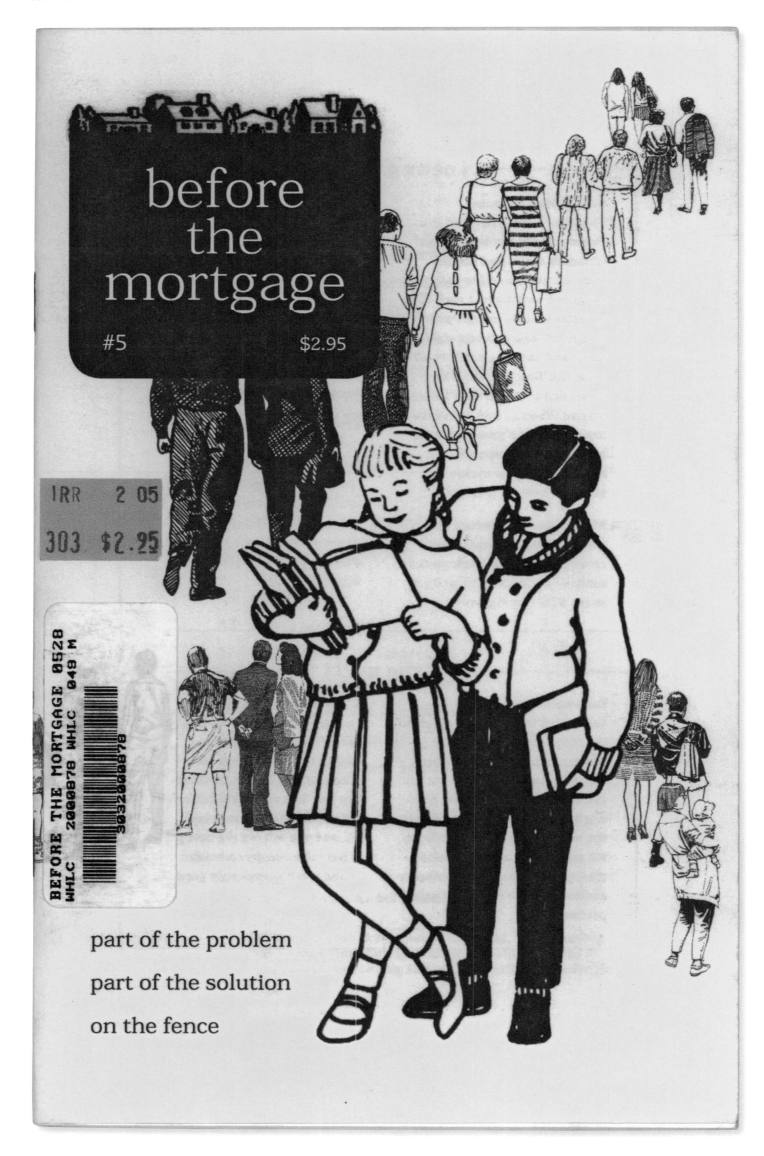

before
the
mortgage

#5 $2.95

IRR   2 05
303 $2.95

part of the problem

part of the solution

on the fence

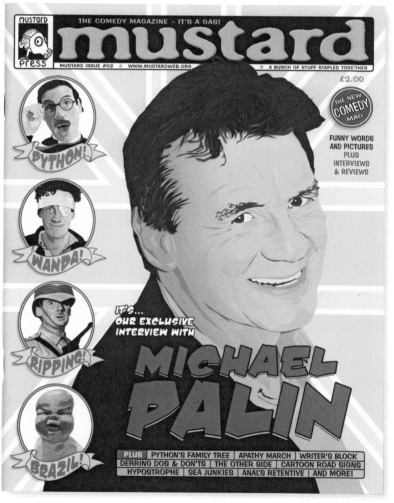

Before the Mortgage (2001-06), edited by Christina Amini and Rachel Hutton, chronicles responsiblity-free life in New York. *Daniel Battams Fan Club Magazine* (2003-n.d.) is a zine about an imaginary celebrity. Australia's *The Alien Invader* (2001-03), by Amin-Reza Javanmard and Jen-Tsen Kwok, was 'intended as a journal dissecting and analysing the Asian-Australian experience'. An annual comedy journal, *The Lowbrow Reader* (2001-) is edited by Jay Ruttenberg and features 'long articles and funny illustrations'. *Mustard* (2007-) edited and designed by Alex Musson, is an indie comedy magazine that features interviews, comic strips and satirical news stories.

SHOREDITCH TWAT
ISSUE 3
he's got a gun

SHOREDITCH TWAT
ISSUE 4
the one in the middle please

SHOREDITCH TWAT
ISSUE 5
standing on the shoulders of midgets

SHOREDITCH TWAT
ISSUE 6
NICE SHADES MATE

SHOREDITCH TWAT
ISSUE 7
STAB IN THE DARK

House Plants

SHOREDITCH TWAT
ISSUE 12
Hot lead for your ass sir

"THE ROAD TO EXCELLENCE IS NEVER ENDING   SO THE SEARCH MUST BE UNRELENTING."

SHOREDITCH TWAT
ISSUE 14
HEAVY ARTILLERY

SHOREDITCH TWAT
ISSUE 18
TOO CLOSE FOR COMFORT

PERVERT LIVES
IN THIS BLOCK
OF FLATS

SHOREDITCH
TWAT HEAD
OFFICE HERE

CHILDREN
PLAY IN
THIS AREA

SCRATCH AND STIFF
ISSUE

Shoreditch Twat (1999–2004) was a satirical
club fanzine edited by Neil Boorman (later
of *Sleazenation* magazine) and art-directed
by John Morgan and Mike Watson (aka design
group Bump). The zine's title was absorbed
into London's urban slang as a term meaning
'a new media, fashion student, photographer-
type person with a privileged digital- or
old-school arts background who lives/works/
socialises in London's East End'. In its heyday
the circulation was 25,000, touting nightclub
333's message that 'partying should be messy,
dangerous and unprofessional, otherwise
it's no fun at all'. It contained edgy satire
and spoof adverts, as well as the club's gig
listings. In 2002 the zine transferred to
television as a one-off comedy special.

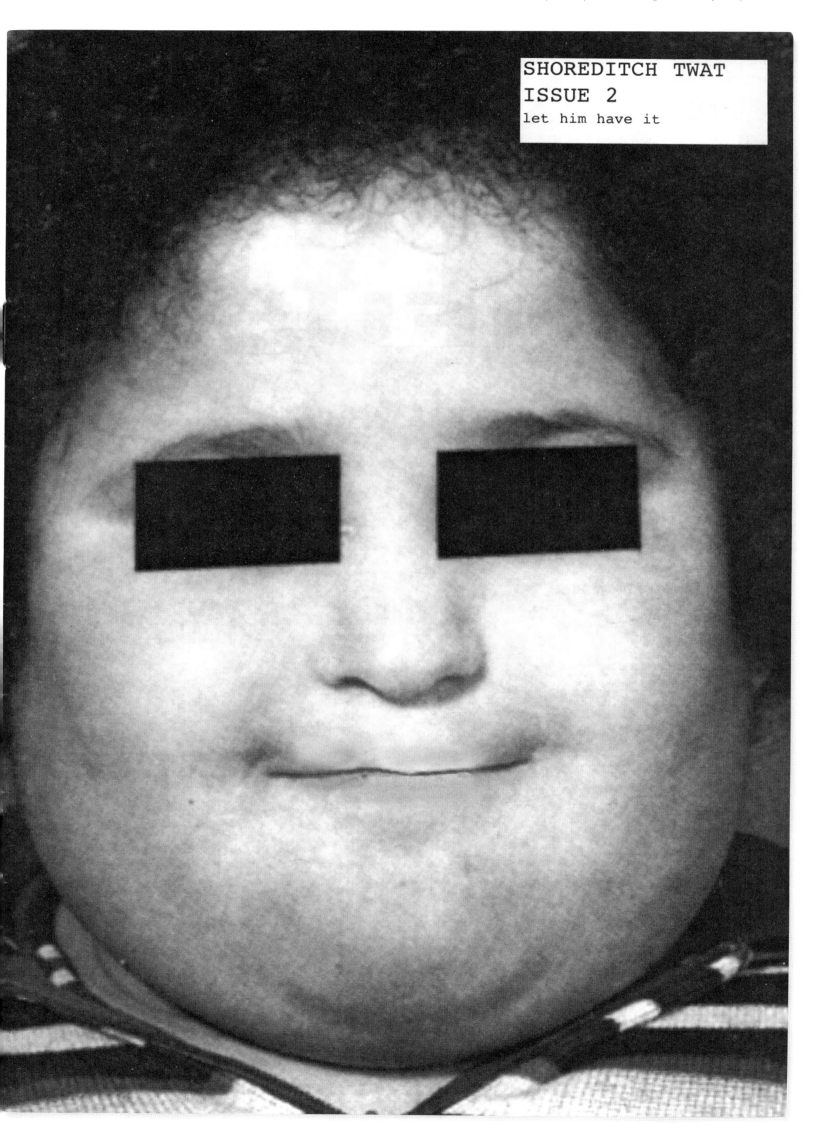

SHOREDITCH TWAT
ISSUE 2
let him have it

Revolution

It's Different For Girls

summer/05 £3

Help She Can't Swim
Jennifer Herrema
The Chalets
Lady Fuzz
The Gin Palace
Michelle Mae
Annie

spilt milkshake

issue #1

spring 2002

RAISE SOME HELL!

a feminist child rearing zine for everyone

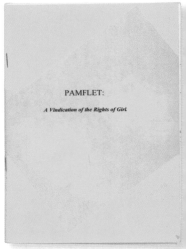

PAMFLET:

A Vindication of the Rights of Girl

Feminist politics links these zines together.
Revolution (2005–n.d.) was edited by club
DJ and music journalist Leonie Cooper, and
featured bands such as Le Tigre and Sleater-
Kinney. *Spilt Milkshake* (2002–c. 2003) by
Rebecca Dyer, is a text-heavy perzine 'not
restricted to any genre or subject matter'.
Raise Some Hell (2008) was a one-off that
emerged out of discussions at a 'feminism
and child-rearing group'. *Pamflet* (2005–)
by 'post-feminists' Phoebe and Anna-Marie,
contained 'feminist rants and bits of quite
frankly libellous celebrity gossip'. *Girls with
Guns* (n.d.–) is a fashion and 'smut' zine out
of Melbourne. *The Pleiades* (c. mid-2000s), a
perzine by Miranda (a college English teacher),
is about 'family history and the frequent
cruelty of life'.

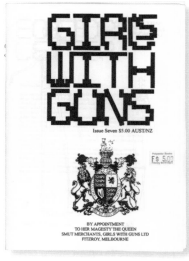

GIRLS WITH GUNS

Issue Seven $5.00 AUST/NZ

BY APPOINTMENT
TO HER MAGESTY THE QUEEN
SMUT MERCHANTS, GIRLS WITH GUNS LTD
FITZROY, MELBOURNE

the pleiades
#14

(this is the blood that we're made of)

Kitty Magik (1996–), edited by Marisa Handren, was looking slick by the time of this issue (2002), but hadn't lost any of its riot grrrl bite. It styles itself as a 'creative outlet dedicated to informing the public about the many different individuals who produce independent, innovative creations…'. *Girls Who Fight* (2009–) by Kathryn Corlett *et al.*, is a collection of writings, illustrations and comics that look at representation, women and celebrity, including 'Nina Simone, Anaïs Nin, Beth Ditto, Virginia Woolf, etc.'. *Muffy!* (2000–n.d.), produced by women from the New College of Florida, was an angry but often amusing feminist zine (sample contents list: 'rape; stalker; rockstar; masturbation; voyeurism; coke').

Queerzines provide a creative space for DIY producers to push the boundaries of accepted 'politically correct' publishing practices. *Butt* (2001–), founded by Gert Jonkers and Jop van Bennekorm out of Amsterdam, is not a fanzine per se (it takes advertising from designer/lifestyle manufacturers), but its pink paper, pocket-size format self-consciously shares qualities with a fanzine approach, and its content is compiled from submissions by readers. *Homobody* (2007–) is by Portland, Oregon, illustrator Tim Batiuk (aka Rio Safari), and is a largely visual (comics and drawings) look at exploration of such themes as gay body fascism and cottaging. *Detroit Queers* (n.d.), produced by a radical queer collective, is a compilation of photocopied pages about inequalities and harassment.

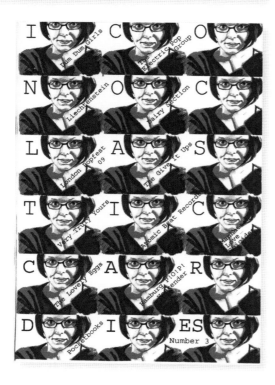

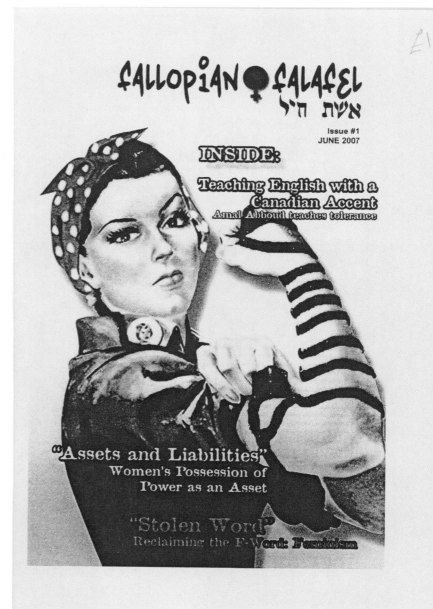

Chica (2001–*c.* 2004) 'celebrates the rudest, crudest, silliest and glitteriest aspects of girlhood' and was produced by Glasgow underground cartoonist and writer Lucy Sweet (also of *Unskinny* fame). This issue features the very bad joke: 'Q: What is worse than a cardboard box? A: Paper tits!' *Fallopian Falafel* (2007–) is edited by Hadass S. Ben-Ari, and is a Jerusalem-based feminist zine that takes 'neither an anti-religious nor anti-Zionist' stance but which 'aims to spread awareness about the ongoing need for feminism to the Israeli public'. Each issue includes a 'riot grrrl corner'. *Iconoclastic Cardies* (2009–) is a 60-page musiczine 'dedicated to all you indiepop wimps, girls, smart kids and weirdos'.

c o p s & r o b b e r s

July

DIY gigs in Leeds

bye bye, duffel boy
number 1 :: summer 2009

"The nice thing is, Indietracks can't grow too much"
Festival visionary Stuart Mackay puts your mind at rest

Yay, interviews!
Jacko from Hull Adelphi
The mighty Horowitz
Jam on Bread

The Deirdres remembered
Sarah Records 20 years on
Post-popshow mornings
Abba vs Helvetica

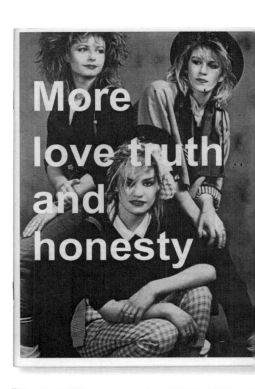

More love truth and honesty

Scotland's Top Punk Rock Fanzine. Issue #7

Runnin' Feart

missing £ 1.50

condemned '84
king prawn
steam pigs
machine gun etiquette
super suckers
argy bargy
runnin' riot
conads
clue
prih
cbh

news
reviews
etc...

Go ahead punk

SUPER WASTE PROJECT 2000

Interviews with Armed with Anger records, Ensign and Unborn + more!

straight edge hardcore

Musiczines remained an important genre into the 2000s. *Cops & Robbers* (c. 2000–) is a monthly that promotes local bands and events in Leeds. *Bye Bye, Duffel Boy* (2009–) is put together on a computer by Pete Green, who apologizes for the perzine looking 'too much like a proper magazine'. *More Love Truth and Honesty* (2007), out of Melbourne, is a perzine by Paul Byron. In the tradition of early punk fanzines, *Runnin' Feart* (c. 2000–) has music reviews and comics, but is a desktop-publishing production. *Super Waste Project* (2000) by Miles is a 'straight edge zine' focusing on hardcore music in the context of a scene without drinking, smoking or drugs. *Taking Dope* (1996–2001) was by ex-Ramones bassist, Dee Dee.

List (2004–) is an illustrated memoir by artist
Ramsey Beyer, and describes her move from
Baltimore to Chicago. *Boredom* (n.d.) came out
of Berkeley, California, and was put together
as a compilation of maps, prose and pictures.
Enthusiasm (c. 2010) is a free 'feel-good' zine
out of Norwich by Susie Rumsby and Tim Wade.
Telegram Ma'am (2000s–) is a mini-perzine by
Maranda, who uses writing to articulate what
it is like being bipolar.

My Evil Twin Sister (1994–) is created by Stacy and Amber, with the former 'doing the design because she has a computer' and the latter providing the words. *Support* (2002) by Cindy Crabb is 'about supporting people who have been sexually abused'. *Not My Small Diary* (2009), with cover art by Frederick Noland tipped into photo-corners, is reminiscent of a photographic album. *I Hate This Part of Texas* (c. 2001–), with its silkscreened cover, is a perzine with meditations on community politics.

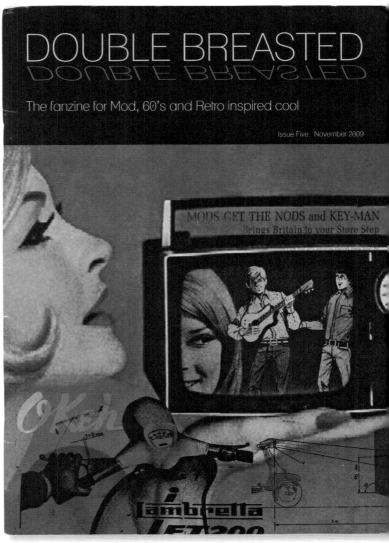

La Bouche Zine (2009–) featured as 'zine of the month' at the Institute of Contemporary Art in London, and is a quarterly critical artzine, this issue including interviews with John Pilger, John Cooper Clarke and Pete Doherty. *Double Breasted* (2009–) is 'the fanzine for Mod, 60s and Retro inspired cool', with a piece on Modernism and a tribute to the 1960s rock band the Small Faces. *Smoke* (2003–) was founded by Jude Rogers and Matt Haynes and is described as a 'love letter to London', featuring reports on everything from the mayor's election to unusual things found in the city's hidden spaces (such as the Stamford Brook warthog).

"Few people laughed, few people
cried, most were silent."

—

J. Robert Oppenheimer
at the Trinity site, 1945

—

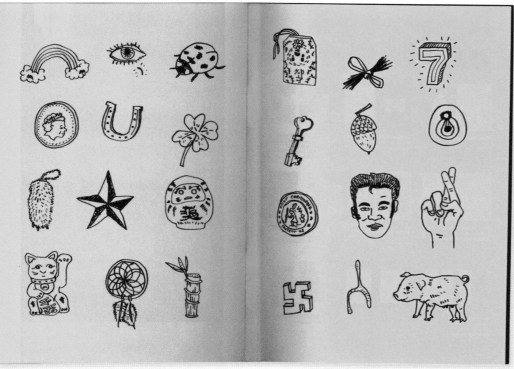

No.Zine (2009–, covers and inside spread)
is an independent arts zine, illustrated,
designed and edited by Patrick Fry, a graduate
of the London College of Communication,
with contributions from others. Fry credits
his father's interest in mathematics as
inspiration for the idea that the content of
each zine should be based on its issue number.
For example, issue 2 riffs on 'my two pence
worth', a watchface with its hands stuck at
2.00 pm, and so on. Each issue is a limited
edition of 500 individually numbered copies,
and the zine maintains a clean, if not
austere, graphic style contrary to most
fanzine aesthetics.

Can You Show Me the Space (2007–08) is a
collection of individually themed fanzines
(e.g. 'the search for a research centre')
created by Public Works — a London-based
art/architecture collective — to foster
discussion around the topic of architecture.
Unemployment (2009), by Aaron Lake Smith,
charts through 44 pages the zinester's
journey through the Kafkaesque experience
of unemployment in the 2000s. Zine 2009 (2009)
was a one-off publication produced during a
letterpress workshop at the London College
of Communication that included students from
the University of Delaware. DIY or Don't We?
(2009) is a zine about community that takes in
a pumpkin farm in the US along with members of
the Cambodian Society. Hardwork Not Paid (2007)
was produced by students in India as a means
of looking at ways to transform the country
and to address cultural plagiarism.

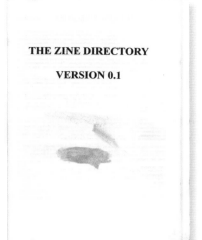

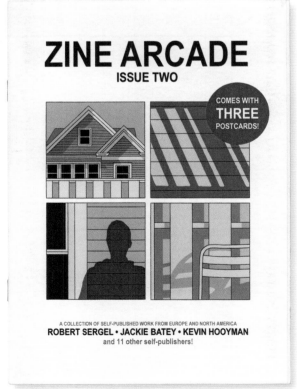

Publications about the distribution and dissemination of information about zines show just how many people are active within the zine network internationally. *The Zine Directory Version 0.1* (2007), produced by Jane Appleby, provided brief but insightful reviews of UK/US zines. *Microcosm Publishing Catalogue* (c. 1996–), with cover artwork by Sarah Oleksyk, was produced by Joe Biel, an independent publisher of zines, books and related ephemera. *Zine Capsule* (2008) contains DIY tips for collecting and archiving. *Zine Arcade* (2007–) is edited by Andrew Owen Johnson and provides a forum for illustrators, artists and zine producers to showcase their work.

Metazines continue to link things together. The *UK Zine Yearbook* (2007) pays homage to the American *Zine Yearbook* anthology (1996–2004), and is a sample of writings and images taken from fanzines produced in the United Kingdom (usefully plotting where they come from on a map). *Australian Zine Resources* (2003) was the result of the producers undertaking a small press project for a professional writing course. *Wasabi Distro Catalogue* (2005) offers primarily English-language zines for sale. *Zene* (*c.* 2000s) from Ely, Cambridgeshire, harks back to the early days of metazine *Factsheet Five*.

NOTES

CHAPTER 1, pp. 6–43

1 Gross, 'Ideas: zine but not heard' (accessed online 15 February 2010). In the following year, the *New York Times* claimed that 20,000–50,000 were published in the USA: Zane, 'Now, the magazines of "me"'.
2 For further details see http://www.zinebook.com/index.html. Rowe's book was released at the same time as R. Seth Friedman's *The Factsheet Five Zine Reader*, and according to one newspaper report, 'their low-key rivalry erupted into a full-blown feud': Stark, 'Smells like zine spirit' (accessed online).
3 Futrelle, 'Been there, zine that' (accessed online 21 February 2010).
4 Ibid. Other producers who jumped into the mainstream media spotlight include Paul Lukas (*Beer Frame*), who went on to have a column in *Fortune* magazine (USA), and Dishwasher Pete (*Dishwasher*), who was asked to appear on David Letterman's late night US television talk show but, famously, sent a friend instead.
5 Duncombe, 'DIY Nike style' (accessed online 15 February 2010). Wieden & Kennedy continue to 'buy into' the subcultural cache of DIY America with their online subsidiary, WKE, with the stated goal of 'negotiating the relationship between art, media, advertising and the consumer': see http://www.wk.com/wke/show/DIY/episode/6
6 See also, a few years later, Sabin and Triggs (eds), *Below Critical Radar*, Farrelly, Zines, Spencer, *DIY: The Rise of Lo-Fi Culture*, Poletti, *Intimate Ephemera* and Piepmeier, *Girl Zines*. Zines have also been published taking up causes for social benefit. Clark (ed.), *Stories Care Forgot* was published in the wake of Hurricane Katrina in recognition of the fact that many originals of fanzines had been lost, including *Chainbreaker* (Shelley Lynn Jackson, c. 2004), *I Hate this Part of Texas* (John Gerken, n.d.) and *Rocket Queen* (Janet, early 2000s). The proceeds from the sale of the book were split among grassroots groups from New Orleans.
7 Jenkins, McPherson and Shattuc (eds), *Hop on Pop*, pp. 161–62.
8 Wertham, *The World of Fanzines*, p. 35.
9 Nicholls (ed.), *The Encyclopedia of Science Fiction*, p. 215; see also Rickards and Twyman, *The Encyclopedia of Ephemera*.
10 Wertham, *The World of Fanzines*, p. 76.
11 Ibid., p. 78.
12 Ibid., pp. 74–5.
13 Trusky, *Some Zines*, p. ii.
14 Atton, *Alternative Media*, p. 55.
15 McKay (ed.), *DiY Culture*, p. 2.
16 Wertham, *The World of Fanzines*, p. 33.
17 Perkins, *Subspace*, p. 1.
18 Poletti, *Intimate Ephemera*, p. 57.
19 Rock, 'Fuck Content' (accessed online 15 February 2010). This was an update to his earlier essay: Rock, 'The designer as author', p. 45.
20 McLaughlin, *Street Smarts and Critical Theory*, p. 54.
21 Duncombe, *Notes from Underground*, p. 127.
22 Atton, *Alternative Media*, p. 23.
23 Ordway, 'A history of zines', p. 157.
24 Hoffman, Allen and Ulrich, *The Little Magazine*.
25 Warner, Sr, *All Our Yesterdays*, p. 3.
26 Ordway, 'A history of zines', p. 157.
27 Wright, *From Zines to Ezines*, p. xxxvii.
28 Johnston, 'What is the history of samizdat?', p. 123.
29 Friedman, 'Editorial', p. 3.
30 Duncombe, *Notes from Underground*, p. 108.
31 Warner, Sr, *All Our Yesterdays*, p. 120.
32 Nicholls (ed.), *The Encyclopedia of Science Fiction*, p. 237.
33 Hansen, letter to the author.
34 Warner, Sr, *All Our Yesterdays*, p. 285.
35 Pustz, *Comic Book Culture*, p. 180.
36 Overstreet, *The Overstreet Comic Book Price Guide*, p. A-68.
37 Williams, email to the author.
38 Shaw cited by Rob Hansen, *Then* (1988–93), http://fanac.org/Fan _ Histories/Then/ (accessed 2 April 2010).
39 Savage, 'Ugly things: music fanzines' (accessed online 23 Feb 2010).
40 McLaughlin, *Street Smarts and Critical Theory*, p. 76.

CHAPTER 2, pp. 44–85

1 Perry, *Sniffin' Glue*, issue 1.
2 Hebdige, *Subculture*, p. 25.
3 Sabin (ed.), *Punk Rock: So What?*, p. 4.
4 McCullough, 'Underground, overground, wandering free', p. 34.
5 Frith, 'Formalism, realism and leisure', in Gelder and Thornton (eds), *The Subcultures Reader*, p. 168.
6 Duncombe (ed.), *Cultural Resistance Reader*, p. 5.
7 Vague, *King Mob Echo*, p. 53.
8 Plant, *The Most Radical Gesture*, p. 1.
9 Jamie Reid, quoted in Kingston, 'Jamie Reid'.
10 Duncombe, *Cultural Resistance Reader*, p. 5.
11 Ewart, interview with the author.
12 Malcolm McLaren, quoted in Marcus, *Lipstick Traces*, p. 9.

CHAPTER 3 , pp. 86–129

1 Mort, *Cultures of Consumption*, p. 5.
2 Marr, 'Privatisation, Consumerism and Thatcherism in the 1980s'.
3 Mort, *Cultures of Consumption*, p. 6.
4 Thornton, *Club Culture*, p. 11.
5 Ibid., p. 12.
6 Deakin, 'Love of nothing', pp. 16–17.
7 Litmus, 'Boy's Own: A History' (accessed online 24 April 2010).
8 Hector-Jones, 'Gareth's aces' (accessed online 24 April 2010).
9 Thornton, *Club Culture*, p. 154.
10 Sharkey, 'My hero the editor' (accessed online 24 April 2010).
11 'The History of Rave Culture' (accessed online 24 April 2010).
12 Reynolds, *Generation Ecstasy*, p. 70.
13 Duncombe (ed.), *Cultural Resistance Reader*, p. 30.
14 Lukas, *Inconspicuous Consumption* (accessed online 24 April 2010).
15 Hoff, *Thrift Score*, p. 3.
16 Duncombe (ed.), *Cultural Resistance Reader*, p. 105.
17 Vale (ed.), 'Temp Slave!', *Zines!*, vol. 2, p. 24.
18 Scott, 'Dishwasher Pete Interview' (accessed online 24 April 2010).
19 Helms, 'Statement of Purpose' (accessed online 24 April 2010).
20 Elliott, 'On Guinea Pig Zero', p. 105.
21 Munroe, Tag line, *Holiday in the Sun*, no. 2, back cover.

CHAPTER 4, pp. 130–69

1 For example, see White, 'Revolution girl style now'.
2 Kate Vickers, quoted in Blase, *Real Girls*.
3 Gina, quoted in *Mental Children*, p. 15.
4 Tucker, *Channel Seven*.
5 http://www.empsfm.org/exhibitions/index.asp?articleID=670
6 Sweet, *Chica*.
7 Ibid.
8 R. K., ' Riot grrrl discourse', p. 17.
9 Leonard, 'Rebel girl, you are the queen of my world', p. 232.
10 Juno (ed.), *Angry Women in Rock*, p. 98.
11 Ladyfest Workshop (Glasgow, 2001).
12 Ladyfest fanzine programme (Glasgow, 2001).
13 Lee Beattie, Ladyfest fanzine programme, p. 19.
14 Ladyfest London (accessed online 3 March 2010).
15 Atton, *Alternative Media*, p. 59.
16 Ladyfest Ten (2010) (accessed online 5 March 2010).

CHAPTER 5, pp. 170–203

Archiving of sites is problematic. The ephemeral nature of the digital means that a website or blog may exist one day and not the next.

1 Labovitz, 'Five years and counting' (accessed online 21 March 2010).
2 Such use of typographic letterforms was not new. The first recorded use of typewritten text as image is Pitman's *The Phonetic Journal* (1898), which reproduced Flora Stacey's butterfly image created from typewriter characters (slashes, hyphens, points, asterisks, etc.): Stark "The History of (ASCII) Text Art" (accessed online 31 March 2010). See also French poet Guillaume Apollinaire's, *Calligrammes* (1918) – his book of shaped poems where letterforms were arranged to form a visual design, figure or pictograph.
3 Cumbrowski, 'The three ASCII art styles of the underground art scene', (accessed online 31 March 2010).
4 *Phrack* (accessed online 31 March 2010).
5 Pore, 'General information about zines and alt.zines' (accessed online 31 March 2010).
6 Labovitz, 'What's "an :e-zine", anyway?' (accessed online 31 March 2010).
7 Duncombe, *Notes from Underground*, p. 197.

8 Secret Nerd Brigade (accessed online 29 April 2010).
9 Atton, *Alternative Media*, p. 75.
10 Duncombe, *Notes from Underground*, p. 230.
11 Blume, 'Zine queen Pagan Kennedy on zines in the age of Web' (accessed online 2 January 2010).
12 McCloud, 'The infinite canvas' (accessed online 2 April 2010).
13 Freedman, 'Zines are not blogs' (accessed online 2 April 2010).
14 'Web log' as a term emerged in 1997 and in 1999 a shortened version was coined, 'blog'. Baron, *A Better Pencil*, p. 165.
15 Smith, 'Strands in the Web', p. 97.

CHAPTER 6, pp. 204–47

1 London Zine Symposium 2006 (accessed online 4 April 2010).
2 Greer, *Knitting for Good!*, p. 10.
3 Metcalf, 'Replacing the myth of modernism' (accessed online 2 April 2010).
4 Metcalf, 'DIY, websites and energy' (accessed online 2 Apri 2010).
5 Wrekk, *Stolen Sharpie Revolution*, p. 5.
6 Ibid., pp. 6–7.
7 Ibid., p. 60.
8 Greer, *Knitting for Good!*, p. 12.

BIBLIOGRAPHY

BOOKS

Chris Atton, *Alternative Media* (London, Sage Publications, 2002).

Camille Bacon-Smith, *Enterprising Women: Television Fandom and the Creation of Popular Myth* (Philadelphia, University of Pennsylvania Press, 1992).

Dennis Baron, *A Better Pencil: Readers, Writers and the Digital Revolution* (Oxford, Oxford University Press, 2009).

Julie Bartel, *From A to Zine: Building a Winning Zine Collection in Your Library* (Chicago, American Library Association, 2004).

Ian Bordon, *Skateboarding and the City: Architecture and the Body* (London, Berg Publishers, 2001).

Ethan Clark, (ed.), *Stories Care Forgot: An Anthology of New Orleans Zines* (San Francisco, Last Gasp, 2006).

Robert Dickinson, *Imprinting the Sticks: The Alternative Press beyond London* (Aldershot, Arena, 1997).

Stephen Duncombe, *Notes from Underground: Zines and the Politics of Alternative Culture* (London, Verso, 1997).

Stephen Duncombe (ed.), *Cultural Resistance Reader* (London Verso, 2002).

Liz Farrelly, *Zines* (London, Booth-Clibborn Editions, 2001).

Nigel Fountain, *Underground: The London Alternative Press 1966–1974* (London, Routledge, 1988).

R. Seth Friedman (ed.), *The Factsheet Five Zine Reader: The Best Writing from the Underground World of Zines* (New York, Three Rivers Press, 1997).

Ken Gelder, *The Horror Reader* (London, Routledge, 2000).

Ken Gelder and Sarah Thornton (eds), *The Subcultures Reader* (London, Routledge, 1997).

Betsy Greer, *Knitting for Good! A Guide to Creating Personal, Social & Political Change Stitch by Stitch* (Boston and London, Trumpeter Books, 2008).

Jonathan Grey, Cornel Sandvoss and C. Lee Harrington (eds), *Fandom: Identities and Communities in a Mediated World* (New York, New York University Press, 2007).

Mike Gunderloy and Cari Goldberg Janice, *The World of Zines: A Guide to the Independent Magazine Revolution* (New York, Penguin Books, 1992)

Dick Hebdige, *Subculture: The Meaning of Style* (London, Methuen, 1979).

Karen Hellekson and Kristina Busse (eds), *Fan Fiction and Fan Communities in the Age of the Internet* (Jefferson, N.C., McFarland and Co., 2006).

Matt Hills, *Fan Cultures* (London, Routledge, 2002).

Al Hoff, *Thrift Score* (New York, HarperCollins, 1997).

Frederick J. Hoffman, Charles Allen and Carolyn F. Ulrich, *The Little Magazine: A History and a Bibliography*, 2nd edn (Princeton, N. J., Princeton University Press, 1947).

Henry Jenkins, *Textual Poachers: Television Fans and Participatory Culture and Communication* (London, Routledge, 1992).

Henry Jenkins, Tara McPherson and Jane Shattuc (eds), *Hop on Pop: The Politics and Pleasures of Popular Culture* (Durham, N. C. and London, Duke University Press, 2002).

Andrea Juno (ed.), *Angry Women in Rock*, vol. 1 (New York, Juno Books, 1996).

Pagan Kennedy, '*Zine: How I spent six years of my life in the underground and finally…found myself…I think* (New York, St. Martin's Griffin, 1995).

George McKay (ed.), *DiY Culture: Party and Protest in Nineties Britain* (London, Verso, 1998).

Thomas McLaughlin, *Street Smarts and Critical Theory: Listening to the Vernacular* (Madison, Wis., University of Wisconsin Press, 1996).

Greil Marcus, *Lipstick Traces: A Secret History of the Twentieth Century* (London, Secker and Warburg, 1989).

Philip Meggs, *A History of Graphic Design* (New York, Van Nostrand Reinhold, 1983).

Nadine Monem, *Riot Grrrl: Revolution Girl Style Now!* (London, Black Dog Publishing, 2007).

Frank Mort, *Cultures of Consumption: Masculinities and Social Space in Late Twentieth-Century Britain* (London, Routledge, 1996).

Peter Nicholls (ed.), *The Encyclopedia of Science Fiction: An Illustrated A–Z* (London, Granada, 1979).

Robert M. Overstreet, *The Overstreet Comic Book Price Guide*, 22nd edn (New York, Avon Books, 1992).

Stephen Perkins, *Subspace: International Zine Show* (Iowa City, Plagiarist Press, 1992).

Mark Perry, *Sniffin' Glue: The Essential Punk Accessory* (London, Sanctuary Publishing, 2000).

Alison Piepmeier, *Girl Zines: Making Media, Doing Feminism* (New York, New York University, 2009).

Sadie Plant, *The Most Radical Gesture: The Situationist International in a Postmodern Age* (London, Routledge, 1992).

Anna Poletti, *Intimate Ephemera: Reading Young Lives in Australian Zine Culture* (Melbourne, Melbourne University Press, 2008).

Matthew J. Pustz, *Comic Book Culture: Fanboys and True Believers* (Jackson, Miss., University of Mississippi Press, 1999).

Steve Redhead, *Post-Fandom and the Millennial Blues: The Transformation of Soccer Culture* (London, Routledge, 1997).

Simon Reynolds, *Generation Ecstasy: Into the World of Techno and Rave Culture* (London, Routledge, 1999).

Simon Reynolds, *Rip It Up and Start Again: Post-punk 1978–1984* (London, Faber, 2005).

Maurice Rickards and Michael Twyman, *The Encyclopedia of Ephemera: A Guide to the Fragmentary Documents of Everyday Life for the Collector, Curator and Historian* (London, British Library, 2000).

Chip Rowe (ed.), *The Book of Zines: Readings From the Fringe* (New York, Henry Holt and Company, 1997); see also http://www.zinebook.com/index.html

Roger Sabin (ed.), *Punk Rock: So What?* (London, Routledge, 1999).

Roger Sabin and Teal Triggs (eds), *Below Critical Radar: Fanzines and Alternative Comics from 1976 to Now* (Hove, Slab-O-Concrete Publications, 2000).

Jon Savage, *England's Dreaming: Sex Pistols and Punk Rock* (London, Faber, 1991, revd 2001).

Amy Spencer, *DIY: The Rise of Lo-Fi Culture* (London, Marion Boyars Publishers, 2005).

Sarah Thornton, *Club Culture: Music, Media and Subcultural Capital* (London, Polity, 1995).

Tom Trusky, with an introduction by Cari Goldberg Janice, *Some Zines: American Alternative & Underground Magazines, Newsletters & APAs* (Boise, Ida., Cold Drill Books, Boise State University, 1992).

John Tulloch and Henry Jenkins, *Science Fiction Audiences: Watching Doctor Who and Star Trek* (London, Routledge, 1995).

Tom Vague, *King Mob Echo: From 1780 Gordon Riots to Situationists, Sex Pistols and Beyond* (London, Dark Star, 2000).

V. Vale (ed.). *Zines!*, vols 1 and 2 (San Francisco, V/Search Publications, 1996 and 1997).

Joan Marie Verba, *Boldly Writing: A Trekker Fan and Zine History 1967–1987* (Minneapolis, FTL Publications, 1996).

Harry Warner, Sr, *All Our Yesterdays: An Informal History of Science Fiction Fandom in the Forties* (Chicago, Advent Publishers, 1969).

Fredric Wertham, *The World of Fanzines: A Special Form of Communication* (Carbondale, Ill., Southern Illinois University Press, 1973).

Sheila Whiteley (ed.), *Sexing the Groove: Popular Music and Gender* (London, Routledge, 1997).

Frederick A. Wright, *From Zines to Ezines: Electronic Publishing and the Literary Underground*, Ph.D. thesis (Kent, Oh., Kent State University, 2001).

ARTICLES

Lee Beattie, *Ladyfest* fanzine programme (Glasgow, Scotland, 2001).

Cazz Blase, *Real Girls*, issue 1 (Stockport, England, 2001).

Harvey Blume, 'Zine queen Pagan Kennedy on zines in the age of Web', *Wired*, issue 4.01 (January 1996), http://www.wired.com/wired/archive/4.01/

Carsten Cumbrowski (aka Roy/SAC), 'The three ASCII art styles of the underground art scene', n.d., http://www.roysac.com/roy-sac _ styles _ of _ underground _ text _ art.asp

Camilla Deakin, 'Love of nothing', *Gear*, no. 2 (1991).

Stephen Duncombe, 'DIY Nike style: zines and the corporate world', *Z Magazine* (December 1999), http://www.zcommunications.org/diy-nike-style-by-stephen-duncombe

Carl Elliott, 'On Guinea Pig Zero', *Tin House* (issue 35, Spring 2008), 103–6.

Joe Ewart, interview with the author (London, January 1997).

Jenna Freedman, 'Zines are not blogs: a not unbiased analysis', originally published in *Counterpoise*, vol. 9, issue 3 (2005), p. 10; http://www.barnard.edu/library/zines/zinesnotblogs.htm

R. Seth Friedman, 'Editorial', *Factsheet Five*, no. 58 (October 1995), p. 3.

Simon Frith, 'Formalism, realism and leisure: the case of punk' in Gelder and Thornton (eds), *The Subcultures Reader*, pp. 163–74.

David Futrelle, 'Been there, zine that', *Salon* (9 June 1997), http://www.salon.com/media/circus/1997/06/09/media/index.html

David M. Gross, 'Ideas: zine but not heard.' *Time* (5 September 1994), http://www.time.com/time/printout/0,8816,981403,00.html

Robert Hansen, letter to the author (27 July 1995).

Richard Hector-Jones, 'Gareth's aces', *City Life for Northern Souls* (26 August 2005) http://www.citylife.co.uk/clubs/news/6470 _ gareth _ s _ aces

Robert P. Helms, 'Statement of Purpose', *Guinea Pig Zero*, n.d. http://www.guineapigzero.com

Gordon Johnston, 'What is the history of samizdat?', *Social History*, vol. 24, issue 2, (1999), pp. 115–33.

Mark Kermode, 'I was a teenage horror fan, or, how I learned to stop worrying and love Linda Blair' in Martin Barker and Julian Petley (eds), *Ill Effects: The Media/Violence Debate* (London, Routledge), pp. 126–34.

Steve Kingston, 'Jamie Reid: Art and Attitude for the 21st Century' [press release] (May 1990).

John Labovitz, 'Five years and counting', *The Art Bin: Articles and Essays,* n.d., http://art-bin.com/art/alabovitz.html

John Labovitz, 'What's "an :e-zine", anyway?'. *E-Zine List* (1993), http://www.meer.net/~johnl/e-zine-list/about.html

Ladyfest London, 'About' (2001), http://www.ladyfestlondon.co.uk/?page _ id=2

Ladyfest Ten (2010), Facebook, http://www.facebook.com/pages/Ladyfest-Ten/298592715550?v=info

Ladyfest Workshop (Glasgow, Scotland, 2001).

Marion Leonard, 'Rebel girl, you are the queen of my world: feminism subculture and grrrl power', in Whiteley (ed.), *Sexing the Groove*, pp. 230–55.

Stephen Litmus, 'Boy's Own: A History', *Resident Advisor* (12 January 2010), http://www.residentadvisor.net/feature.aspx?1139

London Zine Symposium 2006, http://www.londonzinesymposium.org.uk/archives/2006/

Paul Lukas, *Inconspicuous Consumption*, http://www.core77.com/inconspicuous/

Scott McCloud, 'The infinite canvas', http://scottmccloud.com/4-inventions/canvas/index.html

Dave McCullough,. 'Underground, overground, wandering free', *Sounds* (17 March 1979), p. 34.

Andrew Marr, 'Privatisation, consumerism and Thatcherism in the 1980s', ScreamNews.com, http://screamnews.com/privatisation-consumerism-and-thatcherism-in-the-1980s/

Bruce Metcalf, 'Replacing the myth of modernism', first published in *American Craft*, vol. 53, no. 1 (Feb/March 1993), http://www.brucemetcalf.com/pages/essays/replacing _ myth.html

Bruce Metcalf, 'DIY, websites and energy: the new alternative crafts', conference paper (SNAG [Society of North American Goldsmiths], Savannah, Georgia, 2008) http://www.brucemetcalf.com/pages/essays/diy _ websites _ energy.html

Mental Children, issue 1 (London, England, 1980).

Peter Millward, 'The rebirth of the football fanzine: using e-zines as data source', *Journal of Sport and Social Issues*, vol. 32, no. 3 (2008), pp. 299–310.

Jim Munroe, *Holiday in the Sun*, no. 2 (Toronto, Canada, 1999).

Nico Ordway, 'A history of zines', in Vale (ed.), *Zines!*, vol. 1, pp. 155–59.

Mark Perry, *Sniffin' Glue*, issue 1 (London, 1976).

Phrack, no. 67 (July 2010), http://pcworld.about.com/gi/dynamic/offsite.htm?site=http://www.phrack.com/

Jerod Pore, 'General information about zines and alt.zines', (The alt.zines DMZ, The Zine Syndicate, 1995), http://altzines.tripod.com/jerod.html

R. K., ' Riot grrrl discourse', *Fast Connection*, no. 3 (Newcastle upon Tyne, England, August 1996).

Michelle Rau, 'From APA to zines: towards a history of fanzine publishing', *Alternative Press Review* (Spring/Summer, 1994), pp. 10–13.

Simon Reynolds, 'How the fanzine refused to die', *Guardian* (2 February 2009), http://www.guardian.co.uk/music/2009/feb/02/fanzine-simon-reynolds-blog

Michael Rock, 'The design as author', *Eye*, no. 20 (Spring 1996), pp. 44–53.

Michael Rock, 'Fuck Content' (2005), http://2x4.org/

Jon Savage, 'Ugly things: music fanzines' (posted 27 April 2009), http://www.jonsavage.com/journalism/ugly-things-music-fanzines/

Andrew Scott, 'Dishwasher Pete Interview', *Fecal Face Dot Com* (29 May 2007), http://www.fecalface.com/SF/index.php?option=com _ content&task=view&id=629.

Secret Nerd Brigade (Minneapolis, c. 2010), http://secretnerdbrigade.com/zines.shtml

Alix Sharkey, 'My hero the editor', *The Independent* (22 July 1995), http://www.independent.co.uk/arts-entertainment/my-hero-the-editor-1592759.html.

Matthew J. Smith, 'Strands in the Web: community-building strategies in online fanzines', *Journal of Popular Culture*, vol. 33, issue 2 (1999), pp. 87–99.

Jeff Stark, 'Smells like zine spirit', *SF Weekly News* (27 August 1997), http://www.sfweekly.com/1997-08-27/news/smells-like-zine-spirit/

Joan G. Stark, 'The History of (ASCII) Text Art', 1999, http://www.roysac.com/asciiarthistory.asp

Lucy Sweet, *Chica*, no. 1 (Glasgow, Scotland, 2001).

'The History of Rave Culture', TheSite.org, n.d. http://thesite.mobi/drinkanddrugs/drugculture/drugstrade/thehistoryofrave

Teal Triggs, 'Alphabet soup: reading British fanzines', *Visible Language*, vol. 29, no.1, part 3 (Winter 1995), pp. 72–87.

Teal Triggs, 'Look back in anger: the riot grrrl revolution in Britain', *Zed.5* (1998), pp. 8–25.

Teal Triggs, 'Typo-Anarchy: a new look at the fanzine revolution', *Emigre*, no. 46, (Spring 1998), pp. 12–20.

Teal Triggs, 'Girlzines: sex and morality in print' in Steven Heller (ed,) *Sex Appeal: The Art of Allure in Graphic and Advertising Design* (New York, Allworth Press, 2000), pp. 130–37.

Teal Triggs, 'Scissors and glue: punk fanzines and the creation of a DIY aesthetic', *Journal of Design History*, vol. 19, no. 1 (2006), pp. 69–83.

Corin Tucker, *Channel Seven* (Washington, DC, c. 1992).

Emily White, 'Revolution girl style now', *L.A. Weekly* (July 10–16 1992), reprinted in Evelyn McDonnell and Ann Powers (eds), *Rock She Wrote: Women Write about Rock, Pop, and Rap* (London, Plexus, 1995), pp. 396–408.

Paul Williams, email to author (26 July 2000).

Alex Wrekk, *Stolen Sharpie Revolution: A DIY Zine Resource* (Portland, Microcosm, 2003).

J. Peder Zane,'Now, the magazines of "me"', *New York Times* (14 May 2006), http://www.empsfm.org/exhibitions/index.asp?articleID=670

LIST OF ZINES

CHAPTER 1, PP. 6–43

p. 7: **New Worlds**, vol. 1, no. 1 (March 1939), Ted Carnell, cover Harry Turner, Chapman Carnell Publications: London, UK (Terry Carr Fanzine Collection, Special Collections and Archives, University of California, Riverside Libraries). **Exclusively Elvis**, no. 1 (1969), Wendy Murton: Leeds, UK. **Western Trails Magazine**, vol. 1, no. 1 (Jan–Feb 1975), Richard M. Kauffman: Lakeland, GA, USA.

p. 8: **Boomerang**, no. 29 (Feb 1973), John and Jan Ryan: Queensland, Australia. **Aware Magazine**, vol. 2, no. 5 (1977), Steve Kolanjian: Brooklyn, NY, USA. **Crawdaddy!** / The Magazine of Rock 'n' Roll, no. 4 (Aug 1966), Paul Williams and others: Cambridge, MA, USA.

p. 9: **Travellin' Fist**, no. 1 (1989), Dan Koretzky, Rian Murphy and others: Chicago, IL, USA. **Who Put the Bomp!**, no. 14 (fall 1975), Greg Shaw, cover photo Jan & Dean, 1964: Burbank, CA, USA. **Suburban Press**, no. 5 (1972), Jamie Reid: Croydon, Surrey, UK.

p. 10: **Sydney in the Sewer**, no. 2 (Sept 1985), Yolanda, Carol, John and others: Sydney, Australia. **The Exploitation Journal** / The Magazine of Schlock Cinema, no. 4 (1987), Joseph F. Parda and Keith J. Crocker, Cinefear Productions: Levittown, NY, USA. **Ungawa!**, no. 4 (1992), Foss Hagman and Cathal Tohill, cover Aran C.: London, UK.

p. 11: **L'Incroyable Cinema** / The Film Magazine of Fantasy & Imagination, no. 3 (1970), ed. Harry and Marie Nadler, cover illustration Eddie Jones, Orion Press: Salford, Manchester, UK. **TCM The Comedy Magazine**, no. 1 (autumn 1986), Mat Coward: London, UK. **Penetration**, no. 13 (1977), Paul Welsch: Stockport, Cheshire, UK.

p. 12: **Diana Rigg**, no. 1 (1986), Len Theric and Mint Murray, Lenmint Productions: Horsham, West Sussex, UK. **Everyone Needs a Hobby** / The Tim Burton Fanzine with a Sense of Humour, vol. 1, no. 2 (fall–holiday season 1994), Emile St. Claire, cover art Joe 'Magic': Los Angeles, CA, USA. **The Complate Monty Python**, vol. 2 (1979), Howard Johnson: Ottawa, IL, USA.

p. 13: **Passing Wind**, no. 11(1979), Evelyn [Ian Hislop], cover art K.J.A.: Oxford, UK. **The Way Ahead**, no. 1 (1984), Janet: Swindon, UK. **Panda Eyes** / Mini-zine, vol. 2 (2009), Alyssa: Point Reyes Station, CA, USA.

p. 14: **Where's Eric!** / The Eric Clapton Fanzine, no. 15 (April 1996), Tony Edser, cover photo Barrie Wentzell/Star File, Scref Publishing Solutions: Maidenhead, Berkshire, UK. **Weller is Back**, no. 1 (25 Oct 1991), Andy Wyness: Dundee, Scotland. **Pulp** / A Scrapbook Fanzine (summer 2004), Emily Jane Graves: Leeds, UK.

p. 15: **Lobster Telephone** / I am a Product, vol. 1, no. 29 (c. 1989), C.H.A.O.S. Inc: Nottingham, UK. **Lower than Dirt**, no. 3 (1996), Richard Santos, Homicidal Enterprises: Austin, TX, USA. **Crap Hound** / Church & State Part One, no. 7 (2008), Sean Tejaratchi: Los Angeles, CA, USA.

p.16: **Spilt Milk**, no. 1 (winter 1996), Erica and Rebecca Braverman: Prairie Village, KS, USA. **Katy Keene Magazine**, no. 13 (fall 1983), Craig Levitt: Modesto, CA, USA. **Like a Virgin** / Italian Fanzine about Madonna, no. 40 (Dec–Jan 1993), Sauro: Italy. **Danzine**, no. 14 (c. 1998), Teresa Dulce, cover photo Angie C.: Portland, OR, USA.

p. 17: **Outpunk**, no. 7 (1997), Matt Wobensmith: San Francisco, CA, USA. **Lip Gloss**, no. 1 (c. 2009), Chris Gloss: Gosport, Hampshire, UK. **The Filth and the Fury!**, no. 12 (2000), Scott Murphy: Glasgow, Scotland.

p. 18: **Braindeath** including **Slaughtered Trees & Toxic Ink**, no. 3 ½(1997), Pablo, cover Nick Lant: UK and Switzerland. **Culture Slut**, no. 10 (9 July 2007), Amber Farthing: Ontario, Canada. **Hate**, no. 6 (2008), Calvin Holbrook: London, UK.

p. 19: **Seripop/Baltic/Zine** (2009), Patrick Staff and Edward Webb-Ignall, illustration Seripop: Gateshead, Tyne and Wear, UK. **Meat Magazine**, no. 7 (May 2008), James Pallister and Nick Hayes: London, UK.

pp. 20–21: **Shocking Pink**, no. 9 (c. 1990), collective including Katy Watson: Oxford[?], UK. **Kitten Scratches**, no. 1 (1999), Rachel: High Wycombe, Buckinghamshire, UK. **DIY Life Zine**, no. 1 (Jan 2010), Idzie and others: Montreal, Canada. **Beer Can Fanzine**, no. 1 (1999), Jesse Kimball: Portland, OR, USA.

pp. 22–23: **Negative Reaction**, no. 1 (Feb 1977), Jonathan Romney and others, cover photo Paul Cecil: Cambridge, UK. **Nothing is True**, no. 6 (1992), Richard Turner: Liverpool, UK. **Omsk**, no. 4 (May 1996), Peter Smith and others: Ilford, Essex, UK. **Gear** / Boo! (c. 1991), Camilla Deakin, design Fred Deakin: London, UK. **Make Your Own Damn Alcohol** (c. 2005), Jarrod Blatz, illustration Laure: Bowling Green, OH, USA. **The Complete Soapmaker** / Tips, Techniques & Recipes for Luxurious Handmade Soaps / The Abbreviated Version (c. 1997), [adapted from a book by Norma Coney]: [n.p.]. **Chord Easy** / How to Choose Chords, vol. 1 of 3 (2007), Bert Davis, Light Living Library: Philomath, OR, USA.

p. 24: **Novae Terrae**, no. 2 (May 1938), Maurice K. Hanson and Dennis A. Jacques, cover Harry Turner: London, UK (Terry Carr Fanzine Collection, Special Collections and Archives, University of California, Riverside Libraries).

p. 25: **Red Ink** / School Kids' Issue, no. 4 (Oct 1971), Newcastle University Socialist Society Magazine: Newcastle upon Tyne, UK. **Heroes Unlimited**, no. 4 (March 1968), Anthony Roche and others, cover Paul Neary: Dún Laoghaire, Co. Dublin, Ireland. **KRLA Beat** / Los Angeles, California, vol. 1 no. 1 (1965), Bill Finneran: Eugene, OR, USA.

pp. 26–27: **Creep**, no. 10 (1998), Jonnystein: Estacada, OR, USA. **Glamourpuss** / The UK Suede Fanzine, nos. 3 and 4 (c. 1996), Jo Glamourpuss and others, cover Jo Glamourpuss: Cumbria, UK. **Must be the Music**, no. 4 (Feb 1997): Stockton-on-Tees, County Durham, UK. **MaximumRocknRoll**, no. 221 (Oct 2001), Arwen Curry and others: San Francisco, CA, USA.

pp. 28–29: **Slash**, vol. 2, no. 2 (Nov 1978), Steven Samiof and Melanie Nissen and others, photo Stevenson: Los Angeles, CA, USA. **Punk**, no. 2 (March 1976), John Holmstrom and others, cover photos Guillemette Barbet + Rock News, Punk Productions Inc: New York, USA. **International Anthem** / Nihilist Newspaper for the Living (1977), Gee Vaucher and Penny Rimbaud, photo-collages Gee Vaucher, Exitstencil Press: London, UK. **Artcore Fanzine**, no. 23 (spring 2006), Welly: Cardiff, Wales.

pp. 30–31: **The Celestial Toyroom**, no. 7 (July 1979), Gordon Blows, for The Doctor Who Appreciation Society: London, UK. **Your Mornings Will Be Brighter** (May 1990), Richard Murrill: Folkstone, Kent, UK.

pp. 32–33: **Speed Kills**, no. 7 (Sept 1995), Scott Rutherford and others: Chicago, IL, USA. **Things I've Found** / Things I've Lost (Oct 2009), Katie Haegele, drawings Helen Entwisle: Philadelphia, PA, USA. **Straight from the Grooveyard**, no. 2 (c. 1981), Joögen Westman, Johan Kugelberg, Johan Frick and others: Kramfors, Sweden.

pp.34–35: **Freak Beat**, no. 4 (1988), Ivor Trueman and Richard Allen, cover Lyns: Hounslow, Middlesex and Chalfont St. Peter, Buckinghamshire, UK. **Crawdaddy!** / The Magazine of Rock, no. 10 (Aug 1967), Paul Williams and others, cover Paul Rothchild, photograph Racey Gilbert, logo David Flooke: New York City, NY, USA. **Bam Balam**, no. 12 (Nov 1980), Brian Hogg and Jacki, cover logo Nic Dartnell: East Lothian, Scotland. **Sniffin' Flowers**, no. 1 (1977), Sue, Simon, Andrew, Jackie, cover TJH: Romford, Essex, UK.

p. 36: **Serendipity** / Batman at 50, no. 3 (1989), Joseph Dickerson and others, cover Joseph Dickerson, Solarquest Publications: USA. **Fear and Loathing**, vol. 34 (Dec 1995), Andy Pearson: London, UK. **Revolting**, no. 2 (June–July 1993), Ed & Ed, cover Shrub, logo Simon: Kingston upon Thames, Surrey, UK.

p. 37: **Console** / The Heart of the Tardis, no. 1 (1982): Clapham, Bedford, UK. **Typography Papers**, no. 1 (1996), Paul Stiff and others, Department of Typography and Graphic Communication, University of Reading: Reading, UK. **Funk n' Groove**, no. 1 (c. 1995), Ferris and Morgan: Blackhawk, CA, USA.

pp. 38–39: **Punk and Disorderly**, no. 3 (Nov 1991), Mick B., artwork Dave Stonkage: Quarry Bank, West Midlands, UK. **Bugs and Drugs** / A Zine for Scoffers, Screamers, Slackers & Blasphemers, no. 2 (c. 1990s), C. Weston and others, cover Beano Brazdov: Bristol, UK. **Brumble** / Special Brumcon Issue no. 5 (June 1965), C. D. Winstone, cover MiK: Birmingham, UK. **Le Collectionneur de Bandes Dessinées**, no. 68 (1991), Michel Denni, Centre National des Lettres: Paris, France. **Down Under**, no. 1 (1964), John T. Ryan, cover John T. Ryan: New South Wales, Australia. **FOOM**, vol. 1, no. 12 (Dec 1975), editor-in-chief Marv Wolfman, ed. Duffy Vohland, cover John Buscema, Marvel Comics Group, cover Buscema Russell: New York City, NY, USA. **Comics Unlimited**, no. 50 (June–July 1979), Alan Austin, cover Patrick Marcel, Fantasy Unlimited Pubs: London, UK.

pp. 40–41: **Space Times** / Anniversary Issue, vol. 2, no. 6 (June 1953), Eric Bentcliffe, cover Harry Turner, Nor'west Science Fiction Fantasy Club: Manchester, UK. **Thanks for the Memory** / Elisabeth Sladen, no. 4 (1978), Mark G. Knighton, cover Garry O'Hare, Beyond Cygenus: Sutton Coldfield, West Midlands, UK. **Personal Log 01** / Starbase Chicago, no. 1 (1980), Vicki Ashe and Gwen Bolten, cover W. A. Howlett, Tigress Press: Chicago, IL, USA. **Heroes Unimited**, no. 2 (1967), Anthony Roche and others, cover Paul Neary: Dún Laoghaire, Co. Dublin, Ireland.

p. 42–43: ***The Komix***, no. 2 (April 1963), John Wright and thers: Port Elizabeth, South Africa. ***Ka-Pow***, no. 2 (Feb 1968), teve Moore and Phil Clarke: London and Birmingham, UK. ***ightmare***, no. 1 (1969), John Muir and others, cover Mike iggs: Manchester, UK. ***Dead Duck / Corpsemeat Comix*** 991), Savage Pencil [Edwin Pouncey], Shock Imprint, Sexy wastika Productions: London, UK. ***Zum!***, no. 3 (Jan 1992), uke Walsh and Mike Kidson: Liverpool, UK. ***The Golden Age anzine***, no. 2 (Oct 1976), Alan Austin: London, UK. ***Graphic tory World***, vol. 2, no. 3 [no. 7] (Sept 1972), Richard Kyle and thers, cover Norman Mingo: Culver City, CA, USA.

CHAPTER 2, pp. 44–85

. 45: ***Suburban Press*** (*c.* 1970), Jamie Reid, Jeremy Brook, igel Edwards: London, UK. ***Punk*** / *The Legend of Nick Detroit*, o. 6 (Oct 1976), ed. John Holmstrom and others, cover ustration John Holmstrom: New York, USA. ***Sniffin' Glue***, o. 1 (1976), Mark Perry and others: Deptford, London, UK.

. 46: ***Search and Destroy: Rebel Youth Culture***, no. 10 978; repr. 1988), ed. V. Vale and others, cover Kamera Zie: an Francisco, CA, USA (Issue available at www.researchpubs. om). ***Factor Zero***, no. 0 (1980), David Strongos: São Paulo, razil. ***Total Control***, no. 1 (1977) [booklet included in *The strich*], Franz Heribert Bielmeier [Mary Lou Monroe] and Janie Jones: Hamburg and Düsseldorf, Germany.

. 47: ***Ripped & Torn***, no. 4 (April 1977), Tony Drayton and thers: Glasgow, Scotland and London, UK. ***City Fun***, vol. 2, o. 7 (9–22 Jan 1981), Edward P. Nicholls, Martin Heywood, ay Lowry, Tony Wilson, E. C. Martin Rennie, Mark Smith, at Naylor, Bob Dickenson, Liz Naylor, City Fun Publications: alford, Manchester, UK. ***Alternative Sounds***, no. 17 (1980), artin Bowes: Coventry, UK.

. 48: ***In the City***, no. 12 (1979), Pete Gilbert and Francis rake: London, UK. ***Panache***, no. 10 (1978), Mick Mercer: ondon, UK. ***Rebel Rouser*** (late 1970s), Leon Rebel: [n.p.: opy incomplete].

. 49: ***Anarchy in the UK***, no. 1 (1976), Glitterbest, Ltd, rinted by Zig Zag: London, UK. ***Trick***, no. 1 (Nov 1977), ed. . Dallas, contributors Pete of Shrews, Mark of Scum, Kev iles, Jane Suck, cover photo Steve Sparkes, Wishcastle Ltd: ondon, UK. ***Temporary Hoarding***, no. 5 (June–July 1979), ed Saunders, contributors Aruth Shaked, Red Saunders, ndy Xerox, Lucy Toothpaste and others, with photo pages Syd helton: London, UK.

p. 50–51: ***Sniffin' Glue***, no. 3 (1976), no. 4 (1976), no. 5 Nov 1976), / *Christmas Special* (Dec 1976), no. 7 (1977), no. (March 1977), no. 9 (April–May 1977), no. 10 (June 1977), o. 12 (Aug–Sept 1977), Mark Perry and others: London, UK.

p. 52–53: ***Chainsaw***, no. 1 (1977), no. 3 (Nov–Dec 1977), harlie Chainsaw: London, UK. ***Chainsaw***, no. 11 (Feb 1981), harlie Chainsaw, cover Michael J. Weller: London, UK; ***hainsaw***, no. 12 (1981), Charlie Chainsaw, cover Michael J. Veller: London, UK; ***Chainsaw***, no. 14 (Dec–Jan 1984–85), harlie Chainsaw, contributions Kid Charlemagne, Willie D., lichael J. Weller: London, UK.

p. 54–55: ***Panache***, no. 13 (1980), no. 12 (*c.* 1980) [interior age], Mick Mercer: Dunnington, North Yorkshire, UK.

p. 56–57: ***Ripped & Torn***, no. 1 (Nov 1976), no. 5 ([n.d.]), o. 8 (late Sept–early Oct [n.d.]), no. 9 (Nov 1977), no. 10 eb 1978), no. 12 (summer 1978), no. 14 (Oct 1978), no. 15 Nov 1978), Tony Drayton: Glasgow, Scotland and London, UK. ***ipped & Torn***, no. 18 (1979), Steve Abrams: London, UK.

p. 58–59: ***48 Thrills***, no. 1 (1977), no. 2 (1977), Adrian hrills: Essex, UK. ***48 Thrills***, no. 3 (March 1977), no. 6 (*c.* 977), Adrian Thrills: Stevenage, Hertfordshire, UK. ***Bondage***, o. 1 (1976), Shane MacGowan: London, UK. ***London's urning***, no. 1 (Dec 1976), John Ingram: London, UK. ***ayglow***, no. 1 (*c.* 1978), Steve May: Neasden, London, UK.

p. 60–61: ***Kleenex***, no. 1 (1979), Bexleyheath, Kent, UK. ***ada*** / *Zeno Phobia* (late 1970s): London, UK. ***Punkture*** / *The lidlands Punk Scene*, no. 3 (*c.* 1977), Pretty Nasty and Ruthie utrid: Stone, Staffordshire, UK. ***Another Tuneless Racket***, no. (April 1978): East Kilbride, Glasgow, Scotland. ***Confidential***, o. 2 (1977), Pete Nic, Caly, Alexandra Annexe: Watford, ertfordshire, UK.

p. 62–63: ***Situation 3*** (1977), Lofty Rickett and others: ondon, UK. ***Situation Vacant***, no. 4 (*c.* 1978), Glyn and lart and others: Derby, UK. ***Live Wire or Pretty Vacant***, no. 8 :. 1978), Alan Anger, photos Walt Davidson, Eddie Duggan and thers: London, UK. ***Live Wire***, no. 14 (1978), Alan Anger, cover photos Alan Anger and Eddie Duggan: London, UK. ***More-on-Four*** (1977), Sarah Shosubi, photos Crystal Clear: London, UK.

pp. 64–65: ***In the City***, no. 1 (1977), Francis Drake, additional writers Walt Davidson, Adrian and Rob, pictures Walt Davidson, typing and setting-out Peter Gilbert: London, UK. ***In the City***, no. 2 (1977), Francis Drake and Peter Gilbert, additional writer Graham, graphics John Foxx, pictures Walt Davidson: London, UK. ***In the City***, no. 4 (1978), Frank and Pete: London, UK. ***In the City***, no. 5 (*c.* 1978): London, UK. ***In the City***, no. 6 (winter 1979), Frank 'n' Pete: London, UK. ***In the City***, no. 8 (1978), Feet and Plank: London, UK. ***In the City***, no. 10 (April 1979), Frank 'n' Pete: London, UK. ***In the City***, no. 13 (Feb 1980), Frank 'n' Pete: London, UK. ***In the City Special*** / *Ultravox! At the Roundhouse* (1977), Francis Drake, cover pictures Peter Gilbert: London, UK.

pp. 66–67: ***Negative Reaction***, no. 7 (Sept–Oct 1978), Jon Romney and others: Cambridge, UK. ***Positive Reaction***, no. 4 (July–Aug 1979), Ernie B.: Omagh, Co. Tyrone, Northern Ireland (printed SEAN at S.O.S Omagh). ***Kids Stuff***, no. 9 (*c.* 1978), Alastair: Chessington, Surrey, UK. ***Negative Reaction***, no. 3 (Aug–Sept 1977), Jon Romney and Chas Diamond and others, photos Chas, Jon and Jill Furmanovsky: Cambridge, UK. ***Suspect Device***, no. 6 (1979), Pete Gross and others: Northampton, UK. ***Slash***, vol. 1, no. 1 (May 1977) [Mayday issue], ed. Steven Samiof, Melanie Nissen and others, cover photo [Dave Vanian of The Damned] Melanie Nissen: Los Angeles, CA, USA.

pp. 68–69: ***Kingdom Come***, no. 4 (Nov 1977), no. 7 (Feb 1978), no. 9 (May 1978), no. 10 (June 1978), no. 11 (July–Aug 1978), no. 12 (Sept 1978), no. 14 (Jan 1979), no. 15 (March 1979), no. 16 (May 1979), Jonny Waller: Dunfermline, Fife, Scotland.

pp. 70–71: ***Cobalt Hate***, no. 2 (1984), Glyn and others, printed at the Community Workshop: Stevenage, Hertfordshire, UK. ***Blam!***, no. 1 (*c.* 1981), Peter Hall: Chelmsford, Essex, UK. ***Mucilage***, no. 2 (*c.* 1984), Allan, layout Allan and Aidan: St. Albans, UK [front and back covers]. ***4th Wall Theatre of Hate*** (1981), Claire and others, Rhinoceros: London, UK.

pp. 72–73: ***Inx Blotch***, no. 1 (*c.* 1981), Dommo with Andy and Bic: Teddington, Middlesex, and Kew, Surrey, UK [front and back covers]. ***Transformation*** / *The Journal of the Federation of Anarcho-Pacifists* (winter 1989), Jon and the West London F.A.P.: London, and Newbury Park, Essex, UK [front and back covers]. ***Stödge*** ([n.d.]): Oxford, UK. ***NN4 9PZ***, no. 1 (*c.* 1979–80), Chris and others: Northampton, UK. ***Communiqué 2*** / *A System without a System* / *Nihilistic Vices*, no. 2 (summer 1980), Dörmouse and others: London, UK and Amsterdam, Netherlands.

pp. 74–75: ***Vague*** / *Cyber-Punk*, no. 21 (1988), Tom Vague, cover design Jamie Reid and Joe Ewart for Assorted Images: London, UK (printed Aldgate Press). ***Vague***, no. 13 (1982), Tom Vague and others: London, UK; ***Vague***, no. 14 (1982), Tom Vague: London, UK. ***Vague*** / *Back from the Grave*, no. 11 (1982), Tom Vague: London, UK.

pp. 76–77: ***Allied Propaganda***, no. 1 (June 1979), Ray and Mick: Northolt, Middlesex, UK. ***Cross Now*** / *Firework Edition*, no. 2 (1980), cover Cress: London, UK. ***Grinding Halt***, no. 4 (1980), Eddie Snide, Caption Callous and Pig Ignorant: Reading, UK. ***Safety in Numbers***, no. 8 (1980), John Driscoll: Portsmouth, UK. ***Mental Children***, no. 1 (1980): London, UK.

pp. 78–79: ***Guttersnipe***, no. 4 (1978), Guttersnipe Collective: Madeley, Telford, UK [front and back covers]. ***Rapid Eye Movement***, no. 1 (winter 1979), Simon Dwyer. Alan Anger, Mick Dwyer, Lol Loveitt and others, cover picture from screen-print by Michael: [n.p.] [front and back covers].

pp. 80–81: ***Alerta Punk***, no. 3 (1983), Renato Filho: São Paulo, Brazil. ***Espectro do Chaos***, no. 1 (*c.* 1980s): Curitiba, Brazil. ***Atentado***, no. 2 (1983): Brazil. ***SP Punk***, no. 1 (Aug 1982), Meire Martins and Callegari: São Paulo, Brazil.

pp. 82–83: ***Adventures in Reality***, issue J. (*c.* 1981), Alan Rider: Coventry, UK. ***It Ticked and Exploded***, no. 7 (Feb–March 1979), Clive Hollywood: Paisley, Renfrewshire, Scotland. ***Black & White***, no. 1 (1979), Peter Price and Stephen Rapid: Dublin, Ireland. ***The Poser***, no. 2 (*c.*1980), Neil Anderson: London, UK. ***Out of Print***, no. 2 (1979), Chris: Bexhill-on-Sea, East Sussex, UK. ***Leamington's Love Letter***, no. 3 (1981), Gerry O'Brien and others: Leamington Spa, Warwickshire, UK. ***No More Masterpieces***, no. 12 (*c.* 1979), Paul Mathur: Formby, Liverpool, UK. ***Today's Length***, no. 1 (1980), Jessamy Calkin and others, art director Malcolm Garrett Kane: London, UK.

pp. 84–85: ***Jamming!***, no. 14 (1983), ed. Tony Fletcher, design Robin Richards and others, Jamming Publications: London, UK. ***Flipside***, no. 31 (April 1982), Rodney and Christine F., guest commentary Mykel Board: Whittier, CA, USA. ***Jamming!***, no. 7 (1979), ed. Tony Fletcher, Jamming Publications: London, UK. ***Zig Zag***, no. 85 (July 1978), ed. Kris Needs and others, Phoenix Magazines Ltd: London, UK. ***Bomp!*** (Nov 1977), ed. Greg Shaw, managing ed. Gary Sperrazzai: Burbank, CA, USA.

CHAPTER 3, pp. 86–129

p. 87: ***SUREzine***, no. 4 (*c.* 1997), Kane Sure and others: Melbourne, Australia. ***Ben is Dead***, no. 25 (1995), Deborah 'Darby' Romeo and others: Los Angeles, CA, USA. ***Bunnyhop***, no. 10 (2000), Noël Tolentino, Jessica Grüner and others, cover Noël Tolentino: San Francisco, CA, USA.

p. 88: ***Halcyon Daze***, no. 1 (1989): Manchester, UK. ***The Farm***, no. 1 (*c.* 1991), The Staff: Liverpool, UK. ***Debris***, no. 12 (1986), Dave Haslam and others: Manchester, UK.

p. 89: ***Ace of Clubs***, no. 1 (1990), Gareth Jones and others: Manchester, UK. ***The Faced***, no. 4 (July 1992): Exeter, UK. ***Gear***, no. 2 (*c.* 1991), Camilla Deakin and others, design Funny Man Graphic Design (Fred Deakin): London, UK.

p. 90: ***Guinea Pig Zero*** / *A Journal for Human Research Subjects*, no. 6 (31 Dec 1998), Robert Helms and others, design Alexis Buss: Philadelphia, PA, USA. ***Close to You***, no. 11 (July 1999), Salmon Dave and others: Aboyne, Aberdeenshire, Scotland. ***Screaming to be Heard***, no. 2 (1988): Nottingham, UK.

p. 91: ***Dishwasher***, no. 15 (*c.* 1996), Dishwasher Pete (Pete Jordan), cover Sean Tejaratchi: Portland, OR, USA. ***Temp Slave!***, no. 7 (1995), Jeff Kelly and others: Madison, WI, USA. ***Answer Me!***, no. 2 (1992), Jim and Debbie Goad: Hollywood, CA, US.

p. 92: ***CGBC*** / *The Journal of the Incredibly Good Looking*, no. 7 (1998), Chelsea White and others: Oakland Park, KS, USA. ***Cometbus***, no. 47 (2005), Aaron Cometbus (Aaron Elliot): Berkley, CA, USA. ***Beer Frame*** / *The Journal of Inconspicuous Consumption*, no. 8 (March 1988), Paul Lukas and others: Brooklyn, NY, USA. ***The Duplex Planet***, no. 183 (2005), David Greenberger, managing ed. Barbara Price: Saratoga Springs, NY, USA.

p. 93: ***Boing Boing***, no. 7 (1992), Mark and Carla Frauenfelder and others: Boulder, CO, USA. ***Plotz Notes***, no. 16 (2002), Barbara Kligman: New York City, NY, USA. ***Crap Hound***, no. 6 (1999), Sean Tejaratchi: Portland, OR, USA. ***Tiki News***, no. 16 (2000), Otto von Stroheim, cover Dave Wong: San Francisco, CA, USA.

pp. 94–95: ***Murder Can Be Fun***, no. 7 (1987), no. 11 (1989), no. 14 (1992), no. 17 (1996), no. 20 (2007), John Marr: San Francisco, CA, USA. ***Murder Can Be Fun*** / *1997 Datebook* / *Special 10th Anniversary Edition* (1997), John Marr: San Francisco, CA, USA. ***Mystery Date***, no. 5 (1997), Lynn Peril: San Francisco, CA, USA. ***Teen Fag Magazine***, no. 3 (spring 1994), no. 4 (spring 1995), Gordon Gordon: Seattle, WA, USA. ***Teenage Gang Debs***, no. 5 (May 1993), Don and Erin Smith: Bathesda, MD, USA.

pp. 96–97: ***Thrift Score***, no. 1 (spring 1994), no. 3 (fall 1994), no. 4 (winter 1994), no. 5 (spring 1995), no. 6 (1995), no. 7 (1996), no. 8 (1996), no. 9 (1996), no. 12 (1998), Al Hoff and others: Pittsburgh, PA, USA. ***Details***, vol. 2, no. 2 (Oct 1983), ed. Annie Flanders and others, art director Lesley Vinson, cover art Ian Worpole, Details Publishing Corp.: New York City, NY, USA. ***Cheap Date***, no. 4 (summer 1998), Kira Jolliffe and others, art directors Liz Harris, Minnie Wiesz, cover Fergadel-IC for Hysteric Glam: London, UK. ***i-D***, no. 2 (Nov 1980), ed. Al McDowell, Terry Jones and Perry Haines, T.J. Informat Design Ltd: London, UK.

pp. 98–99: ***A.O.B. Zine*** / *The Bumper Book of B.M.X. for Little Boys & Girls*, no. 5 (1995), M Farrington, B. Shell and others: Exeter, UK [cover and inside spread]. ***Skatedork***, no. 1 (*c.* 1998), Steve Voss and others: Berkeley Heights, NJ, USA. ***Oscar's Eye***, no. 1 ([n.d.]), Joe Tindall: Haslemere, Surrey, UK. ***Sauce***, no. 007 (*c.* 2008), Pod, cover Pod: Portland, OR, USA. ***Not the View*** / *Celtic Fanzine*, no. 34 (March–April 1992), J. B. Banal and others: Glasgow, Scotland. ***Johnny Miller 96 Not Out*** (May 1992), Dave Cotton, Martin Fey, Phil Harris, Peter Tovey and others: Bristol, UK.

pp. 100–101: ***Blow Football***, no. 4 (*c.* 1990): Birmingham, UK. ***When Saturday Comes***, no. 7 (April–May 1987), Mike Ticher, Andy Lyons and others: London, UK. ***The Shankill Skinhead***, no. 8 (1991), Tim Glynne-Jones, Stan Griffin, Nigel Scanland and Toddy: Purley, Surrey, UK. ***Someone Likes Us***

(Feb 1991), Mr Knife: London, UK. ***Through the Wind & Rain***, no. 1 (autumn 1989), Steven Kelly and others: Liverpool,UK. ***Hail Mary!***, vol. 2, no. 1 (1992), Ian Corbett: Runcorn, Cheshire, UK. ***NBA Update***, vol. 1, no. 5 (1991), Darren Edwards and Stephen R. Ashmore, art director Mark G. Wolfe: Rugby, Warwickshire, UK. ***Murtaugh***, no. 11 (*c.* 1994), Spike Vrusho, cover woodcut Daisy DeCapite: Brooklyn, NY, USA. ***Waiting for the Great Leap Forward***, no. 8 (1991), I. Mulvey, R. Steward, N. Taylor and others: Strathclyde, Scotland.

p. 102: ***Severely Twisted!***, no. 1 (June 1994): London, UK. ***Holiday in the Sun***, no. 2 (June 1999), Jim Munroe: Toronto, Canada. ***Question Everything Challenge Everything***, vol. 3, no. 2 (1998), Larry Nocella: Collegeville, PA, USA. ***U.K. Resist***, no. 3½ (autumn 1990), design TW: Surbiton, Surrey, UK. ***Hoax!*** (1992), John C. S. Quel [Johnny Datakill]: Brecon, Powys, Wales.

p. 103: ***Ker Boom***, no. 1 (*c.* 1994): London, UK. ***Protest Magazine***, no. 1 (*c.* 1992), Ian Russell: Bedhampton, Hampshire, UK. ***Nil by Mouth*** no. 3 (*c.* 1990s), Reza and others: London, UK.

pp. 104–05: ***Combat Zone***, no. 1 (1985): Bristol, UK. ***Skins***, no. 5 (*c.* 1982): London, UK. ***Boredom Images***, no. 2 (1991): London, UK. ***Nosebleed***, no. 8 (1993), Boz: Dublin, Ireland. ***Strong & Proud***, no. 3 (autumn 1997), Nestor Matilla and The Crew: Vigo, Spain. ***Revenge*** with ***Skinhead Liberation Organization*** and ***Unite for Unity***, no. 2 (Jan 1992), Steve, Mucky, Nazzi and others: Telford, Shropshire, UK, Pittsburgh, PA, USA, and Baltimore, MD, USA.

pp. 106–07: ***Go Go***, no. 1 (April 1985), no. 2 (May 1985), no. 3 (June 1985), no. 4 (July 1985), no. 8 (Nov 1985), no. 12 (May–June 1986), no. 14 (Aug 1986), no. 6 (Sept 1986), Jackie Toby and Bernie Taylor: Dagenham, Essex, UK.

pp. 108–09: ***Smashed Blockhead***, no. 2 (*c.* 1986), Bill Luther and others: Jamesburg, NJ, USA. ***The New Stylist***, no. 3 (May–June 1983),Flecky the K.: England [back cover]. ***Hip 'n' Groovy***, no. 1 (*c.* 1986), Judy Thomas: Bognor Regis, West Sussex, UK. ***Real Emotion***, no. 1 (*c.* 1983), Dev and others: Dublin, Ireland. ***The Inset***, no. 3 (*c.* 1985), Matt Cannock: Bournemouth, UK. ***Passion, Pride and Honesty***, no. 2 (1985), Paul Moody and Robin Stubbs: Chichester, UK. ***Time Moves Us On*** ([n.d.]), Robin King, Piers and others: Chichester, UK.

pp. 110–11: ***Mohawk Beaver***, no. 1 (1997), Gritt Uldall-Jessen, design BADgirl Design: Copenhagen, Denmark. ***FF Magazine*** (1992): London, UK. ***Holy Titclamps***, no. 17 (1999), Larry Bob: San Francisco, CA, USA. ***Kim Wilde*** / *Fan Club News*, vol. 3, no. 3 (1984), Kim Wilde Fan Club: London, UK.

pp. 112–13: ***Subterranean Pop***, no. 1 (1980), Bruce Pavitt: Olympia, WA, USA [cover and inside spread]. ***Sub Pop***, no. 8 (1982), no. 3 (1981) [inside spread], no. 2 (1980), no. 4 (1981), no. 3 (1981), Bruce Pavitt: Olympia, WA, USA.

pp. 114–15: ***Sub Pop***, no. 6 (Feb 1982), no. 5 (1981) [cassette], no. 7 (1982), no. 9 (1983), Bruce Pavitt: Olympia, WA, USA.

p. 116: ***Long Live Vinyl***, no. 5 (1994), Brian: Nottingham, UK. ***Big Muff***, no. 3½ (1991), Neil Boyd and others: London, UK. ***Rebel Sound***, vol. 1, no. 3 (1991), cover art Erick 'Frica-Boy' Backus and others: Pittsfield, MA, USA. ***117***, no. 8 (Sept 1993), J. Faulkner: Hitchin, Hertfordshire, UK. ***Blaster!***, no. 2 (*c.* 1992): Bristol, UK.

p. 117: ***Då***, no. 3 (summer 1993): Stockholm, Sweden. ***Calling Dr Cranklin!***, no. 1 (spring 1989), Steve: London, UK. ***Datakill***, no. 2 (1989), Johnny Datakill: Swansea, Wales. ***Lil' Rhino Gazette***, no. 19 (Feb 1992), K.K.R. North and others, cover J.D. Burdge: Dallas–Fort Worth, TX, USA. ***Commodity***, no. 4 (1995), Josh Hooten, Tony Leone and others: Medford, MA, USA.

p. 118: ***Boy's Own***, no. 6 (1988), Terry Farley, Andy Weatherall, Cymon Eccles and Steve Maize, cover Dave Little: England. ***Beach Boys Stomp***, no. 95 (Feb–March 1993), Michael Grant and others, cover art Nick Guy: Tonbridge, Kent, UK. ***Teenage Depression***, no. 8 (1978), Geoff Banks and others: Enfield, Middlesex, UK. ***The Farm Fanzine*** (early 1990s), Farm Info Service: Liverpool, UK. ***Moonlight Drive***, no. 2 (1981), Rob and others: London, UK.

p. 119: ***T Mershi Duween Zappa Fanzine***, no. 26 (*c.* 1992), Fred Tomsett and others: Sheffield, UK. ***Boomshackalacka***, no. 7 (Aug–Sept 1991), L. Bell-Brown, BSL Productions: London, UK. ***Morri'Zine*** / *A Publication for Morrisey and Smiths Fans*, vol. 4, no. 5 (winter 1992), Nicole Garrison and others: Sacramento, CA, USA. ***Pick of the Bunch***, no. 71 (1997), Mark Boyle: Renfrewshire, Scotland. ***Omaha Rainbow***, no. 8 (*c.* 1978), Peter O'Brien: Wallington, Surrey, UK. ***Rockrgrl***, no. 15 (May–June 1997), Carla de Santis and others, design Jeffery Kennedy: Mercer Island, WA, USA. ***Offering***, no. 21 (Nov 1993), Marilyn: Hertfordshire, UK.

pp. 120–21: ***The TV Collector***, vol. 2, no. 15 (Oct 1984), Stephen W. and Diane Albert: Needham, MA, USA. ***No Remakes***, no. 4 (*c.* 1998): Glasgow, Scotland. ***TV Times*** ([n.d.]), Institute of Social Disengineering: Oxford, UK. ***Totting Times***, no. 2 (Sept 1999), Mark Pearson and others: London, UK. ***Femme Flicke***, no. 4 (1995), Tina Spangler and others: Cambridge, MA, USA [cover and inside spread]. ***Theme '70 Fanzine***, no. 2 (March 1994), Mark Banville, Amateur Fanzine Workshop: UK.

pp. 122–123: ***Fish Piss***, vol. 1, no. 5 (1999), Louis Rastelli and others, cover Siris, The Archive: Montreal, Canada. ***Pop!*** / *Short for Popular*, no. 4 ([n.d.]), Joe Pop!: London, UK. ***Chicken is Good Food*** / *The Beauty Issue*, no. 5 (1999), Summer Stickney and others: San Francisco, CA, USA. ***The White Dot***, no. 6 (summer 1997), Jean Lotus, David Burke and others, layout Gordon Mayer, illustration Sarah Lyons: Chicago, IL, USA. ***Nancy's Magazine***, vol. 9 (winter 1993–94), Nancy Bonnell-Kangas: Columbus, OH, USA. ***Chip's Closet Cleaner***, no. 11 (fall 1994), Chip Rowe: Washington, DC, USA. ***Giant Robot*** / *Asian Pop Culture And Beyond*, no. 21 (2001), Eric Nakamura and Martin Wong and others: Los Angeles, CA, USA. ***Robot Power*** / *Version 20.5* (2000), Eric Nakamura and Martin Wong and others, cover photo Bob Hamilton: Los Angeles, CA, USA. ***Oriental Whatever***, vol. 2, no. 2 [no. 9] (fall 2008), Dan Wu and others, art director Julia Keel: San Francisco, CA, USA.

p. 124: ***Gothique***, vol. 1, no. 3 (Jan 1966), David Griffiths, Stanley Nicholls, Bram Stokes: Dublin, GA, USA and Brentford, Middlesex, UK.

p. 125: ***Psychotronic Video***, no. 12 (spring 1992), Michael J. Weller and others, art director Fred Brockman: New York City, NY, USA. ***Vincent Price File*** (1996), Simon Flynn: London, UK. ***Ain't Bin to No Art School*** ([n.d.]), Mike Weller: London, UK. ***Lip Service***, no. 4 (Aug 1981), Simon and others: Welwyn Garden City, Hertfordshire, UK. ***Zine Zone***, no. 1 (1 Nov 1994): London, UK.

p. 126: ***MaximumRocknRoll***, no. 159 (Aug 1996), Tim Yohannan and others: San Francisco, CA, USA. ***Punk Planet***, no. 11 (Jan–Feb 1996), Dan Sinker and others, layout Josh Hooten: [n.p.]. ***Profane Existence***, no. 34 (1998), Dan Duke, Jon and others: Minneapolis, MN, USA. ***Revolting***, no. 6 (*c.* 1995): Kingston upon Thames, Surrey, UK. ***H.A.G.L.***, no. 20 (*c.* 1980s), Trev Hagl: Newcastle upon Tyne, UK.

p. 127: ***Open Up and Bleed***, no. 8 (summer 2000), Catherine Laz and David Reynolds: London, UK. ***Your Flesh***, no. 7 (1984), Peter Davis and others, cover Lee Ellingson: Minneapolis, MN, USA. ***Ruptured Ambitions***, no. 10 (June 1992), Chris Wheelchair: Tavistock, Devon, UK.

p. 128: ***Factsheet Five***, no. 48 (July 1993), R. Seth Friedman: San Francisco, CA, USA. ***All Genre***, vol. 11, no. 2 (April–June 1992), Hillel Cooperman and others: Washington DC, WA, USA. ***Amok*** / *Third Dispatch* (*c.* 1989), Brian King, Stuart Swezey and others, cover Lori Wierzbicki: Los Angeles, CA, USA. ***Action Resource Guide Cata-zine*** including ***Prisoner's Speak*** (1994), Ashley Parker Owens and Guy Hensel, Soapbox Junc: Chicago, IL, USA.

p. 129: ***Bypass***, no. 3 (*c.* 1994), Bruce and James: Oxford, UK. ***Book Your Own Fuckin' Life***, no. 7 (1999), The Amoeba Collective: East Palo Alto, CA, USA. ***Broken Pencil***, no. 6 (winter 1998), Hilary Clark, Hal Niedzviecki, design Jon Hodgkins, cover Marc Bell: Toronto, Canada. ***The Zine***, no. 9 (July–Aug 1994), Bo Maggs and others, cover Luke Foreman, Power Publications Ltd (UK): Guildford, UK.

CHAPTER 4, pp. 130–69

p. 131: ***Bikini Kill*** / *A Color and Activity Book* (early 1990s), Toby Vail, Kill Rock Stars: Olympia, WA, USA. ***April Fool's Day***, no. 1 (spring 1995), Kathleen Hanna: Olympia, WA, USA. ***Spiderplant***, no. 8 (Aug 2000), Casino: Baddesley Ensor, Warwickshire, UK.

p. 132: ***Kitten Carousell*** / *Special Nail Varnish Edition* (early 1990s), Doncaster and Barnsley, UK. ***Bombshell*** (early 1990s), Anna: Merseyside, UK. ***Ablaze!***, no. 4 ([n.d.]), Karren Ablaze, cover art by Potet!: Manchester and Leeds, UK.

p. 133: ***Starlet*** (1994), Angel: London, UK. ***Twinkle Eye Fizzy***, no. 1 ([n.d.]), Rainy: Essex, UK. **Programme for Le Tigre and Las Sin Fronteras** (2000), Sarah and others: Tucson, AZ, USA.

p. 134: ***Botramaid*** / *Fanzine with Manners*, no. 1 (1996), Gail Douglas and Lorraine Douglas: Glasgow, Scotland. ***Bamboo Girl***, no. 8 (Jan 1999), Sabrina Margarita Sandata: New York City, NY, USA. ***Pretty Ugly***, no. 2 (spring 2002), Pretty Ugly Collective (ed. Kelly Elizabeth, art ed. Lepa, cover image Cameron): Lilydale, Victoria, Australia.

p. 135: ***Ladyfest Glasgow 2001***, UK events programme (2001): Glasgow, Scotland. ***UK Ladyfest Artwork 2001–2008*** (2008), ed. Heather Crabtree and Melanie Maddison: Leeds, UK.

pp. 136–37: ***Bikini Kill*** / *Girl Power*, no. 2 (early 1990s): Olympia, WA, USA. ***Leeds & Bradford Riot Grrrl!*** (1993), Karren, Simone, Lianne, Elizia, Maxine, Clare, Jane, Sarah and others: Leeds, UK [cover and inside spread]. ***Dancing Chicks***, no. 4 (June 1999), Helen Wray: Reading, UK.

pp. 138–39: ***Riot Girl London*** / *Newsletter*, call for zines (Jan 2001), Riot Girl London: London, UK. ***The Jigsaw***, no. 5½ (*c.* early 1990s), Tobi Vail: Olympia, WA, USA. ***[The] Jigsaw***, no. 5 (*c.* early 1990s), Tobi Vail: Olympia, WA, USA. ***Girl Germs***, no. 3 (1992), Allison Wolfe and Molly Neuman: Portland, OR, USA. ***Riot Grrrl***, manifesto (*c.* 1991), Riot Grrrl: Washington, DC, USA. ***Channel Seven*** (*c.* 1990s), Corin Tucker and Erika Reinstein: Olympia, WA, USA.

pp. 140–41: ***Reggae Chicken***, no. 1 (*c.* 1993): UK [cover and inside spreads]. ***Drop Babies*** (April 1993), Elizabeth, Layla Gibbons and others, cartoon by Layla Gibbons: London, UK [cover and inside spreads].

pp. 142–43: ***Vaginal Teeth*** (1998), Maddy, Geraldine, Aisha, Kat, Clare, Vic, Andy, Simone, Karren and Cazz, ed. Clare von Stokes, Simone Ivatts and Cazz Blase: Stockport, Cheshire, UK (printed Cazz). ***Aggamengmong Moggie***, no. 5 (June–July 1994), no. 7 (Oct–Nov 1994), no. 10 (April–May 1995), no. 11 (Aug–Sept 1995), no. 13 (Dec 1995–Jan 1996), no. 16 (June–July 1996), no. 29 (July 1999), no. 15 (April–May 1996), Cazz Blase: Stockport, Cheshire, UK.

pp. 144–45: ***Rebel Grrrl Punk***, no. 1 (1997), no. 2 (1997), no. 3 (1999?), no. 5 ([n.d.]), no. 4 (2000), Kirsty: Wilmslow, UK. ***Sista Yes!***, no. 3 (*c.* 1997), Sophy: Canterbury, UK.

pp. 146–47: ***Junk Food***, no. 1 (Aug–Sept 2003), Judy: Syracuse, NY, USA [cover and inside spread]. ***Toast and Jam***, no. 1 (1997/98), Rachel Kaye and others: London, UK [cover and inside spread]. ***Il pleut des gouines!***, no. 2 (April 2005), Lolagouine (dyke), France [cover and inside spread]. ***Pirate Jenny*** / *A saucy little zine for your inner feminist revolutionary*, vol. 1, no. 4 (summer–fall 2001), cover Adrienne Jan, vol. 1, no. 3 (late summer–fall 2000): Santa Barbara, CA, USA.

pp. 148–49: ***Radium Dial***, ([n.d.]) Ilona Jasiewicz: London, UK, (1995) Ilona Jasiewicz: Chicago, IL, USA. ***Radium Dial*** (spring 1999) [focus on Los Angeles], Ilona Jasiewicz: London, UK. ***Radium Dial***, no.8 (autumn 2001) [full-time work], Ilona Jasiewicz: [n.p.]. ***Radium Dial*** (spring 2003) [personal life], Ilona Jasiewicz: [n.p.] [cover and inside spreads]. ***Radium Dial*** no. 4 (1997/98), Ilona Jasiewicz: [n.p.]; ***Radium Dial*** (summer 1998), Ilona Jasiewicz: [n.p.].

pp. 150–51: ***Radical Cheerleader Handbook***, no. 3 (2000), various: Lake Worth, FL, USA [front and back covers]. ***Ladyfest Cheerbook*** (Aug 2001), Haymarket Hussies: Chicago, IL, USA ***Shag Stamp***, no. 6 (Oct–Nov 1996), Jane Graham: Sheffield, UK and Denmark.

pp. 152–53: ***Hysteria Action Forum*** / *Love and Romance*, no. 5 (1994), Gabby Gamboa, Puppy Toss: Berkeley, CA, USA ***Revolutionary Women*** / *Stencil Book* (2005), Tui, Cherry Bomb Comics: New Zealand. ***Rote Zora*** / *Interview with two members of the German Women's Armed Struggle Group* (June 1984): [n.p.] [pamphlet]. ***Bark + Grass*** / *Revolution Supper*, no. 2 (*c.* 1991): Chicago, IL, USA. ***Drum Core***, no. 1 (1993): Brooklyn, NY, USA. ***What's This Generation Coming To?*** no. 2 (1992), Anon.: Newcastle upon Tyne, UK.

pp. 154–55: ***Heavy Flow***, no. 6 (May 1996), Saskia Hollins, cover girl Melanie Wright: [n.p.]. ***Chart Your Cycle*** (2005), Chella Quint: Yorkshire, UK. ***Heavy Flow***, no. 5 (Sept 1995), Saskia Hollins and others, cover Saskia Hollins and Melanie Wright: Edinburgh, Scotland. ***Red Alert***, no. 2 (1999), Blood Sisters and others: Montreal, Canada. ***Period; A Menstru-Rama!!*** (2001), Veronica Del Real, Las Sin Fronteras for Ladyfest: Glasgow, Scotland. ***Adventures in Menstruating***, no. 1 (Aug 2005), Chella Quint: Yorkshire, UK.

pp. 156–57: ***Electra***, no. 4 (summer 2002), Jane Collins: Llandudno, Wales [cover and inside spread]. ***Kitty Magik***, no. 5 (summer 2000), Marisa: New Jersey, USA. ***Rollerderby***, no. 20 (1997), Lisa Carver: Dover, NH, USA. ***Popgirls***, no. 2

999), Amanda MacKinnon (Manda-Rin): Glasgow, Scotland over and inside spread].

.158-59: ***Big Bums*** (Aug 2008), Charlotte Cooper, Kay yatt, Simon Murphy and Bill Savage: London, UK. ***Nipples nd Bits***, no. 1 ([n.d.]), Brackin': New Orleans, LA, and attiesburg, MS, USA. ***Bust*** (spring–summer 1997), ed. elina Hex and Betty Boop, art director Laurie Henzel, cover noto Andrea Gentl: USA. ***Punktum*** (2002), Rachel House: ondon, UK [cover and inside spread]. ***Unskinny Bop***, no. (2004), Tamsin and Ruth: London, UK [cover and inside read]. ***Unskinny***, no. 8 (*c.* 1996), Lucy Sweet: Glasgow, cotland.

. 160–61: ***Fat!So?*** / *Spare Tires*, no. 4 (1995), Marilyn enrietta 'Hank' Wann, cover photo Marilyn Wann: San rancisco, CA, USA. ***Girl Cult Girlkulturzine***, vol. 3, no. 1 . 1998), Joan Brennan: London, Ontario, Canada. ***For our Own Good / a zine about mothers, daughters and body nage*** (*c.* 2004), Kate, cover by Jeremy Dennis: London, UK. ***irlFrenzy*** / *Fat Lib*, no. 4 (1993), Erica Smith: Hove, East ussex, UK. ***Fat Girl*** (April 1996), Twyla Stark, cover photo eth Peckman: San Francisco, CA, USA.

162: ***Catch that Beat!*** vol. 9 (1999), Yayoi: Tokyo, Japan over and inside spread]. ***Asian Girls are Rad*** / *Lucky issue*, . 7 (June 1994): Austin, TX, USA.

163: ***Girly Transgender Zine*** (Oct 1996), Mona Compleine: ondon, UK. ***Sky High Heels*** ([n.d.]), Mona Compleine: ondon, UK [cover and inside spread]. ***Girly Transgender Zine***, . 7 (winter–spring 1997), Mona Compleine: London, UK.

. 164–65: ***Amp Minizine*** / *Fashion for the Fickle*, no. 11 n.d.]), Miss Amp (Anne-Marie Payne), contributors Francis organ, Alice BS Rooney, Kit Milings, Suki Kent: London, UK over and inside spread]. ***Red Hanky Panky 7*** [combined with *ormone Frenzy 3.5*] (Aug 1999), Rachel House: London, UK. ***mp Minizine*** / *Girls Rock Out*, no. 10/10 ([n.d.]), ed. Miss mp (Anne-Marie Payne), design Look At Me, contributors achel House, Joe Popi, Rebecca Cherkoss, Suki Kent, Charlie ucas: London, UK. ***The Pamzine*** / *Your Guide to the World Pam Savage*, no. 1 (Jan–Feb 2000), no. 7 (winter 2003–)04), Pam Savage: London, UK. ***Honeypears***, no. 1 (summer)02), Heather Middleton: Glasgow, Scotland. ***Vacuum Boots***, . 4 (2000), Miss Rachel, Angel: London, UK.

166: ***Incest*** (1990s), Tammy and others, Desperate Times all for Desperate Zines: London, UK. ***Incest*** / *The Age of Love*, . 3 ([n.d.]), Tammy and others: London, UK [cover and inside read].

167: ***Notes & Errata*** (*c.* 2008), Suzy Pow!: Lewisham, ew South Wales, Australia [cover and inside spread]. ***Pink monade***, no. 3 (2000), Victoria Yeulet: London, UK. ***Gun ounds Again?*** (1997), Emily Sessions: [n.p.].

. 168–169: ***Slampt Underground Organisation*** / *Distro atalogue* (May 1997), Rachel Holborow and Pete Dale: ewcastle upon Tyne, UK. ***Riot Grrl Press Catalogue*** (July, rly 1990s), May and Erika (Marika): Arlington, VA, USA. ***ord is Born: a Riot Grrrl Dissertation?*** (2004), Julia Downes: eds, UK. ***Barnard Zine Library Zine*** (fall–spring 2005–)06), Alexa Antopol, ed. Jenna Freedman: Barnard College, ew York City, NY, USA. ***Riot Grrrl*** (2005), Yuka Ogaki: Japan ack and front cover]. ***I'm not waiting / Doin' it yrself now*** 004), Melanie Maddison, artwork Lucy Sweet: Leeds, UK ssertation].

CHAPTER 5, pp. 170–203

171: ***E-Zine List*** (1993–*c.* 2005) [website], John Labovitz: SA. ***Drummer Con*** (1995–[n.d.]) [networking site]: iladelphia, PA, USA.

172: ***The Zine*** (3 Feb 2004–[n.d.]) [website], Mr Maul: USA. ***ipRowe.com*** (1995–) [website], Chip Rowe: Chicago, IL, SA.

173: ***Mystery Date Online*** (1 May 2001–) [website], Lynn ril: San Francisco, CA, USA. ***Duplex Planet*** (*c.* 2000s) ebsite], David Greenberger: Saratoga Springs, NY, USA. ***Little Poetry*** / *A Perpetual Po-e-zine?* (1996) [website], ed. acee Coleman: UK. ***Blind, Stupid and Desperate*** / *A Watford Fanzine* (late 1990s–2006) [website], Ian Grant and Matt owson: London, UK. ***Jersey Beat*** ([n.d.]) [website], Jim Testa: eehawken, NJ, USA.

174: ***The Flaneur*** (2009) [website], Jonathan Powell and hers: London, UK. ***Stolen Sharpie*** (May 2008) [blog], Alex rekk: Portland, OR, USA. ***To-Do List*** (2005) [blog], Sasha agen: San Francisco, CA, USA.

p. 175: ***Broken Pencil*** ([n.d.]) [website], ed. Lindsay Gibb: Toronto, Canada. ***Irish Books and Zines*** (June 2008) [blog]: Ireland.

pp. 176–77: ***Digizine***, no. 1 (fall 1995) [CD ROM], creative director/writer Timothy R. Zuellig, Ahrens Interactive Inc.: Chicago, IL, USA. ***Cyber Rag*** / *For the Macintosh*, no. 3 (1991) [HyperCard floppy disk], Jaime Levy: Hollywood, CA, USA.

p. 178: ***Pixel This*** (2003–*c.* 2009) [website]: Nicosia, Cyprus. ***Pixel This*** / *Connected Urban Retreat*, no. 006 (Sept 2006): Nicosia, Cyprus.

p. 179: ***Tenderfoot*** (2006–[n.d.]) [website], Jenna Weiss: Fanwood, NJ, USA. ***Sandylovesyou*** ([n.d.]) [blog], Sandy Lim: Perth, Western Australia. ***10 Things Zine*** / *Jesus Wants You to Know* (July 2007–) [blog], Dan Halligan: Seattle, WA, USA. ***10 Things Zine*** / *Jesus Wants You to Know*, no. 15 (*c.* 1995), Dan Halligan: Seattle, WA, USA.

pp. 180–81: ***The Black Cloud***, no. 1 (8 Jan 2007), no. 3 (Nov 2009), Bret Liebendorfer: Columbus, OH, USA. ***Punks Is Hippies*** / *The Online D.I.Y. Punk Fanzine Archive* (Sept 2007–) [blog], Tony Gunnarsson and others, Slobodan Burger: London, UK. ***Kissoff*** (2007–2009) [website], Chris Kiss: Toronto, Canada. ***The ChickenFish Speaks*** (2002–) [website], Grog Mutant (Greg Simerlink) and others: Dayton, OH, USA.

p. 182: ***Loserdom***, no. 16 (June 2007), Anto McFly & Eugene and others: Dublin, Ireland [cover and inside spread]. ***Loserdom***, ([n.d.]) [website], Anto McFly & Eugene and others: Dublin, Ireland.

p. 183: ***Kill Your Pet Puppy*** (Oct 2007–) [website], Tony Drayton: London, UK. ***Attack!***, no. 2 (*c.* 2004), Wes White, Man With A Gun Press: Glastonbury, Somerset, UK. ***Cartilage*** ([n.d.]) [website], Wes White: Glastonbury, Somerset, UK. ***Woofah*** (2007–) [website], John Edne and Paul Meme, design The Droid: London, UK.

p. 184: ***Doris***, no. 26 ([n.d.]), Cindy Crabb: Athens, OH, USA (printed 1984 Printing, Oakland, CA). ***Doris***, no. 19 (*c.* early 2002), Cindy Crabb, cover Sarah Danforth: Ashe, NC, USA. ***Doris***, no. 25 ([n.d.]), Cindy Crabb: Athens, OH, USA (printed 1984 Printing, Oakland, CA). ***Doris Zine Blog*** (May 2007) [blog]: Athens, OH, USA.

p. 185: ***Savage Messiah*** ([n.d.]) [website], Laura Oldfield Ford: London, UK. ***Savage Messiah***, no. 4 (April–May 2006), Laura Oldfield Ford: London, UK. ***Ricochet! Ricochet!***, no. 1 (2005), Paffy and Colly, cover Cat: London, UK. ***Ricochet! Ricochet!***, ([n.d.]) [website], Paffy and Colly: London, UK.

pp. 186–87: ***Supersweet*** (2008), cover Paula Kopecna: London, UK. ***Supersweet Digital*** (2007) [website], editorial coordinator Gemma Dempster, creative director Choltida Pekanan, design Ralph: London, UK. ***Morgenmuffel*** / *A Sort of Compilation* ([n.d.]), Isy Morgenmuffel: Brighton, UK. ***Morgenmuffel*** / *Bits and Pieces* (April 2008), Isy Morgenmuffel: Brighton, UK. ***Morgenmuffel*** / *Cartoons and More*, no. 14 (Jan 2006), Isy Morgenmuffel: Brighton, UK. ***Morgenmuffel*** ([n.d.]) [website], Isy Morgenmuffel: Brighton, UK.

pp. 188–89: ***Rancid-News***, no. 2 (June–July 2003), Edd Baldry: London, UK. ***Last Hours*** (2008) [website], Edd Baldry and others: London, UK. ***Last Hours***, no. 14 (autumn 2006), Edd Baldry and others: London, UK. ***Last Hours***, no. 10 ([n.d.]), Edd Baldry and others: London, UK [inside spread].

p. 190: ***When Language Runs Dry***, no. 2 (July 2009), Claire Barrera and Meredith Butner: Portland, OR, USA. ***Meredith Butner*** (2008) [blog], Meredith Butner: Portland, OR, USA. ***Karen***, no. 1 (2004), Karen Lubbock: Rodbourne Bottom, Wiltshire, UK. ***Karen*** ([n.d.]) [website], Karen Lubbock: Rodbourne Bottom, Wiltshire, UK.

p. 191: ***PonyBoy Press*** (Jan 2007) [blog]: Portland, OR, USA. ***Oh, Darcy*** ([n.d.]) [website], Brittany Brown: USA. ***The East Village Inky***, no. 8 (July 2000), Ayun Halliday: New York City, NY, USA. ***The East Village Inky*** ([n.d.]) [website], Ayun Halliday: New York City, NY, USA. ***Ghost Pine Fanzine*** (2007) [blog], Jeff Miller: Montreal, Canada.

p. 192: ***Fever Zine*** (*c.* late 2000s) [website], Alex Zamora, Simon Whybray and others: London, UK. ***Fever Zine***, no. 3 (2007), no. 4 (2008), Alex Zamora, Simon Whybray and others: London, UK.

p. 193: ***Breakfast*** ([n.d.]) [website], Vincent Voelz: San Francisco, CA, USA. ***Clamor*** / *Your DIY Guide to Everyday Revolution* (2006) [website], Jen Angel, Jason Kucsma and others, web designer Derek Hogue: Toledo, OH, USA. ***The La-La Theory*** / *Always Already*, no. 6 (2008), ([n.d.]) [website], Katie Haegele: PA, USA.

pp. 194–95: ***Hack this Zine*** / *Ammo for the Info-Warrior* (summer 2006), project organizer Jeremy Hammond: USA. ***HackBloc.org*** / *Exploit Code Not People* [*Hack this Zine*] ([n.d.]) [website], Hackbloc Collective: USA. ***Rad Dad*** / *A Zine About Parenting* (2005) [blog], Tomas Moniz: Berkeley, CA, USA. ***Rad Dad***, no. 4 (*c.* 2006), Tomas Moniz: Berkeley, CA, USA (printed Artnoose). ***SocialDesignZine*** (2003–09) [website], Italian Association for Visual Communication Design: Milan, Italy. ***She Must be Having a Bad Day*** / *Food Service: The Second Oldest Profession* (2009) [blog], Dana Raidt (Dana Darko): Minneapolis, MN, USA. ***She Must be Having a Bad Day*** / *The Cult of the Female Food Service Worker* (July 2008), Dana Raidt (Dana Darko): Minneapolis, MN, USA. ***Urinal Gum*** (Jan 2008) [blog], James: Eugene, OR, USA.

p. 196: ***Bust*** / *Fight Like a Girl*, no. 19 (spring 2002), Laurie Henzel and Debbie Stoller, editor-in-chief Debbie Stoller, creative director Laurie Henzel: New York City, NY, USA. ***Bust*** ([n.d.]) [website], Laurie Henzel and Debbie Stoller, editor-in-chief Debbie Stoller, creative director Laurie Henzel: New York City, NY, USA. ***Bitchmedia*** / *Bitch: Feminist Response to Pop Culture* ([n.d.]) [website], executive director Julie Falk, co-founders Lisa Jervis, Benjamin Shaykin and Andi Zeisler, editorial/creative director Andi Zeisler, art director Kristin Roger Brown: Portland, OR, USA. ***Ladyfest London 2008*** (2008) [website], banner artwork Nick, images contributed by Rosalind Glennie and Bg: London, UK.

p. 197: ***Lickety Split Smut Zine*** (Oct 2009) [website], Amber Goodwyn and others: Montreal, Canada. ***Ladyfriend*** ([n.d.]) [website], Christa Donner: Chicago, IL, USA. ***Grrrl Zine Network*** (2001) [website], Elke Zobl: Salzburg, Austria. ***Grrrlzines A Go-Go*** (2002) [website], Kim Schwenk, Margarat Nee, Claudia Lucero, Britton Neubacher, Elke Zobl, site design Ari: Encinitas, CA, USA. ***Scum Grrrls 100% Feminist Energy*** ([n.d.]) [website]: Brussels, Belgium.

p. 198: ***Sticky Institute*** ([n.d.]) [website], Luke Sinclair, Richard Hold, Andrew Seward, Simone Ewenson and other volunteers: Melbourne, Australia.

p. 199: ***Our Hero*** (2000–02) [website], Heroic Film Company: Toronto, Canada.

p. 200: ***Xerography Debt***, no. 25 (2009), ed. Davida Gypsy Breier and others, cover Bojan, layout and design Kathy Moseley, Microcosm Publishing: Portland, OR, USA. ***Xerography Debt*** (2008) [website and blog], ed. Davida Gypsy Breier and others: Baltimore, MD, USA. ***Learning to Leave a Paper Trail*** / *Zine Distro* ([n.d.]) [website], Ciara Xyerra: Lawrence, KA, USA. ***Zine Thug*** (2003–09) [website], Marc Parker and others: Portland, OR, USA.

p. 201: ***Zine World***, no. 10 (spring 1999), Doug Holland and others, cover Jeff Meyer, design/layout Susan Boren: San Francisco, CA, USA. ***Zine World*** / *A Reader's Guide to the Underground Press*, no. 19 (summer 2003), Doug Holland, Jerianne Thompson and others, art director Kyle Bravo: Murfreesboro, TN, USA. ***Zine World*** / *A Reader's Guide to the Underground Press* (2008) [blog]: Murfreesboro, TN, USA.

pp. 202–03: ***Library Bonnet*** no. 1 (*c.* late 1990s), Tommy Kovac, Julie Fredericksen: Orange, CA, USA. ***Library Bonnet*** ([n.d.]) [website], Tommy Kovac and Julie Fredericksen: Orange, CA, USA. ***FYP Fanzine*** ([n.d.]) [twitter feed], James Daly and Mark Tyrrell: London, UK. ***The Oatcake*** ([n.d.]) [message board]: Stoke-on-Trent, Staffordshire, UK. ***ZineWiki*** (2006–) [website, open source], Alan Lastufka and Kate Sandler: Chicago, IL, USA. ***Zine Library*** ([n.d.]) [website, open publishing]: London, UK. ***80s UK Zine Archive*** (*c.* 2005–) [website], Sned: London, UK.

CHAPTER 6, pp. 204–47

p. 205: ***Kurt Cobain was Lactose Intolerant Conspiracy Zine*** (May 1998), Sharky Girl: San Francisco, CA, USA. ***Publish and Bedazzled*** / *The Fagzine for the Peter Cook Appreciation Society*, no. 33 (2003), Clinty: London, UK. ***Pull to Open***, no. 9 (2005), Craig Lightowler and Phil Virco, cover illustration Northern Glory: Bradford, West Yorkshire, UK.

p. 206: ***Squeaky Sneakers***, no. 3 (*c.* 2008), Stapler: The Channon, New South Wales, Australia. ***Manzine*** / *A publication about the male phenomenon*, no. 2 (summer 2009), ed. Kevin Braddock and others, The Clapham Mountaineering Society: [n.p.]. ***The Robert Edmond Grant Fanzine*** / *The Grant Museum* (*c.* 2009), ed. Tine Horn, illustration Danielle Berg: London, UK.

p. 207: **Publish and Be Published** (2005), Eddie Wilson: London, UK. **Zine Libs**, no. 1 (2005), Caroline Paquita and Erick Lyle: San Francisco, CA, USA. **Just Say No Thank You**, no. 2 (March 2007), Star: Auckland, New Zealand.

p. 208: **Nervous System**, no. 1, version 1.0 (spring 2006), Anthony and others: London, UK. **BodyTalk** / The Medical Issue (Dec 2009), ed. Joseph Beeman, art direction Sarah Handelman, design Tom Loughlin: Columbia, MO, USA. **Local Anaesthetic!**, no. 29 (May 2007), ed. Cliff Anderson and Tom Noonan, cover art Jenny Jo Oakley: Geelong West, Victoria, Australia.

p. 209: **Office Pup**, vol. 2 (2002–06), ed. Toby Morris and others: Wellington, New Zealand. **You Stink & I Don't**, no. 9 (2007), Ben Hutchings, Green Comix: Canberra, Australia. **The Squareball**, no. 1 (2005–06), Ian Dobson, Ben Hutchinson and others: Leeds, UK.

pp. 210–11: **Sweet Shop Syndicate**, no. 2 (Jan 2006), Richard and Christina: Brighton, UK, and Graz, Austria [cover and inside spread]. **Zine Making: An Introduction** (2003, 2nd edn 2007), Sarah: Halifax, Nova Scotia, Canada. **Stolen Sharpie Revolution** / A DIY Zine Resource (c. 2003), Alex Wrekk, Microcosm Publishing: Portland, OR, USA [cover and insider spread]. **MixTape**, no. 1 (Aug 2007), Nichola Prested and Justine Telfer, design Motor, cover Shannon Lamden: Moorabbin, Victoria, Australia; no. 6 (2008), Nichola Prested and Justine Telfer, design Motor, cover Mandy: Moorabbin, Victoria, Australia.

pp. 212–13: **Dates I've Been On and Not Been On** ([n.d.]), Anon.: Melbourne, Australia. **We Ear it Regular Differently** / The Punk Issue / Special Edition Do It Yourself, no. 2 ([n.d.]), Alex Weird and others: Montreal, Canada [front and back covers]. **Helping You Find the Right Jewellry!** (c. mid-2000s), Sarah Doyle, cover Sarah Doyle: London, UK. **This Is!**, no. 0½ (May 2002), Helen Wickham: London, UK. **D90** / A Mix-Tape Zine (2007–2008), Spurzzine: Carlton North, Victoria, Australia. **How to Make a Super 8 Film** / Super 8 Super Zine (c. 2006): Halifax, Nova Scotia, Canada. **Hey Look! It's a Zine about Cross Stitch!** (c. 2010), Secret Nerd Brigade [Autumn Patterson]: Minneapolis, MN, USA.

pp. 214–15: **Ker-Bloom!**, LXXX (Sept–Oct 2009), Karen Switzer, Crafty Cards (aka Artnoose): Pittsburgh, PA, USA. **The Squares** (c. 2009), Ewuraba and others, Studio Voltaire: London, UK. **28 Pages Lovingly Bound with Twine**, no. 13 (2005), Christoph Meyer: Danville, OH, USA. **In Sickness** (2008), Maddy Phelan: Wollongong, New South Wales, Australia. **The Memory Cloth** / An Exploration into Craft Memory and Contemporary Design (26 July 2006), ed. and design Suzy Wood, Izzie Klingels, Martin McGrath and others: London, UK.

pp. 216–17: **Mix Zine**, no. 1 (April 2009), Miss Fliss: London, UK [cover and inside spread]. **You** (28 Oct 2008), Luke You: Melbourne, Australia. **Pneumatic Catalog** ([n.d.]), Niku Arbabi and Scrappy Zine Coop: Austin, TX, USA [cover and inside spread]. **By the Time You're Twenty-Five** (Oct 2008), Emma, Flying Machine: Enmore, New South Wales, Australia. **Failed Rock Star**, no. 4 (7 Dec 2005), Rob Phoenix, bag design Shaun Peters: Brighton, UK.

p. 218: **Arty** / England, no. 20 (Aug–Sept 2005), Cathy Lomax, cover Cathy Lomax: London, UK. **Blitzkrieg Babylon** (2003), Dan Holliday and Andrew Craig: London, UK (printed The Mangle). **Organ**, no. 70 (July–Aug 2001), Sean Worrall, Shaari Freed and Marina Anthony: London, UK. **Plastasine Fanzine** / Art Writing Beyond Criticism (17 May 2008), David Burrows and others, Article Press: London, UK.

p. 219: **Enough Magazine**, no. 1 (2007), Tom Morrow: Australia. **Intercity Baby** (April 2009), Jennifer, cover Jennifer: Chicago, IL, USA. **Giant Steps**, no. 3 (15 July 2007), Kirke Campbell and others: Houston, TX, USA.

pp. 220–21: **Bang!**, no. 2 ([n.d.]), Manu: Madrid, Spain. **Ugly is the New Sexy**, no. 28 (6 July 2006), Bryce Galloway: Wellington, New Zealand. **Future Fantasteek!**, no. 6 (2009), Jacky Batey, Damp Flat Books: Brighton, UK. **Obsession** / A Zine of Drawing Obsessions (c. 2009), Karoline Rerrie, Gemma Correll and others, cover Gemma Correll, Love to Print: London, UK. **Rivers Edge** / Notes from the Underground (May 2008), Richard Davis, cover Dan Holliday: London, UK [cover and inside spread]. **Screw Crash & Explode** ([n.d.]), Monobrain and Marcel Herms: Dedemsvaart, Netherlands.

p. 222: **Fire & Knives**, no. 1 (2009), Tim Hayward, design and art direction Rob Lowe, Funistrada Ltd: London, UK (printed Buxton Press). **Barefoot and in the Kitchen of Our Own Accord**, vol. 1 (2005), Ashley Rowe: Santa Cruz, CA, USA. **Stand Aside** / Fashion Issue (c. 2000), Polly Brannan and Miss Deepa Naik, The Cube and Public Works: London, UK.

p. 223: **FP: Fashion Projects**, no. 2 (2006–07), ed. Francesca Granata and others, art director Jennifer Noguchi, published Deconstruction Fashion: New York City, NY, USA. **Just Like Candy**, no. 1 (Sept 2008), Oli and Michaela, cover photo Erin Matthews: [n.p.]. **The Chap**, no. 1 (Feb 1999), ed. Gustav Temple, art director Vic Darkwood: London, UK. **Medium Magazine** / People and the Human Body, no. 1 (spring 2005), ed. Laurie Cansfield, cover Piggy by Judith Erwes, graphic design Form in Motion Production, Cansfield Creative Group: London, UK.

p. 224: **Hey, 4-Eyes!** / A Zine about Glasses, no. 3 (spring 2009), Robyn Chapman, cover Jim Medway, Unpopular Comics: USA. **Dame Pipi Comix** / DMPP Almanach 2009, no. 5 (2009), Gérald Auclin, cover Gustav Verbeek: [n.p.]. **Comix Club** / Meeting with John Porcellino, no. 5 (June 2007), Collective/ Publishing Groinge: Nice, France. **From the Tomb**, no. 21 (Feb 2007), Soaring Penguin: Rochdale, Lancashire, UK.

p. 225: **Re V'La Colyis Naody**, no. 3 (c. 1990s), Martin Guimond, Les Éditions du Chien Décrissé: Quebec, Canada.

pp. 226–27: **Juke Box**, no. 1 (c. 2006), ed. Renato Lima, design Luiza Rezende and Igor Machado: Brazil; **Juke Box**, no. 2, 1 (2007), ed. Renato Lima, design Igor Machado, Dado Oliveira and Gullherme Cavalcanti: São Paolo, Brazil [cover and inside spread]. **Cat Quarterly** / Office Love Issue, no. 7 (1997), Annie Lawson: London, UK. **Reality Optional** (Aug 2007), Andrew Stitt and others: Norwich, UK. **Tantrum Comics**, no. 1 (2002), Miriam Engelberg, design Edmond Y Chang: [n.p.].

pp. 228–29: **Bipedal, By Pedal!** (2008), Joe Biel: Bloomington, IN, USA. **Expansion of Life** / Fuck the Border!, no. 12 ([n.d.]): Japan. **Whoosh!** / The Zine for Whale Lovers, no. 1 (Nov 2008), Katherina Audley: Portland, OR, USA. **Cut and Paint**, no. 2 (Dec 2007), Nicolas Lampert, Josh MacPhee and Colin Matthes: Milwaukee, WI, USA (www. justseeds.org). **How Not to Eat Animals** ([n.d.]), Chickpea: Houston, TX, USA.

pp. 230–31: **Before the Mortgage**, no. 5 (c. 2002), Christina Amini and Rachel Hutton, design Kirk Roberts: Ross, CA, USA. **David Battams Fan Club Magazine**, vol. 2, no. 3 (summer 2004), Daniel 'Made Up' Battams, art direction Made Up Studios: London, UK. **The Alien Invader** (Dec 2003), Amin-Reza Javanmard and Jen-Tsen Kwok: Runaway Bay, Queensland, Australia. **The Lowbrow Reader**, no. 5 (summer 2006), ed. Jay Ruttenberg, design Matthew Berube, cover John Mathias: New York City, NY, USA. **Mustard**, vol. 2, no. 2 (May 2008), ed. and design Alex Musson: London, UK.

pp. 232–33: **Shoreditch Twat**, no. 3 (2000), no. 4 (2000), no. 5 (2000), no. 6 (2000), no. 7 (2000), no. 12 (2000), no. 14 (2001), no. 18 (2001), no. 2 (1999), ed. Neil Boorman, design Bump: London, UK.

p. 234: **Revolution** / It's Different for Girls (summer 2005), ed. Leonie Cooper, art direction James Chorley, cover art Lucy Bailey: UK. **Spilt Milkshake**, no. 1 (spring 2002), Rebecca Dyer: Chelmsford, Essex, UK. **Raise Some Hell** / A Feminist Child Rearing Zine for Everyone (2008), Crap Collective: London, UK. **Pamflet** / A Vindication of the Rights of Girl, vol. 1, no. 1 (Sept 2005), Phoebe Frangoul and Anna-Marie Fitzgerald: London, UK. **Girls with Guns**, no. 7 (c. 2009): Melbourne, Australia. **The Pleiades**, no. 14 (March 2005), Miranda Hale: Spokane, WA, USA.

p. 235: **Kitty Magik**, no. 6 (2002), ed. Marisa Handren: Whitehouse Station, NJ, USA. **Girls Who Fight**, no. 1 (2009), Kathryn Corlett: London, UK. **Muffy!** / The Magazine of New College Girly Life, no. 1 (spring 2000), ed. Regina Gelfo, Carly Earnshaw, Shannon O'Malley, design Carly Earnshaw, Regina Gelfo: Sarasota, FL, USA.

p. 236: **Butt** / Hysterical Magazine for Homosexuals, no. 14 (2005), Gert Jonkers, Jop van Bennekorm, photographer Marcelo Krasilcic: Amsterdam, Netherlands. **Homobody**, no. 4 ([n.d.]), Rio Safari (Tim Batiuk): Portland, OR, USA. **Detroit Queers** ([n.d.]), Detroit Radical Queers: Detroit, MI, USA.

p. 237: **Chica**, no. 1 (2001), Lucy Sweet and others: Glasgow, Scotland. **Iconoclastic Cardies**, no. 3 (2009), Pete Bowers, cover Andy Hart: Midlands, UK. **Fallopian Falafel**, no. 1 (June 2007), Hadass S. Ben-Ari and others: Jerusalem, Israel.

pp. 238–39: **Cops & Robbers**, no. 40 (July [n.d.]), Raine and others: Leeds, UK (printed Footprint). **Bye Bye, Duffel Boy**, no. 1 (summer 2009), Pete Green: Sheffield, UK. **More Love Truth and Honesty** (2007), Paul Byron: Melbourne, Australia. **Runnin' Feart**, no. 7 (c. 2000), Callum Masson: Stewarton, Ayrshire, Scotland. **Super Waste Project** (2000), Miles: Aylesbury, Buckinghamshire, UK. **Taking Dope**, no. 1 (1996), Dee Dee Ramone: New York City, NY, USA.

p. 240: **List** / Goodbye, Baltimore, no. 12 (fall 2008), Ramsey Beyer: Chicago, IL, USA. **Boredom** / 3rd Class Junk Mail Oracle ([n.d.]): Berkeley, CA, USA. **Enthusiasm**, no. 2 (c. 2009), Susi Rumsby and Tim Wade: Norwich, UK. **Telegram Ma'am**, no. 1 (July 2008), Maranda: Ontario, Canada.

p. 241: **My Evil Twin Sister** / Greetings from the Endless Highway, no. 1 (1995, repr. 2001), Stacey and Amber: Jacksonville, OR, USA. **Support** (2002), Cindy Crabb, cover Cristy Road: Asheville, NC, USA. **Not My Small Diary**, vol. 1 (2009), Delaine Derry Green, cover Frederick Noland: Trussville, AL, USA. **I Hate This Part of Texas** / Special Disaster (Jan 2006), John Gerken: New Orleans, LA, USA.

p. 242: **La Bouche Zine** / An Alternative News and Culture Zine, no. 2 (July 2009): London, UK. **Double Breasted**, no. 5 (Nov 2009), Jennie and Colin Baillie, Sharon Wood and others: Edinburgh, Scotland. **Smoke** / A London Peculiar, no. 12 ([n.d.]), Jude Rogers and Matt Haynes: London, UK.

p. 243: **No.Zine**, no. 3 (2009), Patrick Fry, cover Elisa Noguera: London, UK [cover and inside spread]; **No.Zine**, no. 2 (2009), Patrick Fry, cover photo Elisa Noguera: London, UK; **No.Zine**, no. 1 (2009), Patrick Fry: London, UK.

pp. 244–45: **Can You Show Me the Space** (2007–08), Public Works: London, UK. **Unemployment** (2009), Aaron Lake Smith: Cary, NC, USA. **Zine 2009** (June 2009), University of Delaware, London College of Communication: London, UK. **DIY or Don't We?** / A Zine about Community, no. 1 (July 2009), Nicki Sabalu and others: Olympia, WA, USA. **Hardwork Not Paid** (3 July 2007), Mrunmayee, Nandini, Necki, Priyanka C., Pushpi, Sargarn, Tanuja, Vishnu: India.

p. 246: **The Zine Directory**, version 1.0 (Sept 2007), Jane Appleby: Newcastle upon Tyne, UK. **Microcosm Publishing Catalogue** (2005–06), Joe Biel and others, cover artwork Sarah Oleksyk: Bloomington, IL, and Portland, OR, USA. **Zine Capsule** / Zine Collecting for the Future (2008), Kim Schwenk and others, Grrrl Zine A Go-Go: Encinitas, CA, USA. **Zine Arcade**, no. 2 (2008), ed. Andrew Owen Johnston, cover artwork Robert Sergel: Birmingham, UK.

p. 247: **UK Zine Yearbook** (Sept 2007), Toby: UK. **Australian Zine Resource** (2003), Louise Angrilli and Anna Masters, Swirlability Productions: Diamond Creek, Victoria, Australia. **Wasabi Distro** / Spring–Summer Catalogue (2005), Andrea: Tokyo, Japan. **Zene**, no. 23 (2000), Nancy Bennett and others: Ely, Cambridgeshire, UK.

ACKNOWLEDGMENTS

As with any endeavour that has spanned a period of time, there are a number of key individuals who have contributed to the completion of this book along the way: Roger Sabin, whose insights into the worlds of zines and comics has helped to inform the basis of this book; Amanda Vinnicombe, Kirsty Seymour-Ure and Amy Visram for editing my work and keeping me on track; Therese Vandling, whose design shows off the zines to best advantage; and to Lucas Dietrich who commissioned this project in the first place and never lost faith.

I could not have completed this research without the significant support and enthusiastic responses of the individual zinesters whose work is included in this book. I owe them a huge debt for their insights, time and access to their communities.

In addition, I would like to thank: Edd Baldry, Caroline Blase, Bill Burns, Charlie Chainsaw, Robert Clarke, Leigh Clarke, Siân Cook, Bob Dickinson, Joe Ewart, Priscila Lena Farias, Simon Ford, Paul Gravett, Dan Halliday, Dan Halligan, Rian Hughes, Jonathan Kemp, Leila Kassir, Jeff Kleinsmith, Christian Küsters, Rex Martin, Claire McAndrew, Anto McFly, Bruce Pavitt, Richard Price, Andy Sawyer, Patrick Staff, Dominic Thackara, Philip Turner, Stephen Voss, Michael J. Weller.

INDEX